the novel art

the novel art

Elevations of American Fiction after Henry James

Mark McGurl

PRINCETON UNIVERSITY PRESS
Princeton and Oxford

Library of Congress Cataloging-in-Publication Data

McGurl, Mark, date
The novel art: elevations of American fiction after Henry James /
Mark McGurl.
p. cm.
Includes bibliographical references and index.
ISBN 0-691-08898-5 (cloth : acid-free paper)—
ISBN 0-061-08899-3 (pbk. : acid-free paper)
1. American fiction—20th century—History and criticism.
2. James, Henry, 1843–1916—Influence. 3. Fiction—Technique.
I. Title.
PS379.M34 2001
813′.509—dc21   2001021131

This book has been composed in Bauer Bodoni

Printed on acid-free paper. ∞

www.pup.princeton.edu

Printed in the United States of America

10   9   8   7   6   5   4   3   2   1

10   9   8   7   6   5   4   3   2   1
(Pbk.)

to my parents

contents

a c k n o w l e d g m e n t s

Most of what is good about this book is owed to my teachers, and to the institutions that have sustained my relation to them. From beginning to end I have been in the best of hands.

At Harvard I had the good fortune to be tutored by Chris Braider, and befriended by Mark Kantor. At Johns Hopkins, where this project began to take shape, Sharon Cameron taught me to try harder, Neil Hertz taught me to think big, Larzer Ziff taught me that it's okay to make sense, Allen Grossman taught me that it would be nice to know everything, Jerome Christensen taught me to profess romanticism by other means, and Frances Ferguson taught me that there are limits to philosophical materialism. Michael Fried, to whom this book quietly owes a good deal, taught me to see what meets the eye more deeply. Unfailingly generous with his time and attention, Walter Benn Michaels taught me many things, including some ways not to be wrong. I trust he will forgive me if, as seems likely, I have forgotten a few of them along the way. I was further schooled by those with whom I shared these lessons, the likes of J. D. Connor, Shelly Eversley, Maria Farland, Cathy Jurca, Alex Love, Larissa MacFarquhar, Dan McGee, Deak Nabers, Michael Szalay, and Joanne Wood.

At UCLA I have found ideal conditions for the completion of this book: interesting colleagues, interested students, palm trees, time. Thanks especially to Thomas Wortham, who has a gift for making junior faculty feel appreciated, to Jen Fleissner, who has been a wonderful colleague and friend, and to Gopal Balakrishnan, who showed me how best to live the life of the mind in Los Angeles. These are only the most recent of the myriad individuals—conference panel members, journal editors, interested friends, and others—who have made contributions to this project over the years.

Versions of two of the chapters of this book have appeared elsewhere. I am grateful to the editors of *American Literary History* and *Representations* for permission to use and expand those materials here. Financial support for this project was provided in a series of research grants from the University of California, and in the form of a generous fellowship grant from Irving and Helga Cooper.

Deepest of all are the debts I owe to my family and lifelong friends.

i n t r o d u c t i o n

The Rise of the Art-Novel and the Question of Class

> Modern art . . . acts like a social agent which segregates from
> the shapeless mass of the many two different castes of men.
> —José Ortega y Gassett, *The Dehumanization of Art*

Certain Novels

What kind of book is Djuna Barnes's *Nightwood*? "Unless the term 'novel' has become too debased to apply," answered T. S. Eliot, introducing a work whose publication in 1936 owed much to his own efforts on its behalf, "and if it means a book in which living characters are created and shown in significant relationship, this book is a novel."[1] But what sort of novel is it, this novel in which so few of the pleasures traditionally associated with novel-reading are likely to be found?

For one thing, it is not the sort of novel likely to be loved by one and all. "A prose that is altogether alive demands something of the reader that the ordinary novel-reader is not prepared to give" (xii), admits Eliot of Barnes's densely written, minimally plotted meditations on desire and damnation among American expatriates and others in Europe. The "ordinary novel-reader" is used to novels that "obtain what reality they have largely from an accurate rendering of the noises that human beings make in their daily simple needs of communication," and that are written in prose "no more alive than that of a competent newspaper writer or government official" (xii). Failing to be simple or to satisfy "simple needs," *Nightwood* is destined to disappoint these readers, who might indeed question whether it should count as a novel at all. It is, however, in Eliot's view, neither a nonnovel nor a bad novel but rather "so good a novel that only sensibilities trained on poetry can wholly appreciate it"(xii). A depiction of human weakness, *Nightwood* is nonetheless a work for the culturally strong, catering to the taste not of the prosaic many but of the poetic few. It is in short what we have learned to call, knowing it to be a slippery term, a "modernist" novel.[2]

Appearing in the late 1930s, Eliot's somewhat defensive promotion of Barnes's unpopular novel was conducted in terms not entirely new. Allowing for the particular attention the modernist poet paid to the "written-ness" of Barnes's prose, his terms are recognizably continuous with a way of thinking about this genre that emerged in the English-speaking world toward the end of the nineteenth century and found its most persuasive spokesman in Eliot's admired expatriate example, Henry James. Working, in turn, with precedents set in France by Gustave Flaubert some decades earlier still, James had most influentially sought to claim the Anglo-American novel from the domain of popular entertainment and to argue for its potential as what he called "fine art." Exactly what it would mean to produce a novel that could be considered art would of course change, sometimes drastically, in the ensuing decades, but James's conception of the novel as an appropriate vehicle for the aspirations of the artist would persist. Buttressed, some years later, by the epochal example of James Joyce, and enabled all along by a broad set of social formations that structured the efforts of these and many other individuals, the status of the novel in the English-speaking world would never be the same. It would now, as a genre, stake a visible claim in the discursive field of the fine arts and, doing so, would encourage certain novels, and certain novelists, to set out after unprecedented heights of artistic prestige.

The chapters to follow will examine some of the circumstances of this rearticulation of the status of the novel, and will trace some of its most important consequences in the subsequent development of American fiction. Working from different angles and with varying emphases, I will be concerned in all cases to show how a newly intensified engagement with the genre's aesthetic status intersected, in the art-novel, with the questions of social status, class, and manners that had been of central thematic importance to the novel since its earliest days. Reading on both sides of the prismatic boundary between modernist *representations of class* and the *class-system of representations* in which they participate, I will show how the art-novel emerged in a series of transformations of the genre's analogical relation, as a generic institution, to other social-institutional, architectural, and geographical spaces, and how these spaces were themselves imagined to construct persons of a certain kind and class.[3] Doing so, I will call attention to the way—whether by direct statement, or suggestion, or in the waking dreamwork of allegory—the art-novel can be made to tell the story of its own emergence as a recognizable generic form.

Although the appearance of the "modernist novel," as the art-novel is sometimes called, evidently partakes of the much larger aesthetic, cultural, and social phenomenon known as "modernism," this study will, by contrast to most of the accounts of modernism from which it has learned, insist on a high degree of generic specificity both in the texts it examines and in the interest of the questions these texts raise. This will be especially true insofar as modernism in literature is here associated, as it so often has been, with an attempt to elevate the literary text over and above the artifacts of mass culture: in my account the modernism/mass culture relation will be crucially mediated by the term "novel." In the decades since the death of Henry James there has been ample time to absorb, even to the point of forgetting, what seemed to James and his contemporaries a relative originality in the notion either that the novel might function as "fine art" or that the novelist might be considered, in the honorific sense of the term, an *artist*.

Henry James, for one—notwithstanding his appreciation of precursors in the "brotherhood of novelists" as various as Nathaniel Hawthorne and George Eliot, and his envious admiration of the tradition of the novel in France—believed that the genre he inherited had been for the most part a disturbingly lowly and unrefined enterprise, "mass cultural" in many of the relevantly pejorative senses.[4] The Anglo-American novel, writes James in the well-known essay "The Art of Fiction" (1884), has been a thing with "no air of having a theory, a conviction, a consciousness of itself behind it"—deficiencies that have disqualified the novel from consideration as fine art.[5] Despite the occasional, serendipitous appearance of the "practical masterpiece" in the history of the novel, the genre has largely been "*naif*," compromised in its artistic dignity by the "comfortable, good-humoured feeling abroad that a novel is a novel, as a pudding is a pudding, and that our only business with it could be to swallow it" (44). Producing this object of thoughtless consumption, the novelist him- or herself has naturally been deprived of "all the honours and emoluments that have hitherto been reserved for the successful profession of music, poetry, painting, architecture"—that is, the "fine arts" (47).

Seconding Walter Besant's suggestion that it is high time for the novelist to be taken, and to take him- or herself, as seriously as the painter, poet, and architect, James agrees that "it is impossible to insist too much on so important a truth," for the object the novelist creates must be—must make itself deserving of being—"reputed artistic indeed" (47). James's ambitions for novel and novelist seemed remarkable, even ludicrous, to his one-time friend H. G. Wells, who, fashioning himself as a popular entertainer and public pedagogue, retained a more utilitarian conception of the genre's aesthetic status and social purpose:

> From his point of view there were not so much "novels" as The Novel, and it was a very high and important achievement. He thought of it as an Art Form and of novelists as artists of a very special and exalted type. He was concerned about their greatness and repute. . . . One could not be in a room with him for ten minutes without realizing the importance he attached to the dignity of this art of his.[6]

Thus, if one plausible way of defining the modernist movement in literature has been to claim that it represents some form of retreat from, or resistance to, mass culture on the part of professional or cultural elites, this definition might at a minimum seem more interesting and eventful when applied to the novel, which toward the turn of the century seemed to have no tradition of elevated discursive status of its own. Whereas the emergence of other modernist genres and art forms entailed (among other things) the continuation and intensification of a centuries-long partnership of the discourse of aesthetics and social elitism, the rise of the modernist novel registers something somewhat different: a moment of maximum collision of aesthetics and its indistinct, unlovely other in literature, the shapelessly dialogic genre that speaks for the "shapeless mass of the many." When the novel did in certain quarters begin to "gentrify," it became tempting to draw analogies between the art-novel and other, more traditionally elevated cultural forms, as Eliot does when he relates *Nightwood* to poetry, and as James does in "The Art of Fiction" when he claims that "the analogy between the art of the painter and the art of the novelist is, so far as I am able to see, complete" (46).[7] Forging analogies—never identities—between the art-novel and the traditional fine arts was one way writers sought to produce distinctions within the genre of the novel, separating the most ambitious artifacts of modernist fiction from the popular fiction that was most nearly—too nearly—proximate in form to itself.

But not only had the Anglo-American novel, according to James, rarely been considered a vehicle for the effects of fine art; its present status in the field of letters suggested even further embarrassments to the would-be artist of fiction: in the late-nineteenth and early-twentieth centuries it could seem, though it was certainly not the case, that almost everyone was writing and reading novels. This produced a crisis of indistinction that, while it echoed elsewhere, was felt with particular force in the domain of the novel. In "The Future of the Novel" (1899), James states the situation of his genre with nervous verve:

> The flood [of novels] at present swells and swells, threatening the whole field of letters, as would often seem, with submersion. . . . There is an immense public, if public be the name, inarticulate, but abysmally absorbent, for which, at its hours of ease, the printed volume has no other association [than with fiction]. This public—the public that subscribes, borrows, lends, that picks up in one way and another, sometimes even by purchase—grows and grows each year, and nothing is thus more apparent than that of all the recruits it brings to the book the most numerous by far are those that it brings to the "story." (*Essays*, 100)

The cause of this growth in the reading public—"the diffusion of the rudiments, the multiplication of common schools"—is clear to James, but its effects are "of a sort to engender many kinds of uneasiness" because "we are so demonstrably in presence of millions for whom taste is but an obscure, confused, immediate instinct" (101). Worried that his genre, the novel, and his profession, novelist, are being further lowered in status by their association with the primitive millions now learning to read, James is able to look with evident fondness to "that admirable minority of intelligent persons" (102) who do not like—and thus do not consume—the novel at all. Perhaps here, in the few intelligent people who refuse to read novels, is an occult source of hope for the Novel.

This is one odd conceptual consequence of James's belief that the novel at the turn of the century was in crisis, and that this crisis stemmed from its suddenly overwhelming popular success. He was not alone in this belief. In "The Novel and the Common School" (1890), Charles Dudley Warner also attributed this success to a spread of public education, which has produced an "almost universal habit of reading," and "nowhere so conspicuous[ly] as America."[8] Associating the rise of the popular novel with a parallel rise of the mass-circulation newspaper, Warner observed that the novel,

> mediocre, banal, merely sensational, and worthless for any purpose of intellectual stimulus or elevation of the ideal, is thus encouraged in this age as it never was before. The making of novels has become a process of manufacture. . . . One has only to mark what sort of novels reach the largest sale and are most called for in the circulating libraries, to gauge pretty accurately the public taste, and to measure the influence of this taste upon modern production. (258)

While, to his chagrin, James himself was largely spared this pain in the later years of his career, the embarrassment of popular success will be crucial to many of the texts I will examine here, which will be discovered to exhibit a nearly constant, if sometimes encoded, awareness of the "many" whom the genre, as a popular form, had always addressed.[9] This awareness is what exercises Eliot, above, as he takes care to distinguish Barnes's difficult prose from that of the newspaper writer or government official. Even in its most experimental instances—conspicuous difficulty being a common, if by no means universal, feature of the genre—the art-novel remained intensely intimate with the idea, if not always the fact, of the "common people—the people of ordinary comprehension," who had typically been touted as the "novelist's true audience" by popular nineteenth-century writers like Margaret Oliphant.[10] It was in dialectical relation to this audience, and working for the most part within the institutions of an expanding mass market, that the novel would attempt to reinvent itself as fine art.[11] The rise of the art-novel thus becomes visible as a version, of sorts, of the widespread contemporaneous phenomenon of product differentiation—that status-conscious aspect of mass consumerism in which, for famous instance, the mass-produced regularity of the black Ford Model T gives way in the 1920s to the multicolored hierarchies of automotive distinction.

Thus, as recent critics have begun to assert of modernism in general, the art-novel's "flight from" or "resistance to" mass culture must be considered a highly qualified and equivocal—though not necessarily a trivial—one.[12] It partakes of a modernist project that appears increasingly, in self-centered postmodern hindsight, always already to have been a "postmodernist" modernism in one of the senses proposed by Fredric Jameson: in its inability or even unwillingness to purify itself of the contaminations of the culture industry, the market, money. Presented with a "Great Divide" between modernism and mass culture—in which, as theorized most prominently by Andreas Huyssen, "modernism constituted itself through a conscious strategy of exclusion" of a mass culture to which it showed "obsessive hostility"—critics have become increasingly interested in accounting for the bridges that continued to pass from one side of the divide to the other.[13] Thomas Strychacz expresses an emergent critical consensus about the constitutive intimacy of modernist and mass cultural forms with admirable force, reminding us that the

> formal strategies of modernism were conceived dialogically; modernism and mass culture, the authentic and the inauthentic, must be theorized together and situated within the authoritative discursive structures of American society. Modernist writers articulate an opposition between them and mass culture only to disguise larger relations of power within which the products and forms of mass culture are vital to the shaping of modernist discourse. (*Modernism*, 7)

Only in the second half of this formulation does it become something of a Foucauldian caricature: the intent of modernism's critique of mass culture was no doubt more complex than "only to disguise" its implication in larger structures of power.[14] Still, the approach followed by Strychacz is exemplary in its critical vigor, amply demonstrating that modernism and its others can and must be "theorized together."

Not least of the virtues of a dialectical approach to modernism, and the one that I hope to make use of here in my account of the emergence of the art-novel, is that it can bring us back into contact with what must count as one of the central mysteries of this cultural form: How and why is it that a project of aesthetic elevation, associated with high demands for readerly intellection, is so tightly braided with a fascination with various forms of stupidity and social simplicity, or "low life"? This aspect of the modernist project has perhaps most often been discussed under the rubric of primitivism—as it is, for instance, in the recent work of Michael North, Ronald Bush, and others.[15] Hoping to conserve the insights produced by these analyses of primitivism, I will demonstrate that primitivism is only one of a range of phenomena, including most importantly a continuation of the unfinished project of literary naturalism, that attest to high modernism's constitutive fascination with the low. This fascination is made manifest in what I will describe, after William Empson, as the modernist novel's characteristically "pastoral" structure.

Historically, of course, pastoral has been understood as the genre of the urban poet's praise of the simple life of the countryside. In *Some Versions of Pastoral* (1960), however, Empson significantly broadens the definition and scope of pastoral such that it becomes a useful concept for understanding the relation of literary culture to hierarchies of social class and education.[16] In Empson's account, which appears to have been provoked by the proletarian literature issuing from the Soviet Union and the European Left during the Cold War, "pastoral" designates not poetry with rustic subject matter but a hierarchical sociocultural relation embedded in certain kinds of literary texts. Whereas for Empson the idea of authentic proletarian literature suggests a work by and about and, most crucially, for an audience of laborers, pastoral rather suggests a "process of putting the complex into the simple" (23). This complexity remains as a framing presence in the pastoral text, linking it to the social world and sensibilities of an educated urban audience. Thus, while the pastoral work may be about places and persons beyond the pale of literary culture, it nonetheless remains an instance of literary culture permeated by the values of a "social world (ideology)" (3) alien to the "simple" social milieu it represents. Discovering this structural hierarchy in and around a wide variety of texts (including, in passing, those of Stein, Hemingway, and Faulkner), Empson argues that even the proletarian novel, produced and consumed mainly by an educated leftist intelligentsia, is in fact typically a species of what he calls "Covert Pastoral" (6).

Whether or not Empson's skepticism could properly be directed toward the works of the 1930s proletarian avant-garde in the United States is an open question; in figures like Jack Conroy, author of *The Disinherited* (1934), one sees a fairly convincing, if agonized, example of the "worker-writer," and of an attempt to forge a workers' literary culture quite apart from mainstream, middle-class institutions of publishing.[17] And indeed, it should be said from the outset that the interpretive models I will develop here become, as applied to the 1930s, not so much weakened as substantially narrowed in their explanatory power, as the appearance of the Popular Front produces class formations and cultural allegiances that may or may not be comprehended adequately in the terms I will be using here.[18] My object in these pages will instead be the Jamesian modernist tradition— that loosely conceived canon, pointedly exclusive of works of the Popular Front, established in the university after the Second World War under aesthetic criteria that had largely been set forth half a century earlier by James himself.[19]

The significance of Empson's expanded conception of pastoral for this tradition becomes clear if one thinks, first, simply of how frequently its major works depart from the relatively sophisticated urban milieux in which they tended to be produced and read in order to represent social worlds pointedly "lower" or less sophisticated than their own.[20] Picking up on this tendency as early as 1927, Wyndham Lewis would refer to this widespread attraction to the "simpleton" on the part of early-twentieth-century literary elites as a "child cult," a phenomenon plainly "connected"—but not necessarily reducible—to "the cult of the *primitive* and the *savage*."[21] Lewis would in turn decode the modernist cult of the simpleton as evidence of the permeation of even the most "intellectualist" literary projects, such as Gertrude Stein's, by the "hysterical imbecility" of the mass market and the modern social mass. This is acute as far as it goes, but what Lewis failed to explain adequately was how this attraction to the simpleton on the part of literary elites could be something other than a plain contradiction of their efforts to produce literary artifacts distinct from those favored by the simpletons themselves. In order for us to gain some purchase on this aspect of the modernist project, Lewis's exuberant evisceration of the child-cult must be supplemented by Empson's revised conception of pastoral. The latter provides the makings of a dialectical account of how "simplicity" and "sophistication" were braided in the relation between modernism's elevated discourses and its abject objects.

Still tied to the novel of manners and to the representation of the Euro-American haute monde, Henry James might seem in respect to the cult of the simpleton a mostly transitional figure. This is partly true and yet in many ways—even in his signature "international theme," which juxtaposes "sophisticated" European and "simple" American culture—we can see in his work the early stages of what will become the characteristically pastoral juxtapositions of the American modernist novel.[22] After James's, however, come works such as, for brief example, Stephen Crane's *Maggie: A Girl of the Streets* (1893), the "simple hearts" of Gertrude Stein's *Three Lives* (1910), and William Faulkner's *The Sound and the Fury* (1929). These works, ranging across a period of some thirty years, are exemplary even in their radically various attempts to produce literary sophistication by representing a marked (if necessarily relative) sociointellectual simplicity. Faulkner's Benjy, the "idiot" Southerner whose stream of consciousness becomes an occasion for among the most difficult pages in the canon of American fiction, might serve as an emblem of the pastoral juxtaposition that produces complex representations of characters hard to imagine as readers, and still less as writers, of the novels in which they appear.

Seen as a technology simultaneously of *identification with* the low—with the authenticity of folk, the vigor of the primitive, the collective power of the social mass—and of *distinction from* the low, Empson's conception of pastoral enables us to begin to sketch the dialectical relation of the art-novel to its various national, social-institutional, and generic contexts: to the low-status generic history of the novel; to the putatively classless, homogenously "democratic" United States; to contemporary institutions of mass print culture in which the popular novel played so evident a part. American modernism, that is, exists in a "pastoral" relation to American mass culture, while the art-novel exists in pastoral relation to the novel as genre. In each case the presence, as a dialectical foil, of the relatively "simple"—naive, stupid, low, primitive, childish, uneducated—becomes a necessary precondition for the experience of the distinctly "complex."

This juxtaposition enables what Friedrich Nietzsche, adopted by H. L. Mencken and others as one of the house philosophers of American modernism, famously called the "pathos of distance," that "protracted and domineering fundamental total feeling on the part of a higher ruling order in relation to a lower order, to a 'below.' "[23] One might also describe it as a dialectic of (merely) intellectual superiority. What needs to be underscored in this use of Nietzsche's formulation is, first, the surprising ontological interdependence implied in this "pathetic" relation between higher and lower orders, where a "below" is necessary for the experience of an "above"; and, second, the deeply uncertain, if not simply imaginary, status of early-twentieth-century modernist writers as a "ruling order" even of the specific domain of print culture. Describing the frequent admixture of relative social and educational privilege and relative political and economic disempowerment in literary elites in France, Pierre Bourdieu has described these groups as a "dominated fraction of the dominant class," and the term seems equally applicable to most (though not all) of the social milieux of American modernism.[24] Accounts of modernism that dismiss these fractional articulations seem to me not so much wrong as unnecessarily blurry. The vicious snobbery one frequently encounters in and around modernism is, if one cares to look closely, a complex phenomenon manifesting both an injured sense of aristocratic entitlement and, at times, a strenuous attempt to resist, so as to mediate, the naked force of capital on behalf of other values.

Elaborating a dialectical account of the art-novel, attending to the way it combines elevated discourses and abject objects, the chapters to follow will attempt, above all, to give some account of how the *social form* of modernism is at once activated by and made manifest in the innovative *aesthetic forms* of the art-novel itself. This is of course a difficult task, but it is a necessary one, since so much of the specificity of the art-novel is gained by a duplication and transposition of realist sociological thematics into the domain of innovative literary form. Indeed, the novelty of the modernist novel, such as it is, could be said to derive in large measure from the way it supplements the depiction of characters inflected by various social norms and class distinctions—a project fully underway in realist

fiction—with an understanding of the art-novel *itself* as a potential producer of these distinctions.[25]

This had of course, since every cultural practice produces social distinctions of some sort, already necessarily been the case with the realist novel,
but neither intentionally nor interestingly. The self-appointed task of the
realist project, most prominently represented in the United States by William Dean Howells, had been to universalize the values of the virtuous and
industrious middle class as valid for one and all. Its purpose, at least by
its own account, had been to provide a literary "commonplace" for the
production of social equality, sympathy, and ideological consensus.[26] While
its emergence is unthinkable except in relation to this democratic-realist
initiative—in which James played an important if ambivalent part—the
modernist art-novel entertained a substantially different conception of its
social function than this. Abandoning an ideal of consensus that happily
asserts, as Howells put it, that "[m]en are more alike than unlike one
another" (87), modernist fiction aspired instead to produce social distinctions and disagreements.

The traces of this aspiration, as I will demonstrate, are registered
throughout modernist fiction in a series of meditations on the novel as
an object in social space. These meditations raise questions not only of
objecthood in the formal sense, though they do indeed do that, but also of
possession and privation: what does it mean to "possess culture"? What
might it look like to possess culture—cultural capital—in the form of the
novel? Alternatively, what would it mean to think of the novel as offering
a kind of imaginary social space, something like a school, where one could
enter into culture? Or, perhaps more pertinently, as offering only an im-
penetrable surface, a kind of bolted door? Thinking of itself in these social-
spatial terms, the art-novel would participate in the modernist project as
it was conceived and unapologetically celebrated by José Ortega y Gassett
in 1927, where modern art "acts like a social agent which segregates from
the shapeless mass of the many two different castes of men."[27]

Mental Labor

Asserting the constitutive intimacy of modernist literature with economically dominant institutions of mass culture, revisionary accounts of modernism have begun in recent years to build on Richard Poirier's account
of modernism as an "attempt to perpetuate the power of literature as a
privileged form of discourse" in a time of expanding literacy and mass
cultural leveling.[28] It did so, argues Poirier, by presenting literary history
with the relatively new "phenomenon of grim reading," in which reading
seems less like an act of pleasurable consumption than a task of difficult
work. Indeed, offering no easy or foolish pleasures, "modernism" in litera-

ture, for Poirier, "can be measured by the degree of textual intimidation felt in the act of reading." The point, then—an idea supported by the metaphors at work in James's fear of an "abysmally absorbent" audience—might seem to be to produce texts that resist "consumption" as such, thus to offer resistance to mass or "consumer" culture as a whole.

I will argue, however, that the case is somewhat more complicated than this; that indeed, rather than merely trading pleasure for work, modernism is also reflective of the notion, associated with professionalism, that there might be pleasure *in* work and, specifically, in the particular kind of intellectual work that reading the difficult modernist text is said to require. This is as much to say that, despite its frequently antibourgeois rhetoric, the emergence of the art-novel in the United States must be situated within—without simply being collapsed into—the much larger context of the expansion of the "new middle" or "professional-managerial" class in the late-nineteenth and early-twentieth centuries.

Identified chiefly by the intellectual or mental work it performed, this emergent class formation suggested a significant transformation of the historical middle class as it had been understood in nineteenth-century social theory. As C. Wright Mills put it, the "major shifts of occupations since the Civil War have assumed this industrial trend: as a proportion of the labor force, fewer individuals manipulate *things*, more handle *people* and *symbols*."[29] The rapid expansion of this class meant that it would be defined not only in opposition to the "masses" conceived as the working class of manual and industrial laborers, but also as a new version of the masses Mills calls the "white-collar mass" (190). The latter term is an important one, for it suggests the close proximity of the modernist literary-mind-worker to the many—too many—others involved, in this period, in one or another form of productive cogitation. The art-novel did not do anything as simple as express or reflect the ideology of the professional-managerial class as a whole; rather, it registered and mediated instabilities in period discourses of class, and was as concerned to produce distinctions *within* the "white-collar mass" as to speak for that mass.

Contrasted with earlier definitions of the middle class, such as Marx's description of the bourgeoisie as owners of the means of production, the professional-managerial class has been defined as consisting of "mental workers who do not own the means of production and whose major function in the social division of labor may be described broadly as the reproduction of capitalist culture and capitalist class relations."[30] In this account, the professional-managerial class arises and expands as a consequence of a large-scale shift from a classical liberal to a "managerial" model of consumer capitalism at the turn of the century, in which production, distribution, and consumption of goods were rationalized so as to be made more efficient and predictable.[31] The omnipresent advertisements that arose in this period to produce and manage consumption—including the practice, new to the publishing industry, of "booming" books for large sale—constituted a large measure the social and symbolic environment in which the art-novel was produced and consumed. As Jennifer Wicke has demonstrated, this environment was both reflected and critiqued in the modernist text.[32]

Long associated with a conception of the mind as an object of value— the worthy target, for instance, of promotional "mind control" on the part of advertisers—the rise of the consumer economy, managed by an expanding class of mental laborers, also meant that mind would come to be perceived as a primary *producer* of value in this economy. This expansion was in turn associated with significant shifts and internal differentiations in the "middle class ideology," which the novel, as a "middle class genre," has frequently been said to embody and express. Building on the seminal arguments of Ian Watt, Michael McKeon has argued persuasively that the novel of the nascent English middle class of the seventeenth and eighteenth centuries tended to propose moral virtue as a supreme social value, thus to combat pretensions of intrinsic superiority or "nobility" on the part of a rapacious hereditary aristocracy.[33] This antiaristocratic, moralizing tendency is carried all but intact into the realist theory of William Dean Howells, but here it meets significant and sustained opposition. Hence, one finds arguments of the sort made by Gertrude Atherton in the *North American Review* in 1904, which criticize the dominance of American fiction by an ethos of middle class propriety:

> It is the expression of that bourgeoisie which is afraid of doing the wrong thing, not of the indifferent aristocrat; of that element which dares not use slang, shrinks from audacity, rarely utters a bold sentiment and as rarely feels one. It is as correct as Sunday clothes and as innocuous as sterilized milk, but it is not aristocratic.[34]

Returning to some of the aristocratic and intellectualist emphases of the romance tradition, the art-novel, as we shall see, is notable for its relative privileging of *intellectual* virtue—smarts—above all other forms of virtue.

Thus one of the earmarks of modernist fiction—perhaps the first thing an informed reader at the turn of the century would have said about it— was its purported obscenity and seemingly unapologetic immorality. The next thing might have been its unpleasant difficulty and plotless tedium. Even Henry James, hardly a pornographer, had come under significant fire for the immoral "perversity" of his subjects. From early in his career he had wryly spoken up for novels, mostly French, that combined "great brilliancy and great immorality."[35] He had been strident in his opposition to the Victorian censorship that, claiming to protect the innocence of a mass readership of young women, excluded the domain of sex-relations from the novelist's analytic purview. That this scandalous—and, as Joyce Wexler has observed, potentially quite profitable—attention to "low" matters would be combined in works such as Joyce's *Ulysses* (1922), James Branch Cabell's *Jurgen* (1919), or indeed Barnes's *Nightwood*, with notoriously high demands for readerly intellection was entirely characteristic of this "pastoral" reversal and reconfiguration of priorities.[36]

Now, it is important to point out that the ever-larger number of educated persons who began to perform the various tasks of mental labor required in the U.S. consumer economy—a highly differentiated group including sales managers, lawyers, educators, administrators, writers of advertising copy, writers of fiction—did not have access to the term "professional-managerial class" as a means of collective self-identification and communal action. Rather, as Thomas Strychacz, Jonathan Freedman, Louis Menand, and others have made clear in their various accounts of literary professionalism at the turn of the century and beyond, the most characteristic mode of self-organization of this new class was the profession, complete with discrete regulatory bodies and institutions, in which practitioners organized themselves in relation to a relatively defined and unique body of knowledge.[37]

Never managing, on the model of the medical profession, to restrict the practice of fiction writing to those sanctioned by an academic degree, the novelist's trade did not manage to organize itself as a profession in this strongest sense. As a result, being able neither actually to restrict competition from unaccredited sources—as the exile of untrained McTeagues from the dental profession does—nor to legally define what would count as the competent practice of fiction, the profession of novelist remained in a relatively unmediated relation to a market where the "patients" could prescribe for themselves more or less any kind of literary medicine they wanted. As George Saintsbury put it in 1892, the "special difficulty which besets the novelist, and of which he not infrequently complains when he aims at excellence," is that he is "at the present moment, perhaps, the only artist whose art is liable to be confounded with the simple business of the ordinary tradesman."[38] Thus the efforts of the novelist to claim the status honor associated with professional distance from pure market forces were of a distinctly provisional and unreliable kind.[39]

Not yet admitted to the university as the "writer in residence," the art-novelist in the first half of the twentieth century received some help in this endeavor from the structures of patronage, generally more important to poetry than to prose fiction, recently examined by Lawrence Rainey.[40] A more common, if even more self-evidently compromised, form of assistance was lent by the various publishing houses associated with modernism, which institutions provided, after all, the writer's most direct and concrete interface with "market forces" as such. A self-consciously genteel enterprise, the book publishing industry has been perhaps unique in American capitalism in the degree to which it has touted itself as a "bad business" with relatively tiny profit margins, a labor not of capitalist greed but of cultural responsibility and love. This was true both of the older, established houses—Harper Brothers, Houghton Mifflin, Macmillan, Scribner's—who published James, Howells, and Wharton, and also of the new generation represented by such as Boni and Liveright, Alfred Knopf, and Random House. Never averse, in practice, to the profitable windfall of a "best-seller"—so designated by the now-familiar "best-seller list" that first appeared in the *Bookman* in 1895—these houses were run by persons who wished to conceive themselves "not [as] merchandisers but [as] business men of letters."[41] On many occasions, then as now, these publishers were willing to print books with scant hope of making a substantial profit.

Be that as it may, authors of the period did not consider themselves to have been spared the insults of the market. The rise in this period of the literary agent and the Society of Authors, promoting the economic interests of authors against publishers, attests to this.[42] Neither, typically, did authors scruple to avoid the market's opportunities, if only they could be had on the right terms. Having been, until relatively late in life, among the least marketable of famous American modernists, Gertrude Stein could not help but look fondly to that "beautiful autumn in Bilignin" when "in six weeks I wrote The Autobiography of Alice B. Toklas and it was published and it became a best seller and . . . I bought myself a new eight cylinder Ford car and the most expensive coat made to order by Hermès. . . . I had never made any money before in my life and I was most excited."[43] Quickly establishing himself, in contrast to Stein, as one of the most reliably marketable modernists, Ernest Hemingway kept simultaneous watch on his portfolio of monetary and of cultural capital from the very beginning of his career. Approaching Horace Liveright with the manuscript of his early collection of stories, *In Our Time* (1925), he presciently promoted the refined simplicity of his prose as something that "would be praised by the highbrows and could be read by the lowbrows."[44]

In any case, the literary market for the writer of modernist fiction was always present as the visible field in which he or she would work, conditioning his or her "art" and structuring the possibilities for his or her career in fundamental ways. Indeed, in the blush of her surprising success as a best-seller, Stein described the dilemmas presented by the author's proximity to market forces as producing a deep "question of identity":

It is funny about money. And it is funny about identity. You are you because your little dog knows you, but when your public knows you and does not want to pay for you and when your public knows you and does want to pay for you, you are not the same you. . . .

> It is all a question of the outside being outside and the inside being inside. As long as the outside does not put a value on you it remains outside but when it does put a value on you then it gets inside or rather if the outside puts a value on you then all your inside gets to be outside. (46–48)

Capable, in this account, of turning the writer inside out, the market arguably exerted more immediate pressures on the literary trade than on professions designed and maintained as legal monopolies. The purpose of the latter was in part to forestall the market valuation of experts by a nonexpert public experienced here by the gratefully enriched, but fundamentally disturbed and altered, Gertrude Stein.

Nonetheless the relevance, as a form of group identification, of a more general climate and ethos of "professionalism" to the art-novel is abundantly clear in Henry James's conception of a novelistic "brotherhood" ideally constituted through the shared development of theories, convictions, and self-consciousness. "Art lives upon discussion," he writes, as though calling for an annual convention, "upon the exchange of views and the comparison of standpoints" (*Essays*, 44–45). Elsewhere, describing the cultural privations experienced by the lonely romancer Hawthorne, he claimed that the "best things come, as a general thing, from the talents that are members of a group; every man works better when he has companions working in the same line, and yielding the stimulus of suggestion, comparison, emulation."[45] Mixing, as the ideology of literary professionalism always did, a strong assertion of the need for group membership with an equally strong assertion of the need for an individual authorial distinction (which identity functions as a kind of brand name), professional group membership is understood by James as the precondition for individual distinction as a producer of "best things."[46]

Thus, the emergent institutions and ideologies of the profession provided at least one means for mental laborers to identify and distinguish themselves as workers of a certain kind. But this was by no means the only form of group identity and socialization relevant to the emergence of the art-novel. Standing at some remove from the bourgeois respectability associated with Jamesian professionalism, but no less concerned to secure the status honor of the writer in the market, were the American bohemian coteries that arose in such places as Greenwich Village, Harlem, Chicago, New Orleans, and Stein's Paris early in the century. While the "alternative life-style" of these groups was generally understood to embody a critique of middle-class conventionality and moral probity, they shared with the wider professional-managerial culture not only a typical similarity of origin in the educated middle class, but also, crucially, an identification of the *mind* as the primary producer of value in contemporary culture.[47] These bohemian writers would typically have been mortified to be associated

with the corny spiritualist boosterism and success-ideology of the popular
New Thought movement that produced such works as *The Law of Men-
talism* (1902), *Concentration: The Road to Success* (1907), or *Brains and
How to Get Them* (1917), and it is important to note these differences.[48]
And yet, from our point of remove we can see the shared premises underlying, and no doubt intensifying, the antagonism of free thinking bohemians,
New Thought boosters (which latter claimed a filial relation both to the
Swedenborgian theology of Henry James, Sr., and to the pragmatist psychology of his son William), and the many others in the new middle class
who were asserting the productive value of the mind in the late-nineteenth
and early-twentieth centuries. The trick is to keep hold of a conception of
the professional-managerial class supple enough to register its many internal differentiations without breaking apart altogether.

In fact, in the period under consideration the meaning and understanding of "class" was—as it arguably always has been in the United States—
somewhat confused. For the art-novel this was a productive confusion.
First, as to its definition, one finds competing (though sometimes intertwined) tendencies in the period to understand class either as an essential
biological, genealogical fact—that is, as "caste"—or, alternatively, as in
the nineteenth-century European utilitarian and Marxist traditions, as an
inherently alterable economic and occupational social position. Emphasizing the former tendency, recent cultural studies accounts of class in this
period have for the most part wanted to apply to it the same conceptual
paradigms already developed around issues of race and gender.[49] But while
it is true that one can hardly understand American discourses of class
without accounting for their parallel articulation with questions of race
(e.g., in twenties nativism) and gender (e.g., in conceptions of a feminized
mass readership), this approach runs the risk of diminishing the specific
questions of occupational position, economic standing, and educational
level that "class" contributed to period debates about identity. As we shall
see, to understand the emergence of the art-novel it will be as important
to see race as one (highly privileged) form of social *classification* as it will
be to see class as a form of quasi-racialization.

Second, as to the objective "facts" of class and class relations in the
early-twentieth century: virtually side by side in the period one finds the
claim that "real" class distinctions, insofar as they can be said to have
existed in the United States, are *disappearing* in the new mass culture, as
class identity becomes a matter of mere purchase and theatrical display
on the part of the white-collar mass and, as one sees in a work like Jack
London's *The Iron Heel* (1907), the claim that class distinctions are being
intensified in a context of widespread labor unrest and vicious corporate
militarism. For the Jamesian modernist tradition the former claim, associated with the problem of social indistinction, was certainly the more im-

portant. Indeed, as we will see in James's *The Princess Casamassima* (1886), which converts late-nineteenth-century anarchist politics into an individual identity crisis for a young man of mixed-class parentage, James was typical in absorbing the second claim, that class distinctions are being intensified, into the first, that they are disappearing. He did so by reading through the agitated demands of the working class all the way to their logical conclusion in a (for him) problematic social leveling.

At the same time, the emergence and expansion of relatively new forms and conditions of labor in a managerial economy called into question at least one relatively reliable means of large-scale social differentiation prevalent in the nineteenth century, that drawn between the manual laborer and the capitalist. The mental laborer was neither a manual laborer nor a capitalist, but was situated somewhere between and might seem to have attributes of both. He or she might thus in any given context identify with, or feel antagonism toward, either one. Perhaps most crucially, by contrast both to the small stratum of the capitalist elite and to the notional "aristocracies" of the South and mainline Northeastern cities, the mental worker's access to and participation in the professional-managerial class came by virtue of education, training, and work.[50] While one might become a member of the leisure class simply by being born into this class, the child of the professional would not automatically qualify as—though he or she might predictably become—a professional.

Thus, even as Thorstein Veblen was producing his seminal theorizations of the leisure class at the turn of the century, the rise of the professional-managerial class was gradually altering the symbolic landscape of class privilege in the United States, shifting the emphasis in social elites from the avoidance of dishonorable productive labor—signified by conspicuous consumption and aesthetic waste—to the relative status honor associated with different *kinds* and conditions of labor. Indeed, by midcentury it was possible for the philosopher and theologian Joseph Pieper (introduced to the English-speaking audience by T. S. Eliot) to decry what he perceived as the domination of Western modernity by an ideology of "total work." Most forcefully signaled by the widespread currency of the idea of "intellectual work" and the "intellectual worker"—which for Pieper are at least partial contradictions in terms—this state of affairs called, in his view, for a reinstitution of classical ideals of leisure embodied in a contemplative leisure class.[51] Instead, subsequent years have seen the rise of the proudly workaholic billionaire, the millionaire computer nerd with a cot in his cubicle, and the "overworked American." Thus a completer account of twentieth-century consumer culture—one that pays adequate due to the obvious persistence of the other, "Protestant ethic" half of the deal—should supplement Veblen's "conspicuous consumption" with its terminological inversion, *inconspicuous production*—the mental labor of the mindworker.

The professional-managerial class was under construction in this period, then, both at the level of collective definition and, constitutively, at the level of individual participation. A class under construction, persons under construction as members of this class: these facts will influence this study in several ways. Foremost among them is that even as I set the emergence and establishment of the art-novel in America against the backdrop of relatively new occupational conditions about which one can make some very basic objective historical claims, I wish to downplay as much as possible the idea that modernist fiction is in any direct or obvious sense the expression of a given, a priori extant, social class identity.

One senses considerable force, especially as regards poetry, in Marcus Klein's assertion that American modernism was produced by writers who "tended . . . to come from old American stock," and from families "which either were wealthy or had been wealthy"—and who may thus have been psychologically predisposed to consider themselves in terms of "beleaguered gentry."[52] This would make them recognizable as a version of what Antonio Gramsci called "traditional" intellectuals—cultural elites left over, as it were, from a precapitalist past—contrasting them with "organic" intellectuals who speak directly on behalf of the ascendant commercial middle class. I will, however, emphasize how the texts I examine participate in the discursive production of "class" itself and, more particularly, in the production of various forms of social distinction and status elevation. Attempting to avoid falsely hypostatized notions of social class identity, Pierre Bourdieu has termed this process "classification struggle," and it is this struggle—fought in the realm of representation by people whose job it was, among other things, to classify people—that is my main object here.[53]

While many of writers I examine were able to entertain notions of their inherited place in American society, the cases of James, Crane, Faulkner, and Hammett and the others are more powerfully suggestive of considerable uncertainty about what kind of traditional class placement, if any, they could or would legitimately claim. Gertrude Stein was almost alone—and, in context, somewhat subversive—in so firmly touting her origins in a virtuously "ordinary middle class tradition."[54] For James, perhaps it was his being a putatively "classless" American living in class-structured England that produced this quandary; for Faulkner it may have been the ambiguous relation of the relatively humble circumstances of his upbringing to his Southern family's illustrious past. In any case, the larger tendency was to construct the very "class," the sociointellectual space, that each would ideally inhabit with his or her readers. While we will sometimes see these writers draw upon ideas of aristocracy in their reconstruction of the novel as fine art, it is almost as common, and typically no less a matter of artifice, to see them drawing upon the "pastoral" imagery of urban poverty and ignorance in their self-construction as literary intellectuals and artists. Taking a cue from Perry Anderson, we might explain this by saying that status differentiations *within* an overarching middle class context are forged by means of imaginary attachments to and identifications with social groups perceived to be *outside* this class, whether above it or below.[55]

What became increasingly clear, however, was that what the novelist had, in common with other mental workers, was his or her *mind*—an entity for which the late novels of Henry James could be said to be very long advertisements. It was one of the tasks of the novel after James to make the productive force of intellection evident.

Methodological Philistinism: From Difference to Distinction

Adopting a literary-sociological approach to the art-novel, this book takes inspiration from a tradition of cultural analysis that could be said to originate in the work of James's younger contemporary, the aforementioned Veblen, to pass through some of the seminal theorizations of Max Weber and Karl Mannheim, and to arrive at its most prominent contemporary exponent in the French sociologist Pierre Bourdieu. Less systematically, but undeniably, it also takes inspiration from the quasi-sociological tradition of the realist novel itself, the literary form from which the modernist art-novel emerged and to which it always remained in intimate dialectical relation. It is an oft-noted fact that despite their obvious differences, the epistemological premises and evidentiary attractions of the realist novel frequently bear a strong resemblance to those of a sociology of a certain kind.[56] It is surely no accident that Veblen's first and most important champion was the novelist and editor William Dean Howells, no accident that a Veblenian tradition still somewhat marginal to the discipline of sociology continues to appeal to literary critics. Sounding something like Veblen, the genteel socialist Howells criticized the "aristocratic spirit" he saw taking refuge in the realm of aesthetics, where "pride of caste" could reinvent itself as "pride of taste."[57] This study, especially insofar as it attempts to read the sociological thematics encoded in modernist formal innovations, could thus be said to be a "realist" reading of modernism.

At a broader level, however, it will be organized by the outlook and emphases of what Alfred Gell has called Methodological Philistinism: "philistine" because it declines to participate openly in the discourse of aesthetic judgment. Instead it adopts an indifferent, analytical relation to aesthetic value, much as the sociologist of religion unobjectionably adopts an agnostic relation to the gods.[58] While it might thus, to some, seem to be founded on an ill-advised and somewhat vulgar betrayal of the premises of its own discipline, philistine literary criticism is perhaps inevitably—insofar as it is still recognizable as literary criticism—working on behalf of the modernist literary values and institutions it strategically refuses to endorse. The air of postmodern populism this study frequently gives off, while not exactly disingenuous, is in part an epiphenomenon of its attempt to attain some measure of critical distance from the aesthetic elitism in which it surely partakes. In other words, this study is not only a realist reading of modernism; it is also necessarily, to a degree, a modernist reading of modernism, an immanent critique. Its sociological "vulgarities," touched with a patina of literary-critical intelligence, might well be perceived as beautiful.

For instance, from a certain perspective the literary career, while it may be understood as a thoroughly self-interested game—the crass underbelly of disinterested literary greatness—might also be seen as an entirely legitimate and satisfying genre of performance art in its own right. The stories told here of how Henry James became "Henry James" and then was symbolically beheaded, how Stephen Crane and Edith Wharton recuperated downward social mobility as a career opportunity, how Anita Loos negotiated the links between Hollywood and the Eastern literary establishment in a novel narrated by a stupid person, how the pulp writer Dashiell Hammett became the darling of that same establishment and then fell silent, how "William Faulkner" came to serve as a sign both of Southern and of international modernist distinction, and so on, are compelling ones, particularly as they are refracted into the stories told in the novels themselves. While they incorporate more than a little of what might be thought of as petty (because narrowly self-interested) careerism, these projects of individual authorization are in fact always collective endeavors, and resonate with one of the deepest existential struggles imaginable—the struggle for *recognition*, the dialectical "desire for the desire of others" as it is narrated, for instance, in G. W. F. Hegel's *Phenomenology of Spirit*.

Furthermore, it is clear that the way of reading employed in these pages to uncover and analyze these refractions—alternating between moments of focused textual attention, intertextual connection, and theoretical discussion—invites an intellectual pleasure that one might fairly call "aesthetic," and that has not entirely departed from the gentlemanly reverence for the literary embedded in New Critical techniques of close reading. So, too, what might have been a sort of realist narrative—a straight history—of the emergence of the modernist novel has in the sequence of chapters, and sections within chapters, of this work cracked under the pressure of higher-order theorizations. What is left is something like a cubist construction of the art-novel, an assemblage of arguments, interpretations, characterizations, and caricatures highly calculated in its analytical progression but only loosely ordered as a chronological narrative.

If this approach owes any apologies it is not to literary studies but to the discipline of sociology, some of whose themes and preoccupations it absorbs in order to stage an intellectually intense, multidimensional, and only minimally routinized encounter with some literary and other texts. Reflecting its comfortable embeddedness in the discourses of academic literary criticism, which are in turn embedded in discourses of aesthetic and literary value, the "sociology" of this study might seem, to some, a flagrantly aestheticized and thus highly compromised one. Nonetheless, taking this risk, accepting this fact, the philistine literary critic poses here as an insensitive bystander to beauty, hoping by means of this negation to throw certain aspects of the art-novel into greater conceptual relief.

Guided thus by philistine premises, even as it persists in finding literature terribly interesting, this study will predictably forgo the unmediated assimilation of its objects to paradigms of aesthetic disinterestedness and artistic nobility, tactfully remaining silent on the question of whether these desirable things actually exist. But it will perhaps even more pointedly, because more sympathetically, refuse to assimilate its objects to the covertly flattering paradigms offered in some recent historicist and cultural studies criticism of a Foucauldian cast.

It might seem odd to describe these notoriously hostile approaches to literature in these terms. To listen to the denigrations they inspire on the part of Harold Bloom–style aesthetes—who tend see in critiques of the social power of representations an obnoxious resentment of greatness—one would have thought they were quite philistine enough. And yet, this flattery seems to me the ironic effect of approaches that read through literary works to the massive formations of racial or national identity they are understood to enact, exemplify, or represent. If nothing else, this tendency to referential amplification lends to the literary work a dignity of effective scale that it does not *necessarily* deserve. It does not, that is, make any conceptual allowance for the potential triviality of the literary work as a historical force, or for the relative peculiarity of the cultural symptoms it might bear. This potential is perhaps especially salient to discussions of *modern* literature, which as a function of the relative autonomy achieved by modern cultural producers from the state, the church, and other traditional patrons, becomes all the more detached from the scene of political and other overt exertions of power. Foucauldian criticism has to a surprising degree remained in thrall to the Eliotic fantasy of literary power so ably analyzed (along with much else) by John Guillory, the "most profound assumption of that fantasy" always having been "that literary culture is the site at which the most socially important beliefs and attitudes are produced."[59] (Indeed, one might observe that T. S. Eliot himself, however great his influence in the restricted domain of literature, was, politically speaking, something of a crank.) While it is perhaps true that the critic relinquishes this fantasy at some cost—perhaps it is the entire legitimacy of academic literary studies—the philistine literary-critical perspective at least makes it possible to savor these intuitions of our pointlessness, to take intellectual sustenance from our proximity to our own extinction (whether real or imagined) in a kind of autonecrophilic ecstasy of self-knowledge.

This is, let me be clear, not to say that the novels I examine cannot be read as symptoms of mass ideology and utopia, or as contributions to larger historical formations of cultural identity and difference—the formation of American, or white American, or African American, or male or female or queer or Southern or indeed "professional-managerial" identity. Of course they can and, on a more comprehensive view of the task of literary criticism, probably should be read in this way. What critical philistinism seeks to do, however, is to shadow various literary constructions of identity and difference with difference's conceptual twin, "distinction." For what is "distinction" but a form of "difference" operating on a middling social scale?

In Pierre Bourdieu's well-known book of this title, "distinction" is not so much defined as multivalently deployed to get at the way the discourse of aesthetics has participated in the production and maintenance of status and class hierarchies. Closely akin to unapologetically discriminatory Classical conceptions of "virtue," "distinction" in its purest form is personal superiority perceived not as the laborious effect of social institutions (including the school), but as an emanation of inborn "aristocratic" essence.[60] Distinction in this sense has played an important, if primarily negative, role in the Anglo-American discourse of the novel, representing a scale of human worth that the "middle class" realist novel must, at least to a degree, call into question in favor of Christian or democratic conceptions of virtue—in favor, that is, of the "morality of the herd."

More generally, though, distinction can be conceived simply as a well-nigh omnipresent and transhistorical social *process*: the making, measuring, and symbolizing of status and class differences among persons. Distinction in this sense bears an obvious formal-logical relation to notions of philosophical difference (the separation of "A" from "Not-A") and cultural difference (the separation of "culture A" from "culture B"). It is, however, a specific manifestation of differential logic that articulates class and status hierarchies even within putatively homogenous cultural groups or entities. The effective scale of "distinction," taken up and deployed in reverse as an analytical tool, is thus small enough to register levels of sociological mediation missed in other forms of criticism. These mediations can now be seen to intervene in the processes by which certain literary works—or indeed literary discourse *as such*—are argued to be representative of an identity category, historical period, or social movement. Seeing things in this way, critical philistinism denies that "literary greatness" (or any other attribution of distinction) should necessarily induce us to see the literary work as being transparent to, a spokesperson for, the very large and heterogenous social-historical constructions with which it might plausibly be associated. It suggests that, if anything, the distinction of a given literary work should logically tend to disqualify it from being seen as representative—the question of course always being "representative of what, exactly?" To draw attention to these questions is, in any case, an important initial step toward understanding the rise of the art-novel. Whatever else it was trying to do, and however representative of *something* it necessarily became, modernist fiction was strongly motivated by the desire to be recognized as distinct from popular fiction.

For lack of attention to this middling domain of social and discursive distinctions, Joseph Frank's classic "Spatial Form in Modern Literature" can appear to be a somewhat outlandish account of the phenomena it so ably brings to light.[61] Frank's long essay, appearing at the end of the Second World War, was one of the first and strongest synthetic accounts of modernism, in particular of modern fiction, to appear since Edmund Wilson's *Axel's Castle* in 1931. Thus situated, it can be seen to stand at a crucial pivot in twentieth-century literary history that will serve as the conceptual end point (and also, in a sense, starting point) of this study, when a modernist project that had been pursued largely outside, and often in direct defiance of, academe began to be absorbed, consecrated, and canonized in the expanding postwar university.

For Frank, the radical formal innovations characteristic of the modernist novel are evidence of "man's" discomfort with the shocking and disorienting contemporary history that produces such things as world wars. The modernist novel rejects realist narrative forms, associated with the "temporal" unfolding of history itself, in favor of an ideal of spatial-representational copresence such as one might experience when looking at a painting. Associated with such thematic elements as the "timeless" world of myth, and with imagist poetry's presentations in an "instant of time," this narrative ideal, as Frank describes it, seems to run contrary to the "time-cult," the submissive acceptance of "flux" that Wyndham Lewis saw, along with the primitivist child-cult, at the center of literature in his time. This depends on how one reads Lewis, who in fact begins his own account of *Time and Western Man* with the admitted "paradox" that while the writers of his period evinced a sloppy attraction to the Bergsonian *duree*, their more explicit theories of culture were almost invariably arguments for "timelessness."[62]

Rejecting realist forms of narration, the literature of "spatial form," in Frank's account, also asks for a conspicuously difficult mode of reading.

He calls this mode of reading "reflexive reference," in that the reader is asked to maintain an active relation to other moments in the text even as he or she can look only at the one before his or her eyes. The meaning of a given textual moment, in this view, is not to be gained by referring it to a parallel, extratextual domain of reference but to other places in the text. Ideally, Frank argues, one would comprehend the modernist work not consecutively but, as it were, all at once. "As it were," indeed: Frank is careful to remind his readers that this ideal is in denial of what we know necessarily to be the case about reading a text. Conveniently if inconclusively represented by the linearity of type, it unfolds in time.

Borrowing an interpretive scheme made available in Wilhelm Worringer's *Abstraction and Empathy* (1908), Frank argues that the appearance of these modern spatial tendencies in narrative is but one moment in a long history of artistic representation dominated alternately by "naturalistic" and "nonnaturalistic" styles. In the first, the artist "strives to represent the objective, three-dimensional world of 'natural' vision and to reproduce with loving accuracy the processes and forms of organic nature (among which man is included)," while in the second he or she "abandons the projection of space entirely and returns to the plane, reduc[ing] organic nature to linear-geometric forms." These naturalistic and nonnaturalistic styles, each with its own characteristic deployment of representational space, are in turn related to the dominant "spiritual conditions" of the places and periods in which they appear. Naturalism and three-dimensionality are characteristic of times of "equilibrium between man and cosmos," when either "man feels himself at one with organic nature" or he feels confidently able to dominate it (53). Nonnaturalistic abstraction and the flattening of representation occur at times of historical "disharmony and disequilibrium," offering a "stability," "harmony," and "sense of order" unavailable in the external world itself.

As will become particularly clear in chapter 2, where I examine the rethinking of represented or "fictional" space involved in Henry James's attempt to elevate the status of the novel, I think Frank has noticed something important here. Furthermore, he has framed the modernist attraction to "spatial form" in such a way as to make Lewis's critique of the "time-cult" seem somewhat one-sided, since Frank is able to account for the obvious sense in which, for instance, Marcel Proust's "remembrances" signified not only a lazy submission to flux but also an effort to hold time still in the disciplined spaces of text and memory. While the idea of "reflexive reference," as Frank describes it, sounds perhaps too much like a description of one aspect of any reading of any narrative, the modernist novel does indeed conduct an occasional, practical inquiry into the form of the literary object that Frank's spatial terminology is helpful in describing.

The more consequential weakness of his account stems, in my view, from its social generality, whose explanatory limits become visible if one simply remembers that the vast majority of novels produced in the so-called modernist period, as in our period, took a recognizably "naturalistic" or realist form. The briefest glance at the century's best-seller lists confirms this, which in turn suggests that the assertion that modern spatial fiction reflects "man's" discomfort with inharmonious history might be a little blunt. On the evidence of the literary market seen as a wide and highly articulated social field, we would have to say that the fiction of "spatial form" appears only in a relatively circumscribed and, indeed, somewhat rarified position within this field, reflecting the preoccupations, interests, and ambitions of only certain writers and readers.

In its sociological bluntness, Frank's essay shares some of the descriptive weakness of the otherwise powerful critical tradition from which he borrows. The "sociology of genres" or "philosophy of the history of literary forms"—emerging in the general climate of Hegelian aesthetics that produced both Worringer's *Abstraction and Empathy* and Georg Lukács's better-known *Theory of the Novel*—was, in its time, a uniquely powerful attempt to account for the dynamic relation of literary form to historical change.[63] Declining the vulgar formalism that sees literary genres as ideal constructs, or as expressions of timeless structures of the human imagination, this mode of historical analysis made possible the kinds of claims about the novel-form that have become so familiar and, for all their difficulties, so useful to literary critics. Primary among these, no doubt, is Ian Watt's influential claim that its rise as a dominant genre is associated with the ascendance of realist epistemologies and individualist ideologies, and is of a piece with the rise of the commercial middle class.

Nonetheless, the potential limitations of his mode of explanation were clear to Lukács himself by the time he wrote his 1962 preface to *The Theory of the Novel*, when the sheer abstraction of an account like his own—or, we can assume, like Frank's—seemed to him woefully "cut off from concrete sociohistorical realities" (17). Whatever misgivings one might have about the criterion of "concreteness" as a way of judging interpretations, any reader of *The Theory of the Novel* will likely see Lukács's point that a tremendous of amount of potentially relevant detail has been left out of his account of the novel as the "epic of an age in which the extensive totality of life is no longer directly given, in which the immanence of meaning in life has become a problem, yet which still thinks in terms of totality" (56).[64] The same is true, I think, of accounts of the "spatial form" of modern fiction that posit it as an effect of humankind's discomfort with modern history.

Thus, without insisting too much on the extremity of the theoretical renovations entailed in doing so, one can see how the sociology of literary forms can be made, at a minimum, more interestingly sociological by paying closer attention to the specific social groups and institutions in whose loose orbit certain kinds of texts are produced and received (or not). This corrective might then be brought to bear on Frank's reading of the novel that emerges, in his essay, as the prime example of a spatial narrative that asks for the mode of reading termed "reflexive reference," and that leaves behind any aspirations of conventional, "naturalistic" narrative development. This novel is none other than Djuna Barnes's *Nightwood*.

Frank is extremely helpful to any effort to understand this text. Indeed, his patient piecing through of the novel's major themes and his incisive characterizations of its form speak well for the larger project his reading begins to enact: the domestication of gamy modernist narratives like *Nightwood* for the various purposes, pedagogical and otherwise, of the university. And yet, even to situate his reading in this manner is to begin to rewrite—by insisting on a supplementary echo of the term "autonomous structure"—Frank's account of a novel about which we "are asked only to accept the work of art as an autonomous structure giving us an individual vision of reality" (28). It was perhaps only in the relatively autonomous structures of the postwar university, where academic literary criticism was beginning to consolidate around New Critical paradigms, that "the question of the relation of this vision to an extra-artistic 'objective' world" could have been said to have "ceased to have any fundamental importance" (28). I doubt that even Henry James would have countenanced such a severe detachment.

For Frank the central object of this novel, as for the various characters who injure themselves by desiring her, is the young woman named Robin Vote. Described in Barnes's text as a child playing "with her toys, trains, and animals" and as a "beast turning human," this woman who smells of "earth-flesh" and "fungi" symbolizes, for Frank, "a state of existence which is before, rather than beyond, good and evil" (33). Carelessly damaging those who would protect and provide for her, the "primitive" woman Robin "is both innocent and depraved—meet of child and desperado— precisely because she has not reached the human state where moral values become relevant" (33). She is, in short, an "amorphous mass" (34), and as such she is recognizable, from our perspective, as an instance of the pastoral "simpleton" who so often seems to be at the center of the difficult modernist novel. Nora Flood, writes Barnes, "had the face of all people who love the people—a face that would be evil when she found out that to love without criticism is to be betrayed" (*Nightwood* 51). So is Robin to be understood as a personification of the forceful corporeality of "the people"? While Baron Felix Volkbein—the pretentious "Viennese half- Jew" who like his father pays "remorseless homage to nobility"—attempts to assimilate Robin Vote to his theatricalized world of European aristocracy, the "democratic" Nora would accept Robin for the primitive "mass" that she is and that she personifies. Neither, however, is able to raise her from the level of the beast.

That, even while retaining some of his terms of analysis, *Nightwood* might be read in more specific terms than Frank allows is well demonstrated by Erin Carlston, who situates its resistance to realist narrative forms both in the tradition of fin de siècle Decadence and in its most relevant contemporary political context, 1930s Catholic fascism.[65] Resisting the "optimistic positivism and sentimentality of bourgeois Victorianism" (44), Barnes's "Sapphic" discourse also, in Carlston's account, resists normative, procreative sexuality, combining *"l'art pour l'art"* with *"le sexe pour le sexe"* (46). Valorizing sterility as a kind of stasis, a resistance to the transindividual temporality of "generations," Barnes's novel reemerges in Carlston's reading as existing in a remarkably dense network of particular influences and aspirations. Most importantly, by linking it to the tradition of Decadence, she draws attention to a use of language that is, in Arthur Symons's term, "deliberately abnormal" (quoted in Carlston, *Thinking Fascism*, 50)—which is to say incomprehensible except in *active contrast* to what Eliot had called the "daily simple needs of communication" found in the newspaper.

Barnes's novel can be further specified as a distinct form of novelistic discourse if we read these themes in relation to the literary field as it existed when Barnes wrote. First we could say that, representing both the attractions and repulsions of "the mass," Robin's earthy existence in a state "before good and evil" embodies the Nietzschean unseating of conventional discourses of virtue that "obscene" modernist novels, including *Nightwood*, so frequently attempted to enact. Barnes's fascination with deviance had prompted Eliot, in his introduction, to defend the novel in advance against charges that it was, in essence, a freak show. And yet of course it *was* intended, at the very least, as an antibourgeois initiative, borrowing the primitive power of Robin's immorality in order to distinguish itself from the ordinary run of "respectable" middle class realist novels. Barnes's text would then have, from our perspective, one more important piece of business to transact. This is to use Robin as a "pastoral" foil in the dialectical production of a conspicuously intellectualized, sophisticated discourse that would identify the novel as an art-novel.

It first does this intradiegetically, by introducing the bizarre, brilliant, and loquacious American doctor Matthew O'Connor. In his long and difficult monologues, taking up almost half of the novel's pages, Joseph Frank hears the very voice of the "sophisticated self-consciousness" that Henry James hoped would be brought to bear on the genre as a whole. In some ways reminiscent, as we shall see, of James's use of stupid "fools" to throw the intelligence of his featured ruminators into relief, Barnes's juxtaposition of a primitive object, Robin, and a conspicuously intelligent speaking subject, Matthew O'Connor, reproduces at the level of character relations the relation of the "poetic" novel itself to its early-twentieth-century mass cultural context. This, we recall, was the domain of novels that, according to T. S. Eliot, merely mime the "daily simple needs of communication" for "ordinary" novel readers.

For Eliot, writing the introduction to the work, O'Connor's "brilliant and witty" monologues had initially been the thing in the text that had secured his attention and respect for Barnes's novel. Later he began to see them as parts of a larger whole, and in turn began to appreciate the sheer semantic density of its unusual prose. This, though it occasioned a meditation on the status of the novel very similar, in some of its premises, to that initiated by Henry James some decades earlier, was to envision the form of the art-novel in ways that James might barely have recognized.

Though he could turn an impressive metaphor, which metaphor might be intermittently developed across hundreds of pages of text, James's unusual sophistication as an artist was made evident, at the level of the sentence, not by means of intensely "poetic" and tenebrous sentences like Barnes's. Rather, it was by heroically complex exertions of English grammatical structure, and by virtuoso demonstrations, therein, of the mental labor of making distinctions, that James announced himself as Jamesian. To borrow the terminology of structuralist linguistics, he put far more pressure on the axis of combination than on the axis of selection, which latter is the domain of the metaphor and the fascinating word, so much so that Gertrude Stein suspected his sentences of aspiring to the condition of the paragraph. Invested more and more, over the course of his career, in formal structures of arrangement rather than in the particularity of the thing, this increasingly abstract mode of writing harmonized with, even as it produced obvious tensions within, James's efforts to find a "perfect" structure and "rounded" shape for the novel as a whole.

This ideal of novel-as-art-object is remembered in highly charged symbols such as James's own (flawed) "well-wrought urn," the golden bowl in *The Golden Bowl*, and it has no particular purchase on the conspicuously jagged *Nightwood*. Barnes's novel is written after the shattering of the golden bowl and, even more relevantly, after the appearance of such texts as Joyce's *Ulysses* and the "heap of broken images" that was Eliot's own *Waste Land*. It invests itself far more in local intensities of effect than in an overall schema of thematic development, and James might very well have dismissed it on these grounds. Similarly might he have dismissed, though on other grounds, the ponderous, expansive, and incomprehensible repetitions of Stein, as well as most of the novels of William Faulkner. The latter—as chaotic, unfinished "part-objects" of an ever-absent whole, the "apocryphal" history of Yoknapatawpha County—gestured to an ideal unity James would no doubt have preferred to see realized in some way in the individual text-object itself. James, too, valued thought over thing, but he accepted that it was the destiny of his authorial consciousness to become reified as a well-made object—a text.

It is important to register, in this fashion, the various formal alternatives and emphases available to the art-novelist after James, and to give some account of the particular sets of influences and other determinations that made one approach to the art-novel seem more appealing or necessary than another. But so, too, is it important to keep hold of the relative continuity, still so plainly evident in Eliot's introduction to *Nightwood*, of James's more general project of renegotiating the genre's aesthetic status. Indeed, given the remarkable heterogeneity of narrative forms with which it is associated, one of the strongest definitions one can advance of the so-called modernist novel—after one has noted its remarkably persistent interest in the mind and, relatedly, in rigorous experiments in "point of view"—is rather simply, but also powerfully, that it is the novel conceived of as "art," and thus as a bearer of cultural capital. While one can trace strong lines of influence from James into the twentieth century, when a reading of the Master became de rigeur for "serious" novelists (including Dashiell Hammett) setting out on their careers, the Jamesian tradition in the American novel is Jamesian less in its faithful adherence to any given narrative mode than in its effort to produce works that could be, as he put it, "reputed artistic indeed."

Listening to the Jamesian echoes that emerge in Eliot's agonized promotional introduction to *Nightwood*, more transparent in its relation to market forces than Frank's scholarly essay would be, we begin to recover an intentional oddness in Barnes's novel that Frank's account of its representative "spatial form" is allowed to forget. We begin to recover the price of that oddness, a price paid in potential readers lost, as well as the specific forms of honor this oddness—this literary distinction—was intended to win. By extension, the way of reading the Jamesian tradition in American fiction that I pursue in the following pages will, I hope, allow us to recover, so as to ponder, with suspicion but not without fascination, some of the distinction of the art-novel as a whole.

The Mind's Eye and Mental Labor

Forms of Distinction in the Fiction of Henry James

> A receptacle of Revelation and privileged bearer of the
> messianic kerygma, the container benefited over the long run
> from the contents' sacredness, such that "to believe in the
> Book" and to believe in God gradually became synonymous.
> The religions of the Book did indeed dematerialize the divine,
> yet . . . they were not able to do so without rendering divine
> the material tool of this dematerialization, without enthroning
> and ritualizing the access to the Word's sacred place: the
> Codex as house of God.
> —Régis Debray, "The Book as Symbolic Object"

The Novel as Masterpiece

Charlotte and Amerigo take a fateful step: they go shopping. Passing
through the glass doors of a little store in Bloomsbury, they find it inhabited
by "the master," a man "devoted to his business," an uncanny "entertainer" who fixes "on his visitors an extraordinary pair of eyes" while they
themselves examine the succession of "small pieces"—and finally the pièce
de résistance—he offers for sale:

> "My Golden Bowl," he observed—and it sounded on his lips as if it said every-
> thing. He left the important object—for as "important" it did somehow present
> itself—to produce its certain effect. Simple but singularly elegant . . . it justified
> its title by the charm of its shape as well as by the tone of its surface.[1]

The bowl is conspicuous. Is there another artifact in Henry James's fiction
that calls attention to itself in quite the same way? If it is true that James's
novels are littered with meaningful things—M. de Bellegarde's letter (*The
American*), Gilbert Osmond's coin (*Portrait of a Lady*), Chad Newsome's
uncut book (*The Ambassadors*), to name a few—then it is also true that
the "master's" golden bowl in *The Golden Bowl* (1904) is unlike any of
these things in the magnitude of its self-assertion. Indeed, the bowl is "important" enough to have lent its "title" to the object, the novel, in which
it appears. Reciprocally, the novel itself, which might have been mistaken

for something quite different, is strongly associated with this important—though, as we learn, flawed—work of art. Famously, James would "hold the thing the solidest" and most "done" of his productions.[2]

Furthermore if it is true, as F. O. Matthiessen once suggested, that James's novels in the late, difficult "major phase" come increasingly to be organized around static images—a dove, a Palladian church, a pagoda—rather than a plotted succession of events, then it is also true that the golden bowl is not quite like these images, for it is not an image, or not only an image, but an object, too.[3] Maggie Verver's pagoda, for instance, is the private property of her fancy, a metaphor she produces for her "funny" situation, which is why it might alternatively be "some strange tall tower of ivory" (*Golden Bowl*, 327). By contrast the bowl, always a bowl, is understood to be embodied in the same world inhabited by the novel's characters. It is a "solid" production. It has a public role in the story, as a body of evidence, in a way the imaginary pagoda cannot: " 'That bowl,' " Maggie will say, acting the detective, " 'is, so strangely—too strangely almost to believe at this time of day—the proof' " of her husband's adultery (436). It has " 'turned witness—by the most wonderful of chances' " (437), to Amerigo's intimacy with Charlotte. The golden bowl haunts *The Golden Bowl*, but it is curious kind of haunting, having less to do with the rattling of restless spirits than with the hard fact of the object.

Conspicuous, concrete, mysterious—the golden bowl in *The Golden Bowl*, unusual as it may be in the work of James, recalls a long lineage in literary history of similarly uncanny objects. One thinks, for instance, of the marble faun in Hawthorne's *The Marble Faun* (1860), of the moonstone in Wilkie Collins's *The Moonstone* (1868)—even, looking ahead, of the Maltese falcon in Dashiell Hammett's *The Maltese Falcon* (1930). Each of these objects announces what Laurence Holland, referring to *The Golden Bowl*, called an "unbroken analogy between itself as a fictive creation and the action it projects or the life it images"—announces, indeed, a convergence of formal and thematic *mysteries*.[4] Ekphrastic emblems of the "consciousness of self" that Henry James hoped would be brought to bear on the novel genre as a whole, they appear in works that are quite diverse but for their tendency to meditate, not on themselves alone, but on the nature of their relation to the external world in which they will circulate. They ask, that is, not only what kind of object a novel is, but also what social role, if any, this kind of object can play once it is made. They manage this double meditation by resisting the last degree of narrative self-consciousness that would simply collapse the world in which the titular object circulates, admitting that it's all just print, disabling the fictive dream. Rather, they sustain a tension between their primary commitment to realize a fictional world—to tell a believable story about some people and a special object—and their tendency to become arrested by the uncanny fact of their own objecthood. In the interplay of these impulses, social thematics become questions of narrative form and, in turn, formal questions become attached to social thematics.

There is, however, one problem of representation in particular that these texts could be said to manifest in this multivalent sense: what is the relation of the text-object to the image? W. J. T. Mitchell has called this the problem of the "imagetext," in which the respective representational regimes of words and pictures are at once thoroughly entwined and mutually antagonized.[5] The problem with pictures, roughly, is a perceived deficit in their production of discursive meaning, the risk that words will assert themselves in this gap and begin to colonize the picture's representational project. The problem with texts is the gap between what they actually offer to vision, arbitrary signs strung across a page, and the invisible images they would evoke in the mind's eye of the reader. Joseph Conrad's famed call in 1897 for a literary impressionism—"before all, to make you *see!*"—is only a particularly intense moment in a complex history of the text's visionary aspirations.[6] In Hawthorne's *The Marble Faun*, as Joseph Kestner has argued, an invisible political conspiracy is juxtaposed to the equally mysterious origin of fictional illusion, in particular of characters who arise from the flat page upon which they are scripted to assume the sculptural volume represented by the statue of the faun.[7] *The Moonstone* offers an analogy between a diamond—it was once the luminous eye of an Indian idol—threatened with division into several smaller diamonds, and the novel itself, so elaborately broken into the accounts of several different "eyewitness" narrators. In *The Maltese Falcon* the falcon is a kind of grail, a holy object whose absence signals a dispersal of identity in the violent circulation of visible, but existentially counterfeit, representations contained in the detective novel.

As we shall see, versions of these convergent mysteries converge again in James's novel and James's object. Perhaps most notably, however, does the golden bowl in *The Golden Bowl* recall the purloined letter in Edgar Allan Poe's "The Purloined Letter" (1840), which like the bowl is evidence of adultery, and which like the bowl—and faun, and stone, and falcon—lends its title to the text in which it appears. For John Irwin, "The Purloined Letter" partakes of a genre of "symbolist works" of "textual self-inclusion"—his other examples are *Moby Dick* and *The Scarlet Letter*—where "the qualities the text attributes to the symbolic object are for the most part the attributes of the text itself."[8] In the case of the letter, the "distinctive feature" of this object is its "eversion": it is turned inside out and "hidden" in full view. The letter thus "evokes the principal mystery of writing—that letters (written characters) on the surface of a sheet of paper somehow physically 'contain' or 'conceal' something metaphysical" (22). James's version of this eversion takes the form, as we saw above, of his drawing simultaneous attention to the bowl's surface and to its shape. Over a surface of "perfect crystal" has been applied "by some beautiful old process" a layer of gold. And while this may, at a stretch, seem to recall the application of ink to the perfect whiteness of a page, the mystery is how this surface also functions as a vessel, a bowl empty to all appearances but in fact a container of representations.

For Irwin, the self-inclusion of "The Purloined Letter" is echoed, in its structure, not only in the events represented in the story itself, but also outside the text, at its surface, in the famed series of psychoanalytic and deconstructive interpretations of this story by Jacques Lacan, Jacques Derrida, and Barbara Johnson.[9] The text's self-inclusion, Irwin argues, is an act of self-reflection that attempts to totalize identity by allowing consciousness—or in this case representation—to take itself as its own object. This structure is replicated in the story in Dupin's attempts to outwit the Minister, who functions as his double, a visible exteriorization of the self-as-other, an outward sign of internal ontological division. To "outwit" the Minister would be, in an ideal sense, to overcome the logic of identity that decrees that consciousness can represent itself to itself only as other. In the interpretations of the story, similarly, this structure appears as the attempt to outwit a previous interpreter who functions as the critic's double, and in that outwitting to produce an interpretive position—a "third" position, neither subject nor object—so self-transparent as to have transcended the contradictions of consciousness.

But none of these gestures, Irwin notes, can really overcome the antinomy that forces a wedge between the knower and the known, and that leaves a necessary blind spot or residue of otherness in any project of self-knowledge. This, in Irwin's *The Mystery to a Solution*, is the "mystery" that stubbornly persists in any "solution." It is also, importantly, what he uses to justify his reading of the detective story as "high art"—high art being defined for him by its resistance to interpretive closure. Thus the drama of self-establishment Irwin recounts, never truly completed, takes the form of a perpetual agon orbiting around the virtual "high art" object, the letter itself, which is never truly possessed by anyone. For the story's characters as for its critics, the presence of the text as an embodied object suggests the structural availability, or inherent publicity, this text shares with any other visible object (*The Golden Bowl* will get at this idea of availability in the museum, the public space in American City in which Adam Verver's precious objects are destined to show). But at the same time, by insisting upon the gap between this physical presence and the object's esoteric meaning, the text is established as an object of competitive interpretation, where characters and critics alike vie to be the one truly to "see" and therefore to possess—possess knowledge of—the object.

Thus the apparent paradox of the letter's being "hidden" in full view. Running parallel to an ambiguity of "seeing" as either physical sensation or conceptual understanding (where "I see" means "I understand"), this means on one level that eyes will miss the text-object, and on another level that minds will misunderstand or "not get" the text-object. In both cases vision is the primary sensory authorization of knowledge: to see is to know. However, in the first case one is merely an *eyewitness* to the existence of the text, while in the second one is something of a *visionary*. In "The Purloined Letter" the detective figure is distinguished by his privileged relation less to the visible object itself than to the knowledge that object contains. Operating both within the fictive world of the text and at its surface, questions of form are interwoven with themes of social relation: the text represents inequalities of knowledge and also produces (or aspires to produce) them.

The applicability of this model of intellectual distinction and double vision—vision empirical and metaphysical, realist and romantic—to *The Golden Bowl* is suggested early in the novel, when Charlotte Stant and Amerigo meet after a separation during which Amerigo has become engaged to the rich young American, Maggie Verver. Here, however, the reading of this text as "high art" is not something the critic must justify to his readers, but something the text seems to ask for on its own behalf. Registering the text's allegorical self-assertion as a "golden bowl"—as a mysterious instance of fine art—we begin to see the interpretive agon surrounding the text-object not, or not only, as a mechanism for differentiating the individual "in the know" from the one without. It is also a model of the social differentiation of different groups of interpreters—different kinds of readers—in the common space of print culture. The problem of "high art" fiction with which Irwin begins his account of Poe—and which he addresses merely as the capacity of the high art text to support "unlimited rereading"—might, that is, be read back into some of the social and historical contexts of its appearance. When *The Golden Bowl* was published, the idea of the novel's potential as "high art" was not exactly new, but neither could it be taken for granted, and this, as we shall see, had everything to do with how the genre's audience was conceived.

Amerigo sees Charlotte once again: here the object of interpretation is a human body, an object explicitly of interpretive desire. When Charlotte enters Fanny Assingham's parlor, she directs herself to Fanny rather than to Amerigo, and this "discrimination of but a moment" allows the Prince to read the "reference in all her person" at considerable length, given the amount of narrated time in which his reading presumably occurs:

He saw her in her light: that immediate exclusive address to their friend was like a lamp she was holding aloft for his benefit and for his pleasure. It showed him everything—above all her presence in the world, so closely, so irretrievably contemporaneous with his own: a sharp, sharp fact . . . accompanied . . . with those others . . . that Mrs. Assingham had been speaking of as subject to appreciation. So they were . . . and that was the connexion they instantly established with him. If they had to be interpreted this made at least for intimacy. There was but one way certainly for *him*—to interpret them in the sense of the already known. (72)

At first this might seem strange: Charlotte establishes intimacy with the Prince not by speaking to him, but by ignoring him. Saying nothing, establishing her presence only as a body that he can observe, she thereby gives him something to interpret.[10] While the shopman's " 'My Golden Bowl' " seems to "say everything," Charlotte's indirection "show[s] everything." For Charlotte and Amerigo the silent relation of observer to observed seems a more intimate one than can be established by talk, as though in that purely specular relation one is able to reproduce the most intimate relation of all, the relation to the self. Meanwhile Fanny, directly addressed by Charlotte's voice, misses the encoded messages sent by her body. Not so Amerigo, who as he reads Charlotte's body finds that the "sharp, sharp fact" of this body is gradually assimilated, via his eyes, to his mind, where its empirical otherness is mixed with the mental possessions of memory. She has been "known" in the past, has Charlotte, and now she is recognized as his carnal-intellectual property once again. This is why it is "strangely, as a cluster of possessions of his own that these things in Charlotte Stant now affected" (72) Amerigo, the descendant of Vespucci who will find in Poe's Arthur Gordon Pym, voyaging to the obliterating whiteness of the South Pole, an analogy for his own inability to "see"—to understand—the other Americans with whom he consorts.

   Addressed here thematically, the conversion of visible matter into intellectual property that occurs in Amerigo's erotic-phenomenological drama can also be found hovering just at the boundary of the novel's fictive world, where it is an issue for its author. We see this in the 1909 preface to the novel James wrote for the New York Edition of his works. The "collective edition" had been conceived as early as 1904, around the time of the completion of *The Golden Bowl,* and like this novel, though on a much larger scale, it would be intended by James as the creation of a sort of masterpiece. Revised to reflect his latest refinements of style, and supplied with the now-famous prefaces, the volumes in this edition would, James hoped, appear in the form of what he called "Handsome Books"—beautiful, high-quality objects.[11] The New York Edition would be James's artfully reconstructed version of his career as an artist, an ideality manifest materially as a set of handsome and durable things. The New York Edition carried this symbolic burden even as it was also hoped, simply, that it would make James and his publishers at Scribner's some money, as similar editions in this time were known to do. This revisioning was also, as Michael Anesko has detailed, a repackaging, and one attended by considerable wrangling over issues of payment and copyright.[12] Alas, by this point the wide audience that James had begun to lose in the late 1880s could not be lured back to him with handsome books, and the laboriously prepared edition was a miserable commercial failure.

In the preface to *The Golden Bowl* the formation (or recognition) of intellectual property in the meeting of Amerigo and Charlotte is transposed to the relation between the author and the texts he has produced in the past, texts that he must now revise—that is, *see again*. In the task of revision he has undertaken, James explains, he first becomes a reader, or interpreter, of himself. As a reader of a recent text like *The Golden Bowl* he "meets" himself as author "halfway, passive, receptive, appreciative, often even grateful; unconscious . . . [of] any disparity of sense between us. Into his very footprints the responsive, the imaginative steps of the docile reader that I consentingly become for him all comfortably sink." By contrast, in the case of works written long ago, like *The Princess Casamassima* (1886), this begins to look like an encounter with a self who, though bearing his own proper name, has become an other: "nothing in my whole renewal of attention to these things . . . was more evident than that no such active, appreciative process could take place . . . thanks to the so frequent lapse of harmony between my present mode of motion and that to which the existing footprints were due" (26). Revising these earlier works thus becomes, as in the repurloining of the letter in Poe's story, an *"act* of reappropriation" of an alienated authorial self and of intellectual property that seems, with time, to have drifted from his ontological grasp, though perhaps not from his legal one. As a reviser of his own work, James becomes a model of the strong reader—not the eyewitness but the visionary—appropriating the text by reseeing/remaking it his own. In doing so he is not only reclaiming an "other" text as his intellectual property, he is making apprentice texts into masterful ones, novels into art.

But if James, in revision, is the model of the strong reader, then what about the actual readers of his work, for whom it does not signify *intellectual property* so much as—though clearly the two are related, one recognized legally, one socially—*cultural capital*? At this point we begin to see another, more plainly sociological and divisive dimension to the question of intellectual property infiltrating and attaching itself to the art-novel *The Golden Bowl*. We can track this by noting an odd similarity in the preface between the way James describes his writing—it is a "mode of motion" that leaves "footprints"—and, a bit earlier, his account of his walks through London with the photographer A. L. Coburn in search of photographic subjects for the frontispieces of the New York Edition.[13] Speaking of this search, James produces this explicit meditation on the problem of

the imagetext, a problem so important, indeed, that it "may well inspire
in the lover of literature certain lively questions as to the future of that
institution":

> The essence of any representational work is of course to bristle with immediate
> images; and I, for one, should have looked much askance at the proposal . . . to
> graft or "grow," at whatever point, a picture by another hand on my own pic-
> ture—this being, always, to my sense, a lawless incident. Which remark reflects
> heavily, of course, on the "picture book" quality that contemporary English and
> American prose appears more and more destined, by the conditions of publica-
> tion, to consent.(23)

He refers to the increasing tendency of publishers at the turn of the century
to supplement novels with pictures, texts with images.[14] They did so in an
effort to orient fiction to the mass market, to the tastes of a "mass reader"
who, though arguably centuries in the making, was perceived by James
and others to be making a sudden and shocking appearance in the domain
of literature.

The problem of the "picture book" is, in other words, closely tied to a
larger preoccupation James had taken up in essays such as "The Future
of the Novel" (1899), where the fate of that "institution" is explicitly tied
to the new homogenous "multitude," the "total swarm" now able to "possess itself in one way or another of the *book*." James's conception of the
novel, the dominant book genre in mass print culture, as a genre dominated, held hostage to a mass readership for whom "taste is but a confused,
immediate instinct," was shared by his fellow American novelist Charles
Dudley Warner: "This is pre-eminently the age of the novel," wrote Warner. "Everybody reads novels" (169). Like James, Warner attributed this
growth in the reading public to the spread of schooling, but he was as little
impressed by the "level of its intelligence" as James. Noting, as would
T. S. Eliot many years later, the novel's proximity to lowly journalism, the
critic George Saintsbury would in 1892 complain of the novel that "its
substance must always be life not thought, conduct not belief, the passions
not the intellect, manners and morals not creeds and theories"—and would
argue, in the interest of brainier books, for a return to romance.[15]

For James, worried about the future of his beloved generic "institution,"
the crisis of the novel in his time was a crisis of popularity, a state of
affairs that, for all that it was an economic opportunity, suggested a loss
of authorial agency at the hands of the coercive "conditions of publication"
to which the novelist must consent. If the "swarm" demanded pictorial
images more immediate in their effects than the mental images created by
words, then Coburn, as a photographer, was the potential agent of this
swarm. The compound of media and of intentionalities in the illustrated
literary text seems to James a "lawless" confusion not unrelated, we might

surmise, to the lawless social confusions bankrolled by the American money of Adam Verver in the novel.

But while this crisis of popularity suggested a loss of authorial agency it also suggested, in turn, a crisis of stupidity. And illustrations were, in a sense, the visible form of this stupidity, the *graven images* that would sully the spirit-pictures hidden in James's words. Illustrations would not only compete with these mental images, but they would be too easy, like the pictures in children's primers that tie word to image; accurately or not, they would suggest passive consumption and not active mental production (a distinction that would return in debates about the relative intellectual value of watching television and reading). Thus James would argue that "one should, as an author, reduce one's reader, 'artistically inclined,' to such a state of hallucination by the images one has evoked as doesn't permit him to rest till he has noted or recorded them, set up some semblance of them in his own other medium" (23). This "other medium" is of course the reader's mind. Thus the " 'artistic' " reader is an acceptable co-artist, the reader's mind is an acceptable "other medium," but the illustrator and his medium are not.

James believed he had found a satisfactory solution to his problem of the imagetext in the way Coburn's photos did not "keep, or to pretend to keep, anything like dramatic step with their suggestive matter." Instead, "discreetly disavowing emulation," they "were to remain at the most small pictures of our 'set' stage with the actors left out" (24). This is in fact a rather imprecise description of what one actually sees when one looks at the twenty-three frontispieces: many doors, most of them shut tight. Indeed, perhaps because we are given only a tantalizing peek over a high wall, never has a door seemed so massively shut as the one in the frontispiece to *The American*, unless it be the door to the convent into which Christopher Newman's love-object disappears in the novel itself (see fig. 1). One sees mostly doorways in these photographs, a handful of bridges and other arching apertures, a few exteriors of buildings, and one park bench. Given the fully furnished, indoor world that James's characters tend to inhabit, one would have to say that there are in fact very few "stage sets" among the photographs, only one of which is even taken indoors. Rather, with one telling exception, these photographs leave one on the outside of the "house of fiction," unable to see inside (see fig. 2).[16] The question they most interestingly raise is not one of intentionality but of *access*: who will be allowed through these doors into the representation, or "volume," to which they are the literal and figurative entryway? Who will be allowed to see what's inside? But then again, who even *cares* to see what's inside?

It was in part the massive popularity of the novel, in whose bounty James so desperately wanted, did not want, was not able to share that provoked him and others to rethink the formal values of their genre, in

Figure 1. A. L. Coburn's "Faubourg St. Germain," frontispiece to *The American*, volume 2 of *The Novels and Tales of Henry James*. Reproduced by permission of the Harry Ransom Humanities Research Center, University of Texas at Austin.

turn to contribute to a form of social distinction taking place in any number of contexts "outside" their genre: intellectual distinction. The "high art" text may, as Irwin suggests, be characterized by its capacity to support endless rereading, but it was also characterized by its capacity to divide its readership into insiders and outsiders. The reader of James—the Jamesian—was not an aristocrat, exactly, but something else, a certain kind of

Figure 2. A. L. Coburn's "The Court of the Hotel," frontispiece to *The Reverberator*, in volume 13 of *The Novels and Tales of Henry James*. Reproduced by permission of the Harry Ransom Humanities Research Center, University of Texas at Austin.

aesthete-intellectual able to share the Master's endless enthusiasm for the mental labor of making distinctions. This kind of intellectual could lay claim to a superiority to "the mass"—indeed, in a sense that will become clearer in chapter 2, could lay claim to a superiority to matter as such. Indeed, ever-more expansive in consciousness, the Jamesian could turn so much matter into mind it is a wonder he or she had need for any texts at all.[17] Why bother with the book? Why risk this dependence on the vulgar, visible materiality of paper and print? This equivocation would echo through modernism, so preoccupied with the mind, so preoccupied with the nature of the literary object, in its braided fascinations with empirical and metaphysical vision. For one thing, as Debray has argued, even the dematerialized God must assert His presence in the materiality of the Book, which Book then assumes the metaphysical aura of its maker.[18] Similarly, the Jamesian who was James himself needed a commodity to sell, an object to put on the market. Thus it was the destiny of his consciousness to become reified as narratives-of-consciousness, to become embodied in textual things. As Howells would put it, the novelist is "and must be, only too glad if there is a market for his wares."[19] James's hope was that these wares would not be of the same lowly class of commodities as the unmentionable things that have made the Newsome fortune in *The Ambassadors*, and the golden bowl is a strong symbolic assertion that they are not. And the other Jamesians, his devoted readers, were no doubt pleased to see some of their own cultural capital embodied in a tangible, durable book (aren't we all?). Still, it is quite true that James's assertion of the primary value of consciousness, of the power of mind to give form to the material world, meant that the inevitable return of "sharp" matters of fact—the fact of the market, for one—would be experienced as a *concrete haunting*.

James's fiction divides its readers into classes of a sort, but the problem of social class hardly appears in *The Golden Bowl* as an explicit theme, as it does in earlier works like *The American* (1877) and *The Princess Casamassima* (1886). Instead, against the backdrop of a market economy personified by the immensely wealthy American, Adam Verver—whose money, it is suggested, underwrites a "lawless" confusion of individual interests and identities—the distinctions *The Golden Bowl* is most obviously interested in representing and producing are intellectual ones. The novel takes for granted that with the rise of such figures as Adam Verver— with the circulation, in general, of wealthy Americans in the upper levels of European society—traditional modes of class distinction serve, if at all, only in the most obviously compromised way. If it had for centuries been the practice to assimilate commoners with money to European aristocracies, in the world of *The Golden Bowl* this practice has rather conspicuously been reversed: that is why the "real" aristocrat, Prince Amerigo, seems so almost literally to be the property of Adam Verver, another of his authentic works of art.

But that a shift in emphasis from class distinction to intellectual distinction, and back, is not being imposed on the text is suggested by the encounter with the uncanny shopman with which I began:

> Charlotte, after the incident, was to be full of impressions, of several of which, later on, she gave her companion . . . the benefit; and one of the impressions had been that the man himself was the greatest curiosity they had looked at. The Prince was to reply to this that he himself hadn't looked at him; as, precisely, in the general connexion, Charlotte had more than once, from other days, noted, for his advantage, her consciousness of how, below a certain social plane, he never *saw*. . . . He took throughout always the meaner sort for granted—the night of their meanness, or whatever name one might give it for him, made all his cats grey. (114)

We should note both the emphatically specular terms in which Amerigo's snobbery is figured—"he never *saw*"—and the way the "meaner sort" of which the shopman is an example becomes for him an undifferentiated mass of grey cats. This quip will appear again later in the novel from the mouth of Amerigo himself, who, when he is asked to distinguish the characters of Maggie and her father, Adam Verver, will claim with characteristic vagueness that "[a]t night all cats are grey" (259). Thus the *indistinction* of the "meaner sort" is transposed even onto those Americans whose wealth allows them to circulate in the domain of the "royal Personage." We could say, only somewhat prematurely, that Amerigo's mistake with the shopman, as with the Americans, is in his not taking the commercial culture they represent seriously enough, since one of the commodities circulating in it will return to haunt him as a material witness to his crimes. This happens, as we shall see, because this prince is a character in a novel and not a hero of romance.

Epistemologies of Social Class

Review Questions
1. Define the difference between realism and romance.
2. What are the advantages and disadvantages of the realistic method?
3. What are the advantages and disadvantages of the romantic method?
4. Which method is more natural to your own mind?
5. Upon what evidence have you based your answer to the foregoing question?
   —Clayton Hamilton, *Materials and Methods of Fiction*

One of the more surprising things about discussions of the novel in England and America at the turn of the century is the relative lack of originality of the terms in which these discussions were conducted. Dwelling, to all appearances, in a time of considerable ferment in the genre—the dawn of what would in retrospect be called "modernism"—writers of the period continued to revert to categories whose utility and interest, one might well believe, should long since have been exhausted. Prominent among these were "romance" and "realism," terms that took up, as though the literary-historical record had been skipping for two hundred years, the controversial relation of the novel to historical, natural, or probabalistic truth. Although the tedious imprecision, the unwieldy semantic accretions, attendant to these terms was bothersome even to certain writers of the period themselves, hardly a prominent one among them declined to weigh in on the great, awful Realism-Romance Debate.

Tracking an earlier version of this debate in the late-eighteenth century, in such figures as Samuel Richardson and Henry Fielding, Michael McKeon has called the epistemological problems to which these terms are addressed "questions of truth."[20] I will follow McKeon's example here in linking these questions to what he calls "questions of virtue." The latter ask by what standard—genealogical, occupational, moral, behavioral—the worth of the person is to be measured; thus they act, by extension, to interrogate various models of cultural and political authority. Accounts such as McKeon's seem to me to raise important questions that might be directed far afield, temporally and geographically, from the relatively circumscribed domain of the English novel's "origin." For it is the case not only that debate over the respective significances of "realism" and "romance" continues long beyond the end point of McKeon's study, but that these terms have played a central role in American literary criticism in the twentieth century, and have been crucial to the definition of the "American novel" as such.

Granting, as an initial premise, the accuracy of the association of novel with the rise of the middle class in England, we might ask: What parallel arguments might be made for the relation of the novel to the commercial middle class in the United States? What does it signify when the "middle-class novel" becomes, in certain instances, the "modernist novel"? What does it say about the middle class, or about conceptions of "class identity" in general, when the "traditional" form of the novel is subjected by certain early-twentieth-century writers to a period of sustained and, at times, programmatic attack?

Put this way, these questions are too broad, and too complex, to find an immediate and unequivocal answer. And yet, a brief examination of the operation of the terms "romance" and "realism" at the turn of the century will serve as a first step toward the delineation of the epistemological quandaries out of which "modernism" emerges, and also of the social-historical conditions to which modernist forms, in particular the art-novel, respond. In this context, the annoyance of some writers of the period with these terms is not insignificant, suggesting if nothing else a perceived need to move on. After the first decades of the twentieth century, the terms "romance" and "realism" are uttered less frequently by novelists themselves, but they do live an intense and glorious afterlife as they are absorbed into the pedagogical discourse of the school. My central example in this brief archaeological enterprise will be of course be James, a familiar enough switch point between nineteenth- and twentieth-century narrative, between the cultures of "sophisticated" Europe and "simple" America, and between the institutions of fiction and of twentieth-century academic literary criticism. James made his own well-known contribution to the romance-realism debate in the 1907 preface to the New York Edition of *The American*.

McKeon offers his account of questions of truth and virtue in *The Origins of the Novel* as a corrective to Ian Watt's influential assertion, in *The Rise of the Novel*, of the genre's constitutive "formal realism."[21] For Watt, famously, the rise of novelistic realism signals a departure from romance that parallels the rise to power in England of the commercial middle class. Romance, to put it succinctly, had located cultural authority in the past, imagining a world structured by fixed, a priori truths, timeless values, and the permanent claims of social rank.[22] The novel, by contrast, imagines a world whose truth is under continual construction in the present, and which must be discovered, therefore, by close observation of contemporary social conditions. Associated with philosophical empiricism, the novel privileges seeing in the ordinary, not the metaphysical, sense, and has been strongly associated on these grounds with "panoptic" and "policial" projects of surveillance.[23]

In McKeon's view, however, it is not simply the advent of realism, but the dialectical interpenetration of the respective epistemologies of romance and factual narrative, or "history," that produces the relatively stable generic designation of the "novel" by the beginning of the nineteenth century. What the attribution of "realism" alone to the novel fails to take into account is "the persistence of romance." For McKeon the novel is neither romance nor factual history, neither philosophically idealist nor naively empiricist, and it is rather more productive *of* middle class ideology than produced *by* an already-extant middle class. Henceforth novelists might debate the proper relation of the novel to truth, but without seriously disputing that what they are arguing about is indeed "the novel." And this terminological stabilization speaks, for McKeon, of the high level of agreement now underlying these debates, an agreement that extends equally to epistemological questions of truth and to the formation of middle class ideology.

But can this agreement, this generic and ideological stabilization, truly be said to have occurred by the early-nineteenth century? McKeon opens a wedge in Watt's account of the rise of the novel by invoking the difficult case of Fielding, who, contrary to Watt, can be said neither to have departed entirely from romance conventions in his fiction—for instance, the discovery of the aristocratic lineage of the foundling hero—nor, for that matter, to have been a member of the ascendant middle class. And one might easily return the favor, complicating McKeon's account by invoking the example of the United States and, specifically, of Hawthorne, who as late as 1860 makes the notorious claim that the texts he produces are not novels at all, but romances. Hawthorne seems to lend prospective support rather to Watt than to McKeon when, in the preface to *The House of the Seven Gables: A Romance* (1851), he describes the "Novel" he is not writing as "aim[ing] at a very minute fidelity, not merely to the possible, but to the probable and ordinary course of man's experience."[24] Here the novel as a whole is identified with what later commentators, attributing a greater capaciousness to the genre, will specify as the *realist* novel. For Hawthorne the romance remains different in kind, allowing creative license with respect to probability that the novel's constitutive realism will not allow. To take this license, he claims, is no "literary crime," but it is also to write something other than a novel.

One might handle the case of Hawthorne in a number of ways: one might argue that the self-conscious anachronism of Hawthorne's appeal to romance suggests he is a relatively marginal exception that proves McKeon's rule; or that he evinces an anomalous American taste for metaphysics quashed in the British realist tradition of Jane Austen, William Thackeray, and George Eliot. In making the latter argument, one would find support in a long tradition in American literary criticism, as for instance in Richard Chase's classic *The American Novel and Its Tradition* (1957), which sees the exceptionalism of America echoed in its characteristic production of prose romance, or what Chase calls the "romance-novel," rather than the novel as such.[25] Interestingly enough—given that, for McKeon, the stabilization of the term "novel" in England is itself a sign of an achieved consensus in middle class ideology—the American preference for romance over the novel is sometimes argued to follow from the exceptional American gift for consensus: the theory, put briefly, is that the absence of class conflict in America enables the American romancer to shift his focus from society, from the manners in which class distinction is encoded, to questions of "deeper" metaphysical import and to what Chase calls the "extreme ranges of experience" (1).[26]

Though they have some explanatory force, the historical accuracy of
these arguments is heavily compromised by the perspectival distortions of
canon formation. Seen against the backdrop, not of canonized "classic"
American literature, but rather of the popular sentimental tradition represented by Stowe, it might appear simply false to claim that there has been
an "American" preference for romance over realism, a point made effectively by feminist scholars Nina Baym and Jane Tompkins.[27] Similarly, the
claim that English literature has tended toward the production of the realist novel will seem odd if one emphasizes, as does Terry Lovell in her
Consuming Fiction, the Gothic tradition or, alternatively, the romance tradition that emerges from Walter Scott.[28] Edward Bulwer-Lytton, for example, author of *The Last Days of Pompei* (1834), *Zanoni* (1842), *A Strange
Story* (1862), *The Coming Race* (1871), and many other works, was perhaps the best-selling English writer of the Victorian era after Dickens
(himself notoriously difficult to assimilate to the realist paradigm).[29] Span-
ning the better part of the century, Lord Lytton's career evinces an ever-
more-strident promotion both of the aesthetic claims of the romance and
of the political interests of his class, the landowning gentry of Fielding.[30]

This suggests that well after midcentury, even in England, romance retains a degree of generic and ideological autonomy from the "middle class"
novel. The near total eclipse of a writer like Bulwer in most accounts of
nineteenth-century British fiction, paying little heed of the persistence of
romance, may be suggestive as much of the perspectival distortions of
these accounts as of Bulwer's punishing mediocrity: in literary history as
in history, one mainly hears from the victors, and the victors in this case
are those who pursued the realist tradition of Austen through Eliot.

But to say that writers like these were "victorious" is of course to grant
both Watt and McKeon each a significant part of their case. As Watt argues,
and as we have seen confirmed by Hawthorne, the novel as a whole does
indeed come to be strongly associated with probabalistic realism. At the
same time, as McKeon argues, the genre does seem to become, though
perhaps later than he states, confident enough and broad enough in its
reach to perceive romance no longer as its hostile generic other, but as a
minority position within the discourse of the novel itself.[31] A dialectical
counterpart to this incorporation, however—a sign of the disruptive force
romance carries with it into the novel's confines—is the wide dissemination
in this time of the term "realism" to describe a certain kind of literary text.
From the outset this term carried considerable semantic baggage, but in
this period it variously suggested the militant probabalism of Victorian
realism that carries through to William Dean Howells in the United States,
the "vulgarity" of literary naturalism (which defined itself in opposition
to mid-Victorian realism), and the characteristic attention to the social
present, or recent past, common to both. Crucially, however, it seems that

this "realism" is no longer confidently identified with the genre as a whole: in his textbook *Materials and Methods of Fiction* (1908), for example, Clayton Hamilton now must interpolate into his discussion of Hawthorne's "well-known distinction between the Romance and the (realistic) Novel" this qualifying parenthetical term.[32] Thus the price the novel appears to have paid for its generic dominance is an internal splitting into the "realist" and "romanticist" modes so much on the minds of turn-of-the-century novelists.[33]

We are told, we no longer need to be told, that *modernism* critiques the ideologies and narrative forms of nineteenth-century realism; the first critique of realism is made not in the name of modernism, however, but of romance. Risking an association with "popular romance" understood as a kind of low genre fiction—not to be taken seriously because insufficiently realist—the "high" romancer reinstalls within realism a respect for immaterial dimensions of spirit and intellect. Indeed, as late as 1908, in R. A. Scott-James's *Modernism and Romance*, the "modernism" referred to in his title is precisely the set of values—empirical, commercial, scientific, middle class—that one associates with realism, while the "romance" of his title refers to what he perceived as a nascent critique of these values, on behalf of "higher" spiritual truths, in novelists such as Thomas Hardy.[34] So, too, in 1903 we find that

> the reason why one claims so much for Romance, and quarrels so pointedly with Realism, is that Realism stultifies itself. It notes only the surface of things. For it, Beauty is not even skin deep, but only a geometrical plane, without dimensions and depth, a mere outside. Realism is very excellent as far as it goes, but it goes no further than the Realist himself can actually see.[35]

So says Frank Norris, the premier American exponent of literary naturalism, in his short essay "A Plea for Romantic Fiction." That Norris would make such a plea is not incomprehensible: if naturalism was in the view of many contemporaries a grotesquely intense realism, its characteristic attention to the social margins—to the extreme or even improbable cases where the "deeper" truths of society purportedly become visible—could at a stretch suggest its allegiance to romance. As such, it would stand apart from the genteel realism, the "average case" championed by Howells and Bliss Perry.[36]

Indeed, Norris's account of his own naturalist-romance ideal makes it sound very much like Richard Chase's description of the American "romance-novel" as tending "to rest in contradictions and among the extreme ranges of experience." In the latter case, as in the former, there is an explicit attempt to valorize this extremity as a sign of increased intelligence, to find in the romance a vehicle for intellectual distinction. Whereas Norris criticizes realism as comprehending only the *merely visible* geometric plane, or empirical surface, missing a whole realm of experience hidden from the grosser senses, Chase finds in the American romance novel certain "special virtues" that take it above and beyond the "solid moral inclusivity" of the realist novel that merely "serves the interests and aspirations of an insurgent middle class" (*American Novel*, 13). These special virtues are, explicitly, "*intellectual energy*" and the "*virtues of the mind*" (x, emphases added). Romance, in short, is smarter than realism. Modernism would be smarter still. Thus one begins to see a possible link between the rise of the modernist art-novel in the United States and the rise of a class whose worth and virtue would be understood to derive from the mental labor it performs in the twentieth-century managerial-capitalist economy. Perhaps—is it possible?—the "Jamesian" aesthete was a specific class-fraction of these.

Of course, not every writer of the earlier period agreed with Chase that American cultural history presented such a trove of romantic intellectualism. And yet their different assessments of this history tended, even in disagreement, to display precisely the same arguments on behalf of intellectual virtue underpinning the modernist revival of romance. Indeed, one prominent public intellectual of the day argued that until the early-twentieth century, American literature had been unapologetically stupid. This claim is made by John Erskine in the essay "The Moral Obligation to Be Intelligent," which the Columbia English professor first delivered as an address to the Phi Beta Kappa Society at Amherst College in 1914.[37] What Erskine told this gathering of smart people was that English and American literature, considered as a single tradition, had always been a literature of virtuous stupidity. "The disposition to consider intelligence a peril is an old Anglo-Saxon inheritance" (4), he explained, and we "find in the temper of our remotest ancestors a certain bias which still prescribes our ethics and still prejudices us against the mind" (15). We have been taught that a "choice must be made between goodness and intelligence; that stupidity is first cousin to moral conduct, and cleverness the first step into mischief" (5). Had not Milton himself attributed "intelligence of the highest order to the devil" (7), and made God an illogical boob? No wonder, then, that the typical hero of the novel "is a well-meaning blunderer who in the last chapter is temporarily rescued by the grace of God from the mess he has made of his life" (9). These unintelligent heroes are characteristic of a middle class culture that has set too little store by the "things of the mind."

Sounding by turns like a Jamesian, and like an apostle of Progressive expertise, Erskine entreated his listeners to reverse this old prejudice against intelligence and to consider it instead the preeminent "modern virtue." Given the "nature of the problems to be solved in our day," he claimed, "intelligence is the virtue we particularly need" (24), since it is a tool without which our best intentions will remain as though locked in the prison of our stupidity. Not surprisingly, this newly conceived "modern virtue" was precisely the one that the students in his audience would embody as they joined the professions, began to manage business enterprises, or sought political office. It would also, as a potential source of social esteem, form an important portion of their portfolio of cultural capital, one that might be invested in the market of social power. Setting off to take up their expected positions in the professional-managerial world, his audience, Erskine said, would find themselves in the heat of a battle just now being joined: "Between this rising host that follow intelligence, and the old camp that put their trust in a stout heart, a firm will, and a strong hand, the fight is on. Our college men will be in the thick of it" (23). He could not have known, in 1914, how soon American youth would be called to arms of a more literal sort, and how stupidly many of them would die.

The Romance of Romance: Virtue Unrewarded

> James's essential limitation may rather accurately be expressed by saying
> that he attempted, in a democratic age, to write courtly romances.
> —Carl Van Doren, *The American Novel*

Whether as a separate genre or as a minority position within the genre of the novel itself, the *persistent persistence* of romance is a fact that needs to be explained. What social pressures are brought to bear on the novel such that romance remains, or can be revived, as an appealing stance from which to mount a critique of novelistic realism? What, in turn, does the equal distribution of the language of realism *and* romance to both "classless" America and "hierarchical" Britain suggest? But, most crucially, what does the gradual rotation of romance from the outside to the inside of Anglo-American discourse on the novel signify? These questions are worth asking, since it is against this backdrop—a genre more pervasive and powerful than ever, a genre divided—that turn-of-the-century thought on the novel, and in turn the birth of the modernist art-novel in such figures as Henry James, takes place.

One place to search for an answer to these questions would appear to be James's famous invocation of the competing claims of the "real" and the "romantic" in the preface to the New York Edition of *The American*. This novel was written, James tells us, "under the conviction" that he was achieving "a high probity of observation" of his contemporary Parisian surroundings—written, that is, as a self-consciously "realist" text.[38] But in retrospect the novel has turned out "unconsciously" to have been "flying the emblazoned flag of romance," indeed of "arch-romance" (4). And why? Analyses of this preface have tended to focus more or less immedi-

ately on its general claims and definitions, finding in these claims a powerful tool for understanding James's late fiction, which indeed they are:

> The real represents to my perception the things we cannot possibly *not* know,
> sooner or later, in one way or another; it being but one of the accidents of our
> hampered state, and one of the incidents of their quantity and number, that
> particular instances have not yet come our way. The romantic stands, on the
> other hand, for the things that, with all the facilities in the world, all the wealth
> and all the courage and all the wit and all the adventure, we never *can* directly
> know; the things that can reach us only through the beautiful circuit and subter-
> fuge of our thought and our desire. (9)

These definitions suggest James's distance both from realism and from
romance conceived as mutually exclusive positions, though this distance
is measured differently in each case. The idea that there are certain things
we have no grounds for doubting, things undeniable even by art, suggests
how powerful James believes the claims of the "real" to be. This is a fact
of considerable importance in the interpretation both of James and of later
modernism, suggesting that the idea that modernism "critiques" realism
would have to be a highly qualified one. Realist epistemology is criticized,
in James at least, only by recourse to *affect*, where the real in his definition
becomes virtually synonymous with the unpleasant. Thus romance becomes a "beautiful," but self-consciously "impossible," means of registering affective resistance to unpleasant truths that, however, lose none of
their truth-value for being submitted to this affective critique. One is presented with a structure, therefore, in which realist knowledge and romantic
affect operate in dialectical—mutually dependent, mutually hostile—relation, yielding what might properly be called a literary psychology.

Arguably we have the makings here of a primitive definition of the "psychological novel," one of the terminological way stations on the road to the
"modernist novel" that will only come to be defined, and even then without
confidence, after the Second World War: this genre represents a self-con-
flicted realism, shuttling between claims of "thought and desire," on the
one hand, and what Sigmund Freud was at this time calling the "reality
principle," on the other. None of this would be particularly surprising. The
originality of James and later modernist writers, in this view, is only to
insist with unique stridency on the *fact of consciousness*, not necessarily as
it correctly apprehends the real, but as an intractably distorting or simply
"formalizing" feature of the real in the experience of the individual subject.
For modernists, in other words, the confident critique of "Gothic" delusions
on behalf of commonsense realism found in such texts as Jane Austen's
Northanger Abbey is no longer an option, though they were perhaps no
less committed to the "truth" than Austen was.[39] Arguably, in accounting
both for subjectivity and for its object—exemplified by the ekphrastic self-

inclusion of *The Golden Bowl*—modernism rather seeks an ever-more-to-talized representation of "truth." This affective epistemology—or "psychology"—of modernism, however, becomes more interesting insofar as we can specify it as a sociohistorical phenomenon.

And to do this one might well return to the preface of *The American*, and ask again why this novel has come, for its author, to seem like "arch-romance." Confirming McKeon's sense that questions of truth are never far, in the discourse of the novel, from questions of virtue, what produces James's long meditation on "realism" and "romance" in the Preface is rather explicitly a concern with social class. His plan had been to insert a rich, pleasant, but déclassé American, Christopher Newman, into aristocratic Parisian society:

> the point being in especial that he should suffer at the hands of persons pretending to represent the highest possible civilization and to be of an order in every way superior to his own. What would he "do" in that predicament, how . . . would he conduct himself under his wrong? . . . He would behave in the most interesting manner—it would all depend on that: stricken, smarting, sore, he would arrive at his just vindication and then would fail of all triumphantly and all vulgarly enjoying it. (2)

James's novel was to be a tale of class conflict, staging a confrontation between two competing notions of virtue. The virtue of the aristocratic Bellegardes is the innate virtue or "nobility" of social rank. Newman's virtue, by contrast, is "middle class" moral virtue, the product of virtuous acts. Looked at in this light, one can see how deeply embedded in the traditional class problematics of the English novel James's *The American* is. Indeed, absent James's rewriting of the significance of the novel in the preface written several decades later, this text might appear, in the framework offered by McKeon, one of the more militant defenses of the middle class, and of an American nation understood by James to be constitutively "middle class," ever written. From this perspective, the novel can be seen almost programmatically to defuse what had been perceived as a central weak point of the middle class politics of virtue: that this virtue, in Samuel Richardson's famous formulation, is *rewarded*. It was, after all, the fact that Pamela is rewarded for her virtue by marriage into the nobility that had enabled Fielding, in his conservative critique of the grasping commercial "middling sort," to rewrite her purported virtue merely as a form of scheming—that is, to rewrite *Pamela* as *Shamela*.

Establishing, from the outset, that his protagonist will not be rewarded for his virtue—more specifically, that he will not be assimilated, by marriage, into the European aristocracy represented by the Bellegardes—James would seem to protect his hero from the cynical, Fieldingesque, account of his actions: "All he would have at the end," writes James of his initial plan, "would be therefore just the moral convenience, indeed the moral necessity, of his practical, but quite unappreciated, magnanimity" (2). Christopher Newman, that is, is wholly and unproblematically good, a "vulgar" American, to be sure, but not so vulgar that he will ruin the Bellegardes by making a damning letter that has fallen into his hands—a purloined letter—public. Why is he so virtuous? James, in the novel, is pointedly vague on this point: "Whether it was Christian charity or unregenerate good nature—what it was, in the background of his soul—I don't pretend to say; but Newman's last thought was that of course he would let the Bellegardes go" (306). This is an odd, and I think symptomatic, demurral on James's part, evidence perhaps that his realist novel knows, even in 1877, that it is a romance—a romance of goodness.

And yet, by the time of the 1907 preface, this structure will be entirely reversed. James does not question his portrayal of the American capitalist as a benign and selfless Christian. Indeed, as recently as *The Golden Bowl* he had created another such figure in the "selfless" Adam Verver, the staggeringly wealthy American who exhibits none of the predictable characteristics of a man who corners markets. No—what has come to make *The American* seem to James like "arch-romance," we find, is its improbable, if not impossible, assertion that an aristocratic French family like the Bellegardes *wouldn't* accept the rich American Christopher Newman as its newest member. The *unpleasant* truth is that by the laws of realist probability they certainly *would* have done so:

> They would positively have jumped then, the Bellegardes, at my rich and easy American, and not have "minded" in the least any drawback—especially as, after all, given the pleasant palette from which I have painted him, there were few drawbacks to mind. . . . [Their] preferred course, a thousand times preferred, would have been to haul him and his fortune into their boat under cover of night perhaps, in any case as quietly and with as little bumping and splashing as possible, and there accommodate him with the very safest and most convenient seat. (12)

Thus James, in the preface, discovers that his strong defense of the virtuous American commercial class had unwittingly founded itself on a masochistic fantasy—a *romance of rejection*. This, I would argue, entirely reverses the ideological valences of the novel, rewriting its progressive politics of moral virtue as nostalgic conservatism. The romantic dream of this novel, James discovers, is the dream of a world where there exist people committed enough to aristocratic identity and genealogical purity to resist the universal solvent of middle class money. Romance here signifies—as, arguably, it has always done—the "beautiful" appeal of the rigidly hierarchical world that the snobbery of the "Belle-gardes" guards. It would be hard to overstate the significance, for James and for the subsequent development of modernism, of the pun in this French name. For what James will suggest in effect is that aesthetic value must be constituted in opposition to and literally *out of the line of vision* of ordinary members of the expanding middle class of "new men"—the very class on whose behalf, in whose interest, his genre is said to have constituted itself in the first place.[40]

When the aristocratic object of Newman's desire, Mme de Cintre, retires behind the impermeable walls of the convent, never to be seen in public again, this signifies a transformation in the way the "aristocratic value" she represents will be possessed: her possession, as a form of intellectual property, will now be imaginary, a function of consciousness, while the "real" advance of mass cultural indistinction continues unchecked. She will be appropriated not bodily but cognitively, mentally.[41] In the preface to *The American*, that is, the aristocratic romance becomes visible as a romance of consciousness, and social distinctions become a function of intellectual distinctions, which in turn requires a shattering of the idea, in Richard Chase's terms, of a "morally inclusive" common culture based on empirically verifiable "common knowledge." The shattering of these notions of common culture and common knowledge is represented, perhaps, in the shattering of the golden bowl in *The Golden Bowl*. As in the case of the purloined letter, this fragmentation figures the idea that property held in common might, in being understood in different ways, reproduce the social distinctions mass culture threatens to dissolve.

Divisive Perspectivism

Toward the end of *The Golden Bowl*, after Maggie Verver has learned from the uncanny shopman of the intimacy betrayed by Charlotte and Amerigo in their shopping expedition for the bowl, the principal characters of the novel sit down to play bridge in the smoking room at Fawns. Exhausted by the silent complexities and undercurrents of her "funny situation," Maggie excuses herself to do some quiet reading, but "there was no question for her, as she found, of . . . getting away; [her companions] strayed back to life, in the stillness, over the top of her Review; she could lend herself to none of those refinements of the higher criticism with which its pages bristled" (485).

In the preface, we recall, it would be the novel-genre whose "essence" is to "bristle"—not with the refinements of the higher criticism but with "immediate images." Thus if Maggie is incapable of one sort of literary activity, reading criticism, then this is only because there is a more pressing but perhaps equally "literary" task at hand. As her attention strays from the pages of the review, it is as though these pages have become the pages of a novel whose characters have suddenly leapt to three-dimensional life. In their presence, Maggie has found that she must be a strong reader—

indeed an author. In phrasing that takes us directly back to the beginning
of the novel, when Charlotte's body had figured as a "sharp, sharp fact"
for Amerigo, Maggie must ask herself: what to do with "the facts of the
situation" she sees around the bridge table—"the fact of her father's wife's
lover," the "fact of her father," the "fact of Charlotte keeping it up," the
"sharp-edged fact of the relation of the whole group, individually and col-
lectively, to herself"?

The first thing she does, wishing to manage these "facts," is to walk
outside to the terrace, and it might seem, as she does so, that this physical
movement is a figure of her access to the "space apart" that is consciousness:

> [T]hey might have been figures rehearsing some play of which she herself was
> the author; they might even, for the happy appearance they continued to present,
> have been such figures as would by the strong note of character in each fill any
> author with the certitude of success, especially of their own histrionic. They
> might in short have represented any mystery they would; the point being pre-
> dominantly that the key to the mystery, the key that could wind and unwind it
> without a snap of the spring, was there in her pocket. . . . Spacious and splendid,
> like a stage again awaiting a drama, it was a scene she might people, by the
> press of her spring, either with serenities and dignities and decencies, or with
> terrors and shames and ruins, things as ugly as those formless fragments of her
> golden bowl she was trying so hard to pick up. (488)

Maggie's sense of her own authorial power, as she holds the key to the
mystery represented by the bowl, is clear, and her apparent satisfaction in
holding this power and in exerting it in particular over Charlotte is one
thing that has disturbed many readers of this novel.[42] For isn't there a bit
of cruelty in her sudden triumph, a little sadism in her treatment of Charlotte? Is James endorsing her behavior, or is he criticizing it?[43]

These questions, which have engendered a long-standing debate in criticism of the novel roughly divided into "pro-" and "anti-" Maggie camps,
run the risk, I think, of overlooking what is most specific and interesting in
Maggie's exertions of power in *The Golden Bowl*, which is their specifically
intellectual and invisible nature.[44] Maggie's power is an inconspicuous production. The question of how James judges Maggie—what would be a just
response to a best friend who cheats on one's father by sleeping with one's
husband?—is something to ponder, no doubt, but the fact that the novel
does not begin to settle the issue probably follows from the fact that it is
only vestigially, if at all, interested in doing so. Indeed, to read this novel
as primarily a moral drama, and to assume that there must be some moral
to the story, is to miss how pointedly James's fiction had done with moralizing in this traditional sense: for James, as for later modernism, there was
only the moral obligation to be intelligent. Rather, I would suggest, *The
Golden Bowl* is most interested in pointing out how differences between

people are produced by virtue of their different intellectual relations to a set of "facts" that are available to all.

This becomes clear when, after a few minutes, Charlotte joins Maggie on the terrace, where they both can look into the lighted room, and at the "facts" represented by the room's inhabitants, from without. At first this fills Maggie with fear, as it seems that Charlotte's presence with her on the "outside" of the situation might be equivalent to her equal access to the authorial power she only recently has felt able to claim. But it soon becomes clear that a mere physical co-presence and equal ability to survey the "facts" need not compromise the differences that remain in, and that are produced by, Charlotte and Maggie's different and unequal possession of knowledge. And that is important, because the problem of the insufficient differentiation of persons and objects has been one of the novel's central concerns from its first page:

> [Amerigo] had strayed into Bond Street, where his imagination, working at comparatively short range, caused him now and then to stop before a window in which objects massive and lumpish, in silver and gold, in the forms to which precious stones contribute, or in leather, steel, brass, applied to a hundred uses and abuses, were as tumbled together as if, in the insolence of Empire, they had been the loot of far-off victories. (43)

In the commercial crossroads represented by the Imperial city of London, or simply in the shop window itself, objects and persons are "tumbled together" in such a way as to seem indistinct. The novel proceeds to figure this indistinction repeatedly, and in any number of ways, including what has been noted as the virtually "incestuous" relation of Maggie to her father. This suggestion of incest is also at play in the relation between Charlotte and Amerigo, whose "occult" source of connection Amerigo attributes to a common ancestor making "himself felt ineffaceably in her blood and in her tone."[45] Adam Verver, talking to his daughter, states the problem of social indistinction in terms that also seem to connect it to a desire for things: " 'But we're selfish together—we move as a selfish mass. You see we always want the same thing,' he had gone on,—'and that holds us, that binds us, together' " (388).

So how, given this problem, is one to reproduce or to maintain social differences? Maggie and Charlotte stand on the terrace looking in:

> Side by side for three minutes they fixed this picture of quiet harmonies, the positive charm of it and, as might have been said, the full significance—which, as was now brought home to Maggie, could be no more after all than a matter of interpretation, differing always for a different interpreter. (493)

Here, referencing a rhetoric of interpretive perspectivism, James suggests that the solution to the problem of social indistinction may lie in the mind.

No more than that of Friedrich Nietzsche does James's perspectivism imply a "relativism" of value—an equality.[46] Maggie is superior to Charlotte because she is in a position of superior knowledge, having steadfastly frustrated Charlotte's " 'natural desire to know' " (498).

But where, after all, is the mind that makes distinction? Where is the scene of metaphysical vision? Can it actually be put into a book? Or does it hover at the surface of the text, looking down upon it as James looks down upon the characters he has created? That is one of the issues raised by James's representation of Maggie and Charlotte standing on the outside looking in, for though both are physical "outsiders" in this scene, only one of them is also an "insider" to the knowledge that the room, like the novel itself, contains. And, indeed, no less than on the problem of the imagetext was the modernist art-novel founded on the problem of the "volume"— the fictive social space that the novel may or may not contain. As with the shut doors of the frontispieces to the New York Edition, this meant that the question of *access* and *entry* into culture would find itself embedded in the form of the novel—the art-novel—in the profoundest sense. Here, in the rhetoric of spatial relation, we will begin to see how modernism's claims to intellectual superiority were also haunted confessions of dependence on the "sharp fact" of the market.

Social Geometries
Taking Place in the Jamesian Modernist Text

> The ideal for a book would be to lay everything out on a
> plane of exteriority . . . on a single page, the same sheet: lived
> events, historical determinations, concepts, individuals,
> groups, social formations.
> —Gilles Deleuze and Felix Guattari, *A Thousand Plateaus*

The Hidden Dimensions of Class

Where does fiction take place? Edwin Abbott's *Flatland: A Romance of Many Dimensions* (1881) has a surprising answer to this question, which it takes as literally as any novel ever has.[1] For though fiction could, one supposes, be said to take place anywhere an author says it does and, yet, since it is fiction, could as easily be said to take place nowhere at all, *Flatland* constructs a world where events occur across a surface much like a page of the novel itself: "Imagine a vast sheet of paper," the narrator, A. Square, instructs us,

> on which straight Lines, Triangles, Squares . . . and other figures, instead of remaining fixed in their places, move freely about, on or in the surface, but without the power of rising above or sinking below it . . . and you will then have a pretty correct notion of my country and countrymen. (17)

The inhabitants of Flatland exist as "characters" in two senses of that term, both as represented beings and as conventional symbols, somewhat as though the type beneath our eyes has detached itself from the pulp upon which it is pressed and come to life. It is a bizarre form of life, lived laterally, confined to the two-dimensional plane of the page.

Compressing a represented world into what it calls the "second dimension of space," *Flatland* would exempt itself from the rule that fiction evokes from its flat material substrate an illusory sense of volume, the virtual interior of representation that Michel Butor has called "the space of the novel."[2] Butor has not been alone in arguing that while fiction has traditionally been understood as an essentially temporal art, one event following another in narrative succession, these events can occur for a reader only if they are projected into an imaginary location. We implicitly acknowledge this when we pay attention to a novel's setting, where this setting is understood as the relatively stable environment of action and character development.[3] The value in Butor's drawing attention to the "space" of the novel, however, is that he pursues the idea of fictional location to a point where it seems more basic to the novel than its establishment of a particular setting, and more far-reaching in its implications. "When I read a description of a room in a novel," Butor explains,

> the furnishings which are before my eyes, but which I am not looking at, give way to the ones which emerge or transpire from the words on the printed page. This "volume," as we say, which I hold in my hand, sets free as a result of my attention evocations which assert themselves, which haunt the place where I am, displacing me. . . . The novel's space, then, is a particularization of an "elsewhere," complementary to the real space in which it is evoked. (32)

It is, curiously, precisely by abstracting an "elsewhere" from the many places represented in novels that Butor is able here to approach the specific place of the reader. The novel may be set anywhere, but, however far-flung in the imagination, this setting is necessarily held in "complementary" orbit of that reader, wherever he or she may be. Thus Butor's account of the space of the novel appears to lend methodological support, even in its relative abstraction, to the kind of materialist inquiry more interested in hard facts than in fictions: a criticism that asks such questions as, Who is the audience for a novel? To what class or other social group do they belong? By what means did they acquire the artifact they hold in their hands? Where and under what historical conditions is the space of the novel allowed to "emerge or transpire" from the surface of the page? These questions ask us to shift our attention from the novel's interior to its exterior, to the real spaces in which it is received and takes its effect.[4] One could ask similar questions about any kind of commodity. And indeed, the intensity with which Butor pursues the idea of the space of the novel manages ultimately to distract us from the specificity of the "imaginary" and the "fictional" altogether. Clearly the spatializing mechanics to which he draws our attention are features not merely of fiction, but of writing as such. The crucial question for Butor is not the ontological relation of fiction to reality, but the *dimensional* relation of represented to real space.

So too with Abbott's *Romance of Many Dimensions*, which seems from this point of view to test habitual assumptions about the space of the novel by arresting our attention as close as possible at the level of the page— precisely the place, the surface of the text, where it may be unclear whether we are talking about the novel's inside or its outside. Produced by an educator not associated with any particular literary movement, Abbott's romance makes an aggressive, though necessarily asymptotic, conceptual approach to what might be called the primal scene of fiction, where ink and page prepare the volumetric figures that arise when we read. Recalling the roughly contemporaneous poetic project of Stéphane Mallarmé, committed to the dispersal of representational volume across the flat typographic surface of the text in an even more literal sense, *Flatland* appears in this broader context something more than a literary-historical oddity. In fact, I would argue that it may have considerable consequences for our understanding of certain features of the modernist projects to which it appears, in some ways, an eccentric precursor.

This can be seen most immediately, perhaps, by pointing out its remarkable echo not in Symbolist poetry but in painting. In a series of influential essays of the 1940s, Clement Greenberg identified the key force driving the dialectic of modernist abstraction as the gradual flattening of the picture plane in the nineteenth century, where represented objects begin to "flatten and spread" across the "dense, two-dimensional atmosphere" of the canvas.[5] In Greenberg's view the "history of avant-garde painting is that of a progressive surrender to the resistance of its medium; which resistance consists chiefly in the flat picture plane's denial of efforts to 'hole through' it for realistic perspectival space"(34). Now for Greenberg, it is true, this flattening is understood to signal, indeed to assert, something unique to the medium of easel painting: that it is, in essence, paint applied to a delimited support of stretched canvas. The flatter painting becomes, the more it signals an urge to purify itself of the contamination of other media, preeminently of literature, which takes hold in painting to the degree that the canvas produces an illusion of volume in which figures, and ultimately something like narratives, can take place. But while for Greenberg this capaciousness invites the corrupting influence of literature, it also more broadly invites the "infection" of the artwork by the "ideological struggles of society" (28). Thus the flattening of the picture plane, in Greenberg's account, effects both the self-purification of the medium of painting and the avant-garde's "escape from ideas" as such, which ideas "came to mean subject matter in general" (28). Becoming abstract, painting becomes both antiliterary and asocial. But the fact that literature circa 1881 was beginning to flatten itself in oddly similar ways may suggest the overdetermination of the phenomenon Greenberg explains as the self-specification of the medium of painting, and it might at the same time—as he is in any case sometimes ready to admit—call into question the removal of art from ideological debate he takes the flattening of representation to signify.[6]

Does the avant-garde's "purifying" inward turn—taking its "chief inspiration from the medium" (9) itself and not from the realm of social "content"—signal, as Greenberg argues, the avant-garde's "retiring from public altogether," its resistance to the demand that "realistic illusion [be put] in the service of sentimental and declamatory literature"?[7] Abbott's

Flatland suggests that this flattening of representational space, whether in literature or painting, may indeed have been thoroughly involved with social "ideas" and ideological struggles. The flattening of representation appears to be, in Abbott at least, a conspicuous form of *intervention* in public discourse: Abbott's romance is, we discover, invested pointedly, indeed wholly, in the question of class distinction.

In Flatland class identity is a function of the shape of the character-body, where the number of his sides and equality of his angles place each male character in strictly measurable relation to his inferiors and betters. Uppermost is the priestly class, who are circles, while the middle class are squares. Beneath these are the brutal mass of workers, whose "lowness" and stupidity is evident in the unequal angles of their jagged, and thus physically dangerous, isosceles triangle bodies. Females, lowest of all—attached to specific classes, but at the same time an abject class apart—are menacingly phallic straight lines. Lacking our own panoptic view of the page upon which they live, one Flatlander is visible to another only along his or her edges—as though two coins laid flat, with eyes somehow placed in their edges, could view each other across the surface of a table. Founded on the recognition of class identity, the social regulation of Flatland requires the constant measurement of the "dimming" of these lines as they recede at various angles. But this is a difficult process, the subject of much of A. Square's account of his world, which is still recovering, he tells us, from the trauma of the "Colour Rebellion" that occurred years ago: it was discovered in that time that the application of color to the figure-bodies of Flatland makes it impossible to tell their shapes apart. This had been exploited by the leader of the Rebellion who, noticing its enablement of class masquerade, had used the fashion for color to foment revolution. Order has long since been reestablished in Flatland, and color outlawed, but the threat of social indistinction raised by the Colour Rebellion still reverberates in A. Square's two-dimensional world. Geometry in Flatland always implies the construction of a social geometry, a spatialized social order that is also an aesthetic order, and that must be defended at all costs.

But what must be avoided above all, we discover—indeed, even to talk about it is a grievous crime—is the revolutionary idea of a third dimension of space. Though from the point of view of Flatland this dimension is only an imaginary space, hard to credit as real because impossible for Flatlanders to picture, it nonetheless suggests a position of specular mastery—something like the position of the reader of *Flatland*—in which Flatland's strict social geometry might literally be transcended. The threat of the third dimension is the threat of a "higher" space from which point of view the differences of shape so important in Flatland, though still visible, resolve in effect into an equally two-dimensional, equally unimpressive, mass. The ideological significance of the transcendental perspective that produces this leveling effect is still an open question: Does it suggest that seen from a higher dimension, Flatlanders achieve a moral equivalence more important than their class differences, that they are equal in the eyes of an all-seeing God? Or does it rather suggest the existence of an ultraexclusive space that might be inhabited by a few godlike persons—a technology of social distinction that trumps even the rigid hierarchies that avail in two dimensions? The answer, as we shall see, is that it is able to imply both of these positions at the same time. What one must note first is that class identity is not simply important to Flatland's social structure. Rather, along with gender distinction, it is virtually the *only* important thing in its social structure. In this severely restricted visual world all markers of individual identity fall away such that the only recognizable thing about the male Flatlander is his class identity. This is why our middle-class narrator is named "A. Square," the suggestion being that the class identity expressed by his shape virtually exhausts the question of his identity as such. Whether it is conceived as a good or a bad thing, and irrespective of the specific aspirations derived therefrom, the higher-dimensional perspective that discovers a principle of dimensional indistinction underlying these class differences supplies the logic of what we have come to call "mass culture."

Flatland's fascination with dimensions, and the inflection of dimensionality with the question of social distinction, had by Abbott's time a substantial history, stretching at least to Carl Friedrich Gauss (1777–1855), the German peasant who became known as the Prince of Mathematicians, and who initiated virtually every important branch of modern mathematics. Gauss wondered whether—despite the overpowering prestige of Euclid's three-dimensional geometry, earned over two uninterrupted millennia of theoretical and practical demonstration—there might not exist a higher space in which his imagination could, in good scientific conscience, roam.

Gauss kept his "astral" aspirations to himself, leaving credit for the discovery of non-Euclidean geometry to others. He wrote his friend F. W. Bessel in 1829 that he feared, if he took his ideas public, the "clamour of the Boeotians."[8] This was an allusion to the purportedly dull-witted Greek tribe who had lived beyond the pale of classical Attic genius. He meant, more immediately, "the majority of people" around him who "have not clear ideas" about the crucial fifth or "parallel" postulate of Euclid. As Morris Kline has put it, recasting Gauss's Boeotians as a dim-witted German multitude, "Gauss had the intellectual courage to create non-Euclidean geometry but not the moral courage to face the mobs who would have called the creator mad."[9] Had not Immanuel Kant himself, still the dominant intellectual presence of Gauss's time, claimed that Euclidean space is the only conceivable space, and that Euclid's geometry describes the fundamental cognitive form of all experience?

On the other hand, it was Kant's assertion that Euclidean space is the product of cognition, not necessarily a property of the thing-in-itself, that encouraged Gauss to wonder whether reality might in fact contain a dimension not visible to the Euclidean eye. What is remarkable is how Gauss's explanation, by analogy, of the absence of this higher dimension from ordinary vision invents a species of lower-dimensional beings strikingly similar to the clamoring Boeotians and disbelieving mobs. As his first biographer, Sartorius von Walterhausen, recalled in a statement published in the English journal *Nature* in 1869, Gauss reasoned that "as we can conceive beings (like infinitely attenuated book-worms in an infinitely thin sheet of paper) which possess only the notion of space of two dimensions, so we may imagine beings capable of realising space of four or a greater number of dimensions."[10] A few years later, in a lecture published in the journal *Mind* in 1876, Hermann von Helmholtz took up the idea of plane-beings again, noting that if "such beings worked out a geometry, they would of course assign only two dimensions to their space" and therefore "could as little represent to themselves" a solid object "as we can represent what would be generated by a solid moving out of the space we know."[11]

It was probably from Helmholtz that Abbott took the idea for his own plane-beings, who as we see were invented as a means of figuring, by analogy, our own ignorant relation to a higher, four-dimensional space. It is difficult to say, because the fourth dimension had by the later decades of the nineteenth century begun to filter from the specialized discourse of mathematics to become a relatively widespread source of fascination, first in Europe, then in the United States. By 1925, in the essay "Morality and the Novel," D. H. Lawrence is able to assert that the "truth" of representation lies not in the representation itself, the object, but "only in the much-debated fourth dimension. In dimensional space it has no existence."[12] The particular appeal of the fourth dimension was as a potential means of reintegrating the two sides of what has been called the "Omnipresent Debate" in the nineteenth century between empiricism and transcendentalism or, more roughly, between the competing cultural authority of science and religion.[13] Still reeling from the shock of Darwinism, for instance, certain religious writers saw in the fourth dimension a path to transcendence vouchsafed by the prestige of science itself. Gaining some form of access to this occult habitation, humans perhaps could be "higher," godlike beings after all, not merely naked apes.[14]

More broadly, non-Euclidian geometry suggested in its own way the possibility of a "transcendental materialism" similar in some respects to that being developed by figures such as Walter Pater, whose aestheticism merged the traditions of British empiricism and German idealism, and

Henri Bergson, whose phenomenology set out to "affirm" both "the reality of spirit and the reality of matter."[15] Cumulatively—one can see this most clearly in aestheticism—these thinkers drew attention to the idea of the *surface* of the object as the meeting place of matter and spirit. In the poetic project of Mallarmé, for example, obsessive attention to the literal surface of the text—to the apparently vulgar facts of printing, typography, and the shape of the page—enables an aesthetic of absolute transcendence, the idea being that it is *through* matter, not in simple denial of it, that one gains access to a realm of pure Being. Following William Empson, one might describe this as a "pastoral" relation to matter itself. Similarly, Abbott's idea of a world-on-paper encourages the fantasy of multidimensionality, as though a page were not merely flat but two-dimensional, which no solid object is: thus, even as *Flatland* emphasizes the literal spatial relation of the reader's body to the physical ground of representation, readers are encouraged in the fantasy that their position puts them in a higher dimension altogether. Braiding the physical and the metaphysical, the text would produce the "pathos of distance," Nietzsche's "domineering fundamental total feeling on the part of a higher ruling order in relation to a lower order, to a 'below.' "[16]

Seen in this context, even as hastily as I have sketched it here, the contemporaneous flattening of the canvas noticed by Greenberg seems difficult to explain as the self-specification of the medium of painting. The "progressive surrender" of painting "to the resistance of its medium" that he describes becomes difficult to take at face value, since it seems merely a tactical surrender in an overall strategy of overcoming the world of matter altogether. But as the diverse examples of Mallarmé, Pater, and Abbott already suggest, the scientific and religious valences of surface and space also became useful as a means of thinking about the relation of representation to social distinction. In Mallarmé, for instance, the Symbolist steam-rolling of the inviting interior of representation is, among other things, a way of excluding a despised mass reader looking for easy transport from his debased, "materialistic" life. What Abbott's *Flatland* enables us to see, indeed, is how closely associated two senses of the term "mass"—as physical matter and as an undifferentiated social body—could become: the pathos of distance is at once an epistemological and a social "attitude." The flattening of representation in the late-nineteenth century is, it seems, a complex symptom of a concern for "massification" in general, where the advent of mass culture is one symptom of a much bemoaned "materialistic" age. As we might expect from the very generality of the problem to which it responds, the impulse to flatten was susceptible to deployment in any number of specific ideological programs. In Abbott's case the acknowledgment of the unholy power of matter is the necessary first step—the identification of a problem—in proposing the general societal transcendence of materialism in favor of a Christian spiritual ideal. For others, however, the flattening of representation acknowledges the irrevocable facts of mass culture—the problem—while already imagining a reconstruction of social distinction in the form of psychic access to a privileged higher space. This version of the fourth dimension—in contrast to the leftist-socialist potential of the concept, where it could suggest a point of critical remove from the cognitive imperialism of the capitalist status quo—is better described as *supertopia* than utopia.[17]

Enter the versatile figure of the plane-being, an image at once of the flat-minded mass obstructing the spiritual and social advance of humankind but also, more divisively, of the "quarter-educated" idiots with whom literary elites increasingly felt themselves to be sharing cultural space. The convenience of the plane-being, for these writers, was in its allowing the imaginative application of a limitation presumably universal to humans, the inability to see the fourth dimension, to "lower" social groups. So too did it absolve the "higher" beings its flatness threw into relief of the necessity of offering physical proof of their exclusive location: the point was that this location was psychic, occult, and not subject to empirical verification. The plane-being also suggested, however—and not unrelatedly—an uncanny revelation about the nature of fictional character, and by extension about the novel, as such. The plane-being foregrounds the curious fact about fictional characters that their physical existence is realized in real space only as ink on a page, as collections of letters. Otherwise they are as invisible as spirits. From this substrate the character is "raised" into a virtual three-dimensional existence that seems to leave behind its crudely material origins.

This idea had considerably more influence in the development of the novel than one might at first imagine. The mutually implicating importance of dimension and literary character in this period was merely ratified when in 1927 E. M. Forster offered his influential distinction in *Aspects of the Novel* between "flat" characters, who do not change, and "round" (or three-dimensional) characters, who do.[18] His terminology is directly descended from the late-nineteenth-century preoccupation with dimensionality that produced *Flatland*.[19] With more social-historical resonance than he probably realized, Forster called the collections of letters from which character arises "word-masses." His distinction between flat and round characters organizes characters not in terms of the traditionally defined social class to which they belong, but in terms of their greater or lesser complexity. Transposing Bergson's assertion that "our psychic life may be lived at different heights with respect to matter" to the ontology of fictional character, the class or "type" of character is refigured by Forster in terms of this character's dimensional status. The round or "high" character (note how literally one can begin to take the spatial metaphors of "high" and "low") is defined by his or her existence in a mode of becoming rather than of being, his or her identity as an evolving "intelligent" spirit rather than as an inert thing. The flat character, meanwhile, is defined by his or her ontological proximity to the grossly material "word-mass" from which all characters arise.

Pursuing some of the implications of this process, narrative in the late-nineteenth century at once registers, and begins to respond to, the advent of mass culture, a culture that produces what Mallarmé derisively called "Art for All"—that does not distinguish the classes who consume it. Writing in the 1920s, Wyndham Lewis would call this mass culture a "plane-universe, without depth" where "every superlative" is "degraded into a worm-like extension, composed of a segmented, equally-distributed, accentless life."[20] Lewis's own loathing of this state of affairs did not prevent his acute retrospective analysis of the way a writer like Henry James could find a solution to the dilemma of mass cultural indistinction by intensifying his attention to the dimensions of representation and by attaching the class significances of "high" and "low" to a rhetoric of intelligence: "The vulgarity and *stupidity* . . . the *lowness* of the company" kept by popular novelists like Anthony Trollope "genuinely horrified" James, wrote Lewis, though this "low company" was only the company of stupid fictional characters. And

> how easy it is for those unduly sensitive to "lowness" and to "highness" to allow one sort of "lowness" [social] to merge in another [intellectual]—in rather the same manner that, above this melting pot where all the "lows" run into one, the mere old-fashioned snob is apt to converge upon, and is often found to be interchangeable with the "superior person," whose sensitiveness is intellectual rather than social.[21]

What Lewis saw in James was the emergence of the intellectual as a class designation founded not on genealogy or economic standing, but on a higher-dimensional placement with respect to the melting-pot "mass."[22] This was one response to the problem of indistinction in mass culture; and in the light cast backward from the ingenuity of its solution, the problem itself, I believe, emerges from the darkness of a perhaps deadening familiarity. We are prepared now, that is, to set James's work in the context of the institutional mechanisms by which the advent of mass culture was thought, by some, to have occurred; to see how these institutions inflected the old question of the relation of fiction to reality with newly intensified social significance; and, circling back to our beginning, to see why the idea of *dimension* could seem, to James and others, as if it might solve a problem no longer manageable in terms of *fiction*.

Fictions of the Mass

Take, for instance, this moment early in Henry James's novel *The Princess Casamassima*, a text at first glance quite removed from the concerns of Abbott.[23] First published in 1886, this was James's only extended attempt to represent life among the lower classes and, not unrelatedly, the place that his work is most obviously "infected," as Greenberg might put it, with the "ideological struggles of society."[24] His protagonist is young Hyacinth Robinson, the orphaned bastard son of a French laundress and an English aristocrat she has murdered. Early in the novel, before he has offered his services as a political assassin to a group of anarchist conspirators, Hyacinth stands in front of the sweetshop across the street from his humble home in Lomax Place. The shop is

> an establishment where periodical literature, as well as tough toffy and hard lollipops, was dispensed, and where song-books and pictorial sheets were attractively exhibited in the small-paned, dirty window. He used to stand there for half an hour at a time, spelling out the first page of the romances in the *Family Herald* and the *London Journal*, and admiring the obligatory illustration in which the noble characters (they were always of the highest birth) were presented to the carnal eye.[25]

The image here is made unmistakably of the materials of the novel's time, when the illustrated weekly magazine was becoming an ever stronger presence on the scene of English and American print culture. This mass circulation, whose novelistic counterpart was the phenomenon of the "bestseller," became possible in England and the United States for a number of intertwining and complex reasons, including the reduction of printing costs and eventually of product, but perhaps most importantly as a result of the spread of public schooling noted with some distress by Charles Dudley Warner in "The Novel and the Common School."[26] Historians usually point to the Education Act of 1870 as the key event in England: making elementary education the responsibility of the state, the Education Act enabled the extension of literacy deeper than ever before into previously illiterate classes.[27] Though he will quickly become quite a serious reader indeed, young Hyacinth's slow "spelling out" of the romance through dirty glass evokes precisely the transition to literacy of many in this time, reader-consumers whose entry into print culture was encouraged by the "carnal" lure of illustration.[28] Noting, as we saw in chapter 1, the spread of illustration even to bound books like his, James would elsewhere decry the " 'picture book' quality that contemporary English and American prose appears more and more destined, by the conditions of publication, to consent."[29]

What is most fascinating about this passage, however, and no less characteristic of its time, is how James places Hyacinth's act of reading at a threshold between an interior and an exterior space. Pages face outward against the glass, the inside of the sweetshop behind, as though there is real space on the other side of that page where his young reader could go—through the looking glass, so to speak—to claim his sweet identity as an aristocrat. We might dismiss this idea as fanciful if the novel did not proceed to figure it in any number of ways, even until James's preface of 1909, where Hyacinth is described as one of those "condemned to see" higher civilization "only from outside" and "with every door of approach shut in his face" (34), a description all the more interesting, I think, for being obviously inaccurate.[30] Most conspicuously, however, is it figured in Hyacinth's occupation, which literalizes the idea of a "relation to culture" as a spatial relation to its objects. He becomes a bookbinder, a laborer on the *outside* of books, and though he believes "that the covers of a book might be made to express an astonishing number of high conceptions," he has ambitions to make the "transition—*into* literature" as a writer (403, emphasis added).[31] In this manner Hyacinth's actions in *The Princess Casamassima*—constantly described, contrary to the preface, as the penetration of privileged social spaces—start to seem like ventures inside the very book on whose cover he works.

Now in most cases, it is clear, the idea that the masses had invaded fictional space took a more conventional form, relying not on the concept of fictive space but of empirical place. We have seen how in his 1899 essay "The Future of the Novel" James speaks with frightened awe of the new "multitude able to possess itself in one way and another of the *book*," how "the book, in the Anglo-Saxon world, is almost everywhere" and how "it is in the form of the voluminous prose fable"—"aided by mere mass and bulk"—that "we see it penetrate easiest and farthest."[32] Describing the preference of the new "homogenous" reading masses, or "total swarm," for the fat novel over any other kind of book, he suggests a curious similarity between the "monstrous multiplication" of novels and the crowding of humanity itself. Indeed, James seems to transpose a widespread preoccupation in this time with overpopulation directly into the book market.[33]

But this formulation—descriptive, in any case, more of the virtual space of the social imaginary, and of its purportedly crumbling hierarchies, than of any empirical social space—was also capable of being turned inside out, imagining not an empirical place crowded with massive books but a fictional space crowded with masses of readers. The idea was that to read a novel, to be immersed in its space, is to enter a sort of theater. This is how the American novelist Marion Crawford answers the strikingly fundamental question underlying his essay of 1893, *The Novel: What It Is*.[34] Noticing the novel's uncanny reversal of inside and out, and of expected scale, Crawford compliments "humanity" for finding "within the past hundred years" a "way of carrying a theatre in its pocket" (49), of condensing the space in which the theatergoer is contained into a small object, a "marketable commodity" itself capable of being contained in the person of the reader. The classic statement of this conception of the novel, how- ever, had already been offered by the popular novelist Walter Besant in his now famous speech before the Royal Institution in 1884, published as "The Art of Fiction." (It was this speech that occasioned Henry James's response of the same title.) Besant observes that the novel, a

> world in which the shadows and shapes of men move about before our eyes as real as if they were actually living and speaking among us, is like a great theatre accessible to all of every sort, on whose stage are enacted, at our own sweet will, whenever we please to command them, the most beautiful plays: it is, as every theatre should be, the school in which manners are learned: here the majority of reading mankind learn nearly all that they know of life and manners, or phi- losophy and art; even of science and religion.[35]

Although his stated purpose in the lecture is to make a claim for the novel as fine art, worthy of the prestige of painting, drama, and music, Besant's argument is remarkably inflected by a concern for the novel's pedagogical utility. In this he speaks in the long tradition of Samuel Richardson, where as a kind of conduct manual the novel begins to function like a dramatic text from which the virtuous reader takes her cues and learns her lines. William Dean Howells would similarly insist upon the role of the novel as teacher.[36] Crucially, however, Besant grants the reader considerably more agency in this process than the idea of her instruction by the author might suggest. Indeed, while he would restrict authors to writing about the classes they know from personal experience, for the reader there are no such restrictions on his or her class mobility, since the novel is a space of unobstructed *imitatio*, a school staffed with fictional characters, some of them princesses, from whom the reader can learn even the most aristo- cratic manners.

The most efficient way to summarize James's complex response to Be- sant in his own version of "The Art of Fiction" (1884) would be to say that he reverses Besant's evaluations. He insists stridently on the freedom of the author—including the freedom to range across class experience and the freedom from the compromising demands of pedagogical utility— while remaining relatively silent about what fiction does to, or for, the reader.[37] *That* half of James's response is offered subtly, though massively, in the novel composed immediately after his exchange with Besant, *The Princess Casamassima*, which registers the rise of the mass reader in the figure of Hyacinth standing before the sweetshop, and which entertains precisely the notion of blurred class identity that Besant allows to occur in the theater of fiction. In the space of the novel Besant describes, a "little bastard bookbinder" might, in a manner of speaking, befriend a princess.

And this is precisely what James's bookbinder does when he is able to attend a play at the theater, itself described as a kind of sweetshop. The theater, writes James,

> was full of sweet deception for him. His imagination projected itself lovingly across the footlights, gilded and coloured the shabby canvas and battered accessories, and lost itself so effectually in the fictive world that the end of the piece . . . brought with it a kind of alarm, like the stoppage of his personal life. (178)

It is hard to avoid the sense that this passage, written soon after James's debate with Besant, functions as an "allegory of reading," as the phrase goes. For Hyacinth the play has what James in "The Art of Fiction" calls the "sense of reality" he believes is the "supreme virtue of a novel" (*Essays*, 52–53). This sense of reality is betrayed when an author such as Trollope concedes "in a digression, a parenthesis or an aside" that "he and his trusting friend are only 'making believe' " (46). What is odd, though not unpredictable, is how the self-conscious assertion here of the "supreme virtue" of the "sense of reality" seems immediately to produce, in the nearly contemporaneous novel, precisely the threat of unreality it wants to ward off.

As though something about the self-consciousness of realist theory is undermining the realist project itself, right before our eyes, Hyacinth identifies so intensely with the fiction, is "so *friendly* to the dramatic illusion" (178, emphasis added), that the "reality-effect" of the representation starts to compete with his apprehension of reality itself. We begin to wonder whether the cross-class friendship he will moments later strike up with the Princess Casamassima is not itself a continuation of that dramatic illusion; whether we have not found ourselves in a theatrical dimension in which the distinction between the inside and outside of fiction, "personal life" and fantasy, is no longer secure. The "whole proposal" of Captain Sholto that Hyacinth meet the Princess in her stage-box does "make things dance, to appear fictive, delusive" (186). His penetration of concentric spaces, each more exclusive than the last, becomes more difficult to locate in real space. The Princess's expensive stage-box is reached, like a dream-world, only by "traversing steep stair-cases and winding corridors" (189), and when he opens the door to the stage-box his "first consciousness" was of his "nearness to the stage. . . . The play was in progress, the actor's voices came straight into the box, and it was impossible to speak without disturbing them" (190). Here it is as though the fourth wall has fallen, actors and audience, bookbinders and princesses, now dwelling in the same order of space. Hyacinth might well wonder "what kind of princess" this princess is, this fictional person who, James tells us in the preface, is the only one of his major characters to be "revived" after her use in an earlier novel (*Roderick Hudson*). This revival is itself described as a penetration of fictive space, where by some "obscure law" certain "of a novel-

ist's characters, more or less honourably buried, revive for him by a force
or a whim of their own and 'walk' round his house of art like haunting
ghosts, feeling for the old doors they knew, fumbling at stiff latches and
pressing their pale faces, in the outer dark, to lighted windows" (45). Hyacinth at the window of his sweetshop, the ghostly Princess at the lighted
window of the "house of art," befriend each other in the uncanny theater
of fiction.[38]

Precisely at the point in his career when James, with Howells, is making
his strongest claims for the novel's realist verisimilitude, his work begins
to be suffused with the strangeness we find in the scene at the theater, with
its suggestions of a "confusion of fiction with life"—a formula it would be
tempting to extend to the emergence of modernist narrative as a whole.
The epistemological problem of "fiction" begins, in James at least, with
his rotation of the "mass reader" from the exterior to the interior of the
representation. He does so because, as his essays from this time make clear,
the advent of mass readership is the kind of important historical fact he
believes it is the realist novel's task to represent. But as an object of representation, "the reader" has certain unique qualities, in that he or she can
seem to carry an uncanny "other" source of cognitive agency into the representation itself. In James this begins to produce not only the familiar
trope of the novel that seems in an obscure sense to read itself; it also
inflects the distortions of this textual self-consciousness with the question
of class identity. Thus James in the *Princess* seems to be working through
the more dizzying consequences, for the social geometries of his time, of
Besant's conception of fiction as a pedagogical theater. For instance, given
that the novel is a mechanism of class homogenization, the place where
"all of every sort" learn "nearly all they know of life," how can the writer,
himself a reader—or indeed any literate person with access to books—be
restricted to the class experience he knows? Do the writer's experiences as
a reader count, as they seem to for the rest of "reading mankind," as cross-
class experiences? What happens to the "reality" of class distinction when
fiction, as James puts it, has been subject to "monstrous multiplication."
What happens when the privileged knowledge and manners contained in
fiction, falling into the hands of the "total swarm," are now found "everywhere" in public space?[39]

James's answer is that the reality of class distinction threatens to disappear, but with the remarkable consequence that a secure sense of the difference between "life" and "fiction" threatens to disappear as well. It is
the literacy of the masses, in the late-nineteenth-century version of the
Shakespearean idea, that makes all the world a stage. Persons in this confused space have the ontological ambiguity of actors, the kind of "per-
formativity" often said to characterize the modern subject as such, but in
this period inflected with the question of class: thus is the unclassifiable

Hyacinth, without a stable class identity, "destined" to be "every day and every hour, an actor" (109). In this, I would suggest, he is the very emblem of the mass cultural subject. It is not that the traditional markers of class distinction have altogether disappeared from this culture—any more than they do in the three-dimensional view of Flatland, or in the Ralph Lauren semiotics of our own mass culture—but that these visible markers cannot be trusted to signify an essential class distinction. When Hyacinth enters the sweetshop of fiction he begins to read, to somewhat mind-bending sociological effect, the very novel in which he plays a part.

Indeed the omnipresence of "fiction," for James, produces a state of affairs where the effort to write a novel in the "scientific" manner of the French naturalists seems to require that the protagonist himself be, as Hyacinth uncannily is, born of a French mother, so that Hyacinth's trip to Paris in the novel starts to look as much like the novel's search for its own origins as Hyacinth's search for his. So, too, the resistance Hyacinth begins to give to his revolutionary "instincts" is hard to distinguish from the novel's resistance to its own generic naturalism: no less than the illustrated romances young Hyacinth sees in the window of the sweetshop does this novel contain characters "of the highest birth," one of whom might be, as in the tradition of romance, Hyacinth himself. Just as Hyacinth is a creature of "mixed, divided nature," so too is the novel uncannily divided between its naturalist and romantic impulses, and it ultimately traps Hyacinth in its contradictory space, becoming rather more like the "vast interior dimness" of the prison that housed his mother than of the sweetshop.[40] Unable to resolve his internal class division, that is, the novel kills him off.

Near the end of *Princess*, which is also the suicidal end of Hyacinth, the morbidly conflicted bookbinder is once again seen "looking into a window" of a shop, "when a vision" arises "before him of a quick flight . . . for an undefined purpose, to an undefined spot" (584). Here again is the evocation of the "elsewhere" found through the looking glass. From the perspective of the inside-out fictional world that Hyacinth now inhabits, however, that esoteric elsewhere has become precisely the extrarepresentational space he left outside the novel—the novel from which he, and his kind, were initially excluded. But this time, alas, Hyacinth can get neither inside that space nor to the undefined "outside" it miraculously encloses. Only by returning to his humble quarters and killing himself can he rejoin the author who, claiming the space vacated by his sacrificed bookbinder, now floats free as a ghost above the massified materiality of his texts.

In other words, in the *Princess* we see not only a parable of the intrusion of the mass reader into fictive space, and the confusions resulting therefrom, but also the first steps in the imagination by literary elites of various means of reproducing this reader's exclusion: one of these means is to *relocate* the space of privilege from the inside to the outside of fiction, such that privilege is now expressed in the *failure* to appear in, or to inhabit, what is now conceived to be the prison house of social representation.[41] But since the regime of representation now extends equally into real and fictive social spaces, the "outside" of representation has to be located in a space that is neither of these but something entirely new, the "higher" space often literally described, in this time, as an unrepresentable "fourth dimension." In this manner the vocabulary of dimension addresses problems no longer manageable in terms of "reality" and "fiction," even as it concedes the unalterable social (ir)reality of mass culture.[42]

Nowhere is this made more comically clear than in a novel by James's future and one-time friend H. G. Wells, *The Invisible Man* (1897), where the protagonist, Griffin, disappears with the help of a "geometrical expression involving four dimensions," the better to enjoy the "mystery, the power, the freedom" of being unseen.[43] Griffin soon discovers that he cannot deny the continuity of the space he inhabits with the flat stage of the everyday. And this, for literary history, is a crucial point. Griffin realizes this when his unseen naked body, exposed to the elements, is knocked about by passersby on the crowded streets of London. It is only the humiliation of being human, of having to play a social role, that is expressed when the haughty, snobby Invisible Man—in quite the reverse mood of the aspiring Hyacinth in front of his sweetshop—is forced to enter "a dirty fly-blown little shop . . . with a window full of tinsel robes, sham jewels, wigs, slippers, dominoes and theatrical photographs" (104). The confusion of inside and outside his penetration of the shop signifies, however, is precisely the same as Hyacinth's.

This is most obvious in a brief exchange between Mr. Marvel, the bewildered drunk forced to hold on to Griffin's books, and the curious mariner whose mind, in the vicinity of these oddly placed volumes, "wander[s] back again to a topic that had taken a curiously firm hold of his imagination."

> "Books?" he said suddenly, noisily finishing with the toothpick.
> Mr. Marvel started and looked at them. "Oh, yes," he said. "Yes, they're books."
> "There's some ex-traordinary things in books," said the mariner.
> "I believe you," said Mr. Marvel.
> "And some extra-ordinary things out of 'em," said the mariner. (103)

Something has taken a "curiously firm hold" of the mariner's "imagination," language that recalls Hyacinth at the theater, dwelling in a confused mixture of "personal life" and "illusion," empirical and fictive space. And indeed the suggestion here seems almost to be that the Invisible Man, standing unseen near the mesmerized mariner, is an ambiguously placed fictional character, neither within the book nor without.

Keeping hold of the concessions implied in the fourth-dimensional solution to the crisis of indistinction, we are able to make sense of an apparent
paradox in James's biography that has troubled critics of James for a long
time: the fact that his response to the evaporation of his readership, beginning with *The Bostonians* and the *Princess*, was first of all to make his
infamous "assault" on the London theater, an institution even more dependent on mass taste than the novel. In the theater, complained James,
"you write for the stupid," but it was by consorting ever more intimately
with this low company that he sought the economic windfall that would,
paradoxically, protect him from the market.[44] Wells, reviewing James's
Guy Domville on its opening night, agreed that a "play written for the
stage may very well be compared to a pen-and-ink drawing that is to
undergo reproduction by some cheap photographic process. . . . The thing
is to be reproduced on such a scale as to carry across unimpaired to the
pit and gallery"—that is, to the lowlife in the cheap seats.[45] James's play,
opening in early 1895, notoriously failed this test. But too little has been
made of the strange continuity of this real drama—in which, as James said
of the theater in general, his dramatic text *Guy Domville* was "murdered"
in its first performance—and *The Princess Casamassima*, a novel that itself juxtaposes notions of theatricality and murderous political conspiracy.

A rumor developed in the days following the raucous evening—the audience had booed the play and, finally, when he was brought onstage at the
play's conclusion, James himself—that the "roughs" making noise in the
gallery were in fact conspirators of some kind. In his well-known account
of this evening, Leon Edel writes that a "spectator reported" in one of the
papers in which the evening's performance was being hotly debated that
"there were some twenty men in the gallery and as many in the upper
boxes, the 'veriest roughs' who could not possibly have paid four shillings
for their seats. Each set had a leader who gave signals for the hooting"
(*Domville*, 103). This figures the bad manners of the audience as a sort of
anarchist plot: The Revenge of Hyacinth. At the same time—making curious sense of Wells's otherwise unmotivated observation, in his review, that
Guy Domville takes place "in the years immediately preceding the French
Revolution"—it figures James's moments onstage as the staging of a sort
of execution. Pressed flat and blinded by the glare of modern electric lights,
judgment pouring down from somewhere beyond, behind, above—James
inhabited in these traumatic moments a social-aesthetic space that as a
novelist he was accustomed to seeing only from outside and, in the production of text, literally from above. To be brought onto the stage was an
ontological reduction to the status of a Flatlander, as though in a night-
mare he had become merely a character in one of his own novels, no longer
free "to see—to see all over, to see everything" but pinned, now, to the

surface of his own page.[46] Here the readers who no longer bothered with
his novels could, adding a sort of phantasmatic insult to injury, boo him
off the stage of his own representation, realizing in this way a cultural-
political horror that had already been predicted, in remarkably lurid
terms, by James's friend Edmund Gosse:

> One danger which I have long foreseen from the spread of the democratic senti-
> ment, is that of the traditions of literary taste, the canons of literature, being
> reversed with success by a popular vote. . . . Of late there have seemed to me
> certain signs . . . of a revolt of the mob against our literary masters. . . . By de-
> grees [this mob] will cease to support reputations which give it no pleasure and
> which it cannot comprehend. The revolution against taste, once begun, will land
> us in irreparable chaos.[47]

James's response to his cultural beheading at the hands of this revolutionary mob was to abandon the theater—returning, in Edel's felicitous
phrase, "to his old observation post of the mind" (*Domville*, xviii), from
which point of the view the author's failure to appear in the space of representation could become an elaborate principle of composition.[48]

Extraordinary Readers

In one of the last chapters of *The Spoils of Poynton* (1897), the first novel
James produced after his failure as a playwright, Fleda Vetch and Mrs.
Gereth walk through the rooms of Ricks, a much humbler establishment
than the illustrious manor, full of treasures, the two women have lost to
the beautiful, dull-witted Mona Brigstock. It is easy to believe that in this
space that vibrates with defeat what is felt is in some sense the aftershock
of James's own recent failure—his inability to win over the house of riches
that was the St. James's Theatre, his flight back to the comparatively
pocket-sized "house of fiction." It is indeed as a player who has fled, failing
to act her part, that Fleda appears: She has been invited to Ricks by Mrs.
Gereth "because of all" her acquaintances, Fleda is "far away the least
stupid. For action you're no good at all; but"—and here it could be the
failed playwright speaking—"action's over, for me, for ever" (200). Fleda,
as they stroll, proves her intelligence immediately when she senses something subtle and wonderful in the rooms, " 'a presence, a perfume, a touch
. . . a soul, a story, a life' " (203). It may be the ghost of the maiden aunt
to whom Ricks once belonged and who lingers now as a kind of invisible
authorial presence. " 'There's ever so much more here than you and I,' "
says Fleda, traveling up the number line: " 'We're in fact just three!' "
" 'Does it happen,' " Mrs. Gereth asks, " 'to be in your power to give it a
name?' " It is in Fleda's power. She has only to add one to her sum: " 'It's
a kind of fourth dimension' " (203).

Sensing this "fourth-dimensional" presence, Fleda, the narrator tells us, "suddenly became the one who knew most." That for James knowing most means being most like the author seems to be made explicit in the preface to *Spoils* he wrote some years later. For it is here, recalling the tendency of works like *Flatland* to figure the ability to perceive higher dimensions as an invidious distinction, that he names "the very source of interest for the artist" in writing a novel, quite different from the pedagogical utility championed by Walter Besant: "it resides in the strong consciousness of his seeing all for himself . . . that he alone has the *secret* of the particular case, he alone can measure the truth of the direction to be taken by his developed data" (26). For James, it would seem, the value of consciousness derives at least in part from its participation in an economy of scarcity. It is thus a measure of Fleda's quasi-authorial intelligence, her uncommon ability to gain psychic access to his occult habitation, that she too begins to exhibit "consciousness of the whole, or of something ominously like it" (30). And again: the "appreciation, even to that of the very whole, lives in Fleda; which is precisely why, as a consequence rather grandly imposed, every one else shows for comparatively stupid" (31). Similarly did Abbott's A. Square, rising above his two-dimensional world and seeing it whole, experience the comparative stupidity of those living below.

It is often held, and no wonder, that Henry James's late fiction is centrally concerned with problems of epistemology—with how we know what we know, and how valid that knowledge is. So, too, the uncertainty upon which his fiction meditates, and which his readers seem necessarily to inherit, is one feature of his later work that is said to mark it as so plausible a progenitor of modernism. The title alone of *What Maisie Knew* (1897), the novel that followed directly upon *Spoils*, suggests the plausibility of the first claim, while the last sentence of the same work—"[Mrs. Wix] still had room for wonder at what Maisie knew"—suggests the "ambiguity" at which James's epistemological inquiries are so often said to arrive.[49]

It is true that James in his later fiction often develops the theme of ignorance-becomes-knowledge, and that he develops a narrative technique—the filtering of action through a relatively delimited "center" of perception and consciousness—seemingly well suited to fictional phenomenologies. The argument I have elaborated in the first two chapters of this book, however, linking James first to the social problem of the imagetext, and now to the intersecting rhetorics of geometry and social hierarchy, suggests that it would be wrong to let these facts obscure the degree to which this began as a project of somewhat more manifestly "social" intent than the representation of thought as such. It began—and I would argue continued throughout modernist fiction—as an attempt to distinguish the intelligent from the stupid.

The apparent "inward turn" of James's work after the "political" novels of the 1880s could not truly manage either for himself or for the texts he would continue to produce the "escape" from society—from its "ideas" and "ideological" struggles"—that Greenberg found in the avant-garde painter's flattening of representation. Rather, this turn represented, among other things, the aftermath of James's discovery of the geometric limitations of realist forms of social representation whose efforts to anatomize class differences become confused by the proximity, intimacy, and capacity for imitative theatricality of different persons circulating in the same dimension of space. *Flatland*'s fictional elaboration of social geometry, presenting both old threats of social indistinction and new opportunities for social exclusion, became in James's intensified turn to the novel of consciousness an alternative approach to, rather than a dismissal of, the problem of class. Rising, somewhat like A. Square, above the flatlands of the realist novel, James in his later fiction began to construct restricted avenues of access to a higher dimension, a higher consciousness, where a more reliable form of distinction could take place.

This mode of distinction was no less useful, in its way, for partaking of an ideal of authorship stridently opposed to the idea that novelists must be useful to the common reader. For one thing, the hypertrophy of rumination in James's late fiction succeeded to a degree in distinguishing his vestigial contemporary readership from other consumers of fiction. While it occasioned a long tradition, beginning with the obnoxious apostasy of the once-respectful H. G. Wells, of ridicule of James's work as absurdly and punishingly boring, and of his characters as monstrously and unrealistically brainy, to be a "reader of Henry James" began in this time to mean something significantly different—and no doubt, for some, better—from one who was a reader of novels. It meant, even as James's commercial failure was recuperated as artistic honor by James himself, and by worshipful early critics such as Ford Madox Ford, Percy Lubbock, and others, that one was particularly subtle and thoughtful—a Jamesian. In 1926, Floyd Dell would explain the cachet of James for his generation with considerable candor:

> [W]e came to honor and love Henry James, irrespective of our ability to make head or tail of his sentences, simply because those sentences notoriously and haughtily ignored the demands of the ordinary reader for an ordinary meaning.[50]

But no doubt the most ingeniously useful aspect of Jamesian conception of the class of the intelligent who dwell among the flat-minded mass was its sheer practicality. Refiguring class distinction as intellectual distinction, James found a way not only to accept the presence of the stupid masses in the space of culture but to figure the *necessity* of that presence: a model, perhaps, of high modernism's "pastoral" relation both to the vulgar matter—the ink and paper, paint and canvas—it reconstitutes as art and to the undifferentiated social masses with which this matter is metaphorically aligned.[51] In the preface to *Spoils*, for instance, the "spectator of life" is offered the "general truth" that "the fixed constituents of almost any reproducible action are the fools who minister, at a particular crisis, to the intensity of the free spirit engaged with them," a spirit whose intellectual superiority these idiots throw into relief (30). By this logic of contrast, we could say, the intellectual model of social distinction whose emergence I have been tracing appears not so much a rejection of mass culture as an effect of mass culture.

three _____

Downward Mobilities
The Prison of the Womb and the Architecture of Career in Stephen Crane

> By the time he reached her door he had confided to her that,
> in secret, he wrote: he had a dream of literary distinction.
> —Henry James, *The Princess Casamassima*

House of Fiction, House of Shame

I have been arguing that the modernist novel is the novel conceived as art, and that the art-novel is the novel conceived, among other things, as a bearer of cultural capital. What this means is that the question of status, a central preoccupation of the novel since its earliest days, is addressed by the *modernist* novel in two overlapping dimensions: it is a question not only of internal, thematic interest but also of external, formal interest—that is, self-interest. What does the novel's form say about the novel's status as a bearer of cultural capital? What must the novel be, what must it do, to be recognized as "art"?

These questions were embedded in the foundation of modernist fiction and guided its establishment in any number of ways. In chapter 1 we saw how the novel's cultural capital was imagined in the form of a visible art-object, a golden bowl one might hold in one's cognitive grasp, while in chapter 2 we saw how it was made to disappear, an invisible entity resident in a kind of non-Euclidean social space. Gaining access to this space, the modernist intellectual was understood to stand in the position both of a privileged "insider" to cultural knowledge and as an "outsider" to the humiliations of social representation. In this chapter we will begin to see how, implicating itself so literally in the question of *access*, the modernist novel extended and developed analogies between itself and other social spaces—architectural, biological, geographical—of more obviously inhabitable kinds.

Here, too, we will see that a desire for access, for the status of insider, is tightly braided with an opposing metaphorics of escape, or liberation. In the realist and naturalist writing associated with New York City this liberation is often figured as a kind of birth, an escape from the maternal prison of the womb into the masculine space of career. Indeed, it partici-

pates in what has been described by several critics as a general masculini-
zation of novelistic prestige, over and against a feminized mass market
fiction, that extends at least from Howells's realism through Crane's impressionism and Wharton's antisentimentalism, on to the exaggerated
modernist masculinities of Ernest Hemingway and Dashiell Hammett discussed in my final chapter.[1]

Some of these analogies are already visible in Henry James's experiment
in literary naturalism, *The Princess Casamassima*, when, early in the
novel, the "little bastard" Hyacinth Robinson is taken by Amanda Pynsent
to see his dying mother in prison. Before he sees this Frenchwoman, Hyacinth first must encounter the structure that houses her, and it can seem,
as James describes it, as though this "big, dark building . . . lift[ing] its
dusky mass from the bank of the Thames, lying there and sprawling over
the whole neighborhood, with brown, bare, windowless walls . . . and a
character unspeakably sad and stern"—is something of a maternal figure
in its own right. "It looked very sinister and wicked," Amanda thinks,
"about as bad and wrong" as the women "who were in it." But, already
having confronted the "sullen walls" of the prison, Amanda feels "they
had already entered into relation" with their sullen inmate, and so must
continue inward even though she has "no confidence that if once she
passed the door of the prison she should ever be restored to liberty."[2]

It is "not on her own account" that Amanda is most nervous, however,
"but on that of the urchin," Hyacinth, "over whom the shadow of the
house of shame might cast itself" (79). And indeed, as he enters the "dark
corridors" and "vast interior dimness" of the prison, it can seem that Hyacinth is undergoing a sort of reverse birth, a return to the defiled and
disgraced womb from which he, both organically and socially, has
emerged. The question for Hyacinth is whether and to what degree the
"circumstances" of his birth, figured here as the shameful prison of the
womb, can be differentiated, ultimately, from the various spaces in which
he has been, as we say, "socially constructed" as a person. In his immensely
powerful characterization of late-nineteenth-century culture, Mark Seltzer
has traced this sort of uncertainty to what he calls the period's "body-
machine complex," its twin fascination with organic and artificial reproduction: Is it Hyacinth's point of biological origin, imagined as a kind
of architectural space, or rather the social spaces of his adoptive society,
themselves subject to being understood as a maternal womb, that hold the
key to his destiny?[3] The question is one to which neither the bookbinder
Hyacinth Robinson nor the author Henry James will be able to provide a
satisfactory answer.[4]

For Hyacinth, as we have seen, this confusion has drastic consequences,
for having committed himself both to the cause of anarchist revolutionaries, whose aspirations to social equality he gradually understands to be

fantasies, and to his fantasies of social distinction, which he uncannily
begins to realize, he finds himself not only morally but epistemologically
trapped, a victim, we might say, of the conflicting imperatives of realism
and romance. The Princess Casamassima, whose name suggests an architectural space, a house that might make room for the mass, can no longer
shelter him. His quandary—a confusion of class conflict and class defer-
ence, fixed identity and social mobility—can be resolved only by killing
himself.

For James, the consequences of this confusion were not quite so dire.
He merely produced a novel frequently judged to be bad, an unconvincing
attempt to represent a social milieu of which he had little direct knowledge,
and thus a weak attempt to produce a naturalist text in the manner of
Zola. But if this novel has had little success with latter-day critics, still less
was it a success with its first potential readers, who stayed away from it
by the millions. James's misjudgment seems to have been to think that the
commercial viability of naturalism in France—a viability he wished to
emulate, even as he was somewhat uncomfortable with Zolaesque grotes-
queries—would extend to his own work. In this view James's novel looks
doubly unfortunate, a sellout that didn't sell.[5]

Rather than continue in this tradition of aesthetic judgment, however,
we will find it more useful to attend to what the text most convincingly
and compellingly reveals, a project ably taken up in the earliest work of
Seltzer. In Seltzer's Foucauldian account of James, his fiction is said to
reveal the "ways in which the novel, as a form and as an institution,
reinscribes and supplements social mechanisms of policing and regulation."[6] It reveals, that is, the thorough complicity of the Jamesian realist
novel in a more general project of panoptic surveillance that makes persons
accountable to social norms and to the law. While I will take issue with
some of its emphases, Seltzer's reading is bound to seem a considerable
advance upon accounts which argue that James's "art" has nothing at all
to do with "power." Accepting James's aspirations for his aesthetic project
at face value, these accounts can seem to grant to James the fulfillment of
what can only, one assumes, be a wish: the absolute removal of art from
more worldly and practical domains.

And yet it is possible, even granting Seltzer much of his case, to find in
this sort of analysis of James's "fantasy of surveillance" its own fantastic
component, "power" itself. As a heuristic abstraction, residing in no particular subject or social group, "power" has considerable power, presiding
over Foucauldian literary criticism as a beacon to which virtually any feature of a text can be mapped.[7] For Seltzer, that is, James's art has *everything* to do with power, always, and never more so than when it seems to
disclaim this relation. Thus, symptomatically, "one reason for suspecting
this link between art and power" in James is that he "works so carefully

to deny it" (*Art of Power*, 16). Protesting too much, the Jamesian aesthetic
enterprise only manages to betray its complicity with the more visible and
vulgar brutalities of the policial regime. This regime is characterized by
its dispersal of power through "tutelary" social institutions that do not
admit to the dominations they covertly enact. Indeed, insofar as this "ruse"
is taken as the very essence of modern techniques of discipline, the Jamesian aesthetic institution can seem, if anything, *more* powerful than the
institutions of politics, the military, and the law. Having the considerable
disadvantage of wearing power on, rather than up, their sleeves, these
institutions start to seem oddly marginal to their own ends.[8]

If this suspicious account of the aesthetic is by now somewhat familiar,
less so are the means by which it can be made more credible without
reasserting an absolute difference between art and power. One might begin
by restoring to accounts of this period something that historicist criticism
frequently ignores: the relative autonomy, after midcentury, of what Pierre
Bourdieu has called "the field of cultural production" from contig-
uous institutions of politics and government. This relative autonomy is no
less significant for being misperceived, at times, as the possibility of absolute autonomy from these institutions. Drawing attention to the specificity
of cultural production, and to the specific forms of value (and power) circulating around aesthetic objects, the sociological perspective enables a
form of analysis that pauses at the level of institutional mediation long
enough to register the fact of discursive differences. So, too, are we encouraged to attend to differences even within the novel's relatively delimited
field, so that "naturalism," for instance, becomes legible not merely as an
instance of "culture," or even of the "novel," but as a genre with a specific
set of significances for its various producers, champions, detractors, and
consumers.[9]

By contrast, the tendency of the Foucauldian account is to assimilate
different forms of cultural production to each other, in turn to assimilate
cultural production to vigilantly "caring" institutions such as medicine
and public health, in turn to assimilate all of these to "social mechanisms
of policing and regulation" whose operations they "reinscribe and supplement" (Seltzer, *Art of Power*, 19). One effect of this spiral of assimilations
is to suggest that "power," because it is everywhere, exerts itself on different social groups with equal force. One need not attempt to dissuade those
who want to believe in a citizenry "policed" by the novels of Henry James
to note something that the Foucauldian account makes virtually invisible:
that to be a "reader of Henry James," in his own time as in ours, was also
to lay claim to cultural capital. One might of course read the very desire
to acquire cultural capital as evidence of a submission to a social imperative; at the same time, it might seem worthwhile to keep hold of the sense
that certain forms of "submission" are experienced as more enabling, or

even empowering, than others. Thus, even as Seltzer, in his reading of James's *Princess*, convincingly documents how the supervision of the urban underclass in late-nineteenth-century documentary texts is performed by a higher class that reifies and pathologizes the poor, the comprehensive power of "power" in his argument leads him ultimately to minimize the significance of this social difference.

Elsewhere, explaining how this might be so, he describes what he calls the "law of reversibility," whereby the subject's "power of seeing," becoming transfixed by its object, "opens the possibility of a violent loss of balance or *dis*empowerment" on the part of the supervising subject him- or herself. Generalized as an account of social supervision, this suggests a remarkably democratic "seeing machine in which everyone is caught" (Seltzer, *Bodies*, 97). Again, there is an important element of truth here. Even the most economically and culturally empowered persons are subject to structures of socialization. One need look no further than the highly scrutinized worlds of the Jamesian society novel, or novel of manners in general, to see that this is so. However, this perhaps only goes to show how banalizing the Foucauldian abstraction can become: located everywhere, and thus nowhere in particular, power is hardly to be differentiated from the force of "the social" as such. Following this line of argument, Seltzer is left with no convincing means—or, rather, desire—to account for the unequal or qualitatively different distribution of power to historically situated individuals and groups.

And yet it is at the level of *discursive* difference—distinctions between the institutions of literature and other institutions; distinctions within the field of literary production itself—that the occlusions enacted by Foucauldian criticism become most evident. As many critics have noted, and as the previous chapters of this work have confirmed, the writing of this period is profoundly marked by a concern for distinctions—social, generic, and otherwise—between different kinds of cultural objects understood to be bearers of different amounts and kinds of capital. Taking into account the fact that in this period (though not only in this period) different kinds of writing are defined in opposition to competing forms, the pages to follow will track some of these constitutive relations. Doing so, I will attempt not so much to critique as to retexture the Foucauldian account of certain texts of this period by paying attention to the specifically *literary institutional* power relations in which they are engaged. I will demonstrate how certain texts of the period, working with the architectural analogy, internalize these relations, representing the social structures, productive of social and cultural differences, that are their mirror image and ultimate cause.

Thus, for instance, while *The Princess Casamassima* might be assimilated at a certain level of abstraction to French naturalism, in turn to be assimilated to other social institutions of policing and power, this vertical trajectory leaves unexamined what might seem, upon closer examination, to be more specifically at stake in this text: the complex relation between the genre of naturalism and other forms of the novel, including the Jamesian realist novel of the 1880s. In *The Princess Casamassima*, the social relations the novel represents become all but indistinguishable, at certain moments, from generic and literary-institutional relations.[10] For example, if, for many critics, James's *Princess* has seemed insufficiently committed to the project of literary naturalism, then it seems important to note that the novel virtually declares its lack of commitment to this genre as the fear of being trapped in the dark, maternal space that the genre of French naturalism, for James, represented. This fact, supported by the evidence of James's own criticism of Zola, is lost in the voraciously assimilative Foucauldian reading of the novel.[11] Indeed, in Seltzer's account, a mirror reversal of those who judge unkindly the *Princess*'s failure to instance naturalism, the form of the major-phase fiction is explained in terms of the novel's all-too-visible *success* in achieving naturalism's policial ends. Thus "James, in his later fiction," is forced to "reject . . . this too-evident narrative policing and elaborate . . . a more tactful and more comprehensive style of supervision" (*Power*, 18).

    It will seem that the novel has always already been troubled by its relation to naturalism, however, when we note the simple but extraordinary fact that Hyacinth's grotesque mother is represented as a *Frenchwoman*. It is as though Zola's form cannot be transposed onto an English setting without dragging along one of its disturbing objects, and also some of its language: by the time Hyacinth sees her, his mother has lost her ability to speak English. Thus she reverts to the "mother tongue," which erupts in the prison scene in a long series of untranslated sentences (a unique occurrence in James's fiction). Borrowing a phrase from Fredric Jameson, we could say that this maternal prison is a "prison-house of language," a real space and also a *discursive space* that James must enter to emulate Zola. In this view James's novel does not, as Seltzer would have it, *exemplify* naturalism; rather, it represents a *relation* to the generic abstraction, "naturalism," by turns invested and repelled, and it does so in remarkably literal architectural terms. Indeed, James's work suggests how "novelistic" is the increasing tendency, in contemporary cultural criticism of various kinds, to become fascinated by the question of institutional, social, private, public, cultural, or literary "space."

    Among the most productive of these has been Bourdieu's sociological account of distinction. Thus, for instance, even as Bourdieu's work—suffused with metaphors of the "field," of the "space of positions," and the like—provides a useful way to reread James's novel, this novel can in turn seem to lend to Bourdieu's spatial metaphors something more than a heuristic force. This is the result, perhaps, of the many shared premises of the discipline of sociology and the realist/naturalist novel, both of them committed to *seeing* the abstraction that is "social structure." Take, for instance, Bourdieu's analysis of Flaubert's *Sentimental Education*, his most sustained attempt to perform a reading of a literary text. Like Hyacinth, Flaubert's Frederic is a would-be novelist but, also like Hyacinth, fails to realize his literary aspirations. Without denying the important differences between the two novels, one immediately sees how Bourdieu's characterization of Flaubert's project might find an echo in James's own:

> One is thus led to the true site of the relation, so often evoked, between Flaubert and Frederic. In place of the customary complacent and naive projections of an autobiographical type, one should in fact perceive an enterprise of objectification of the self, of autoanalysis, of socioanalysis. Flaubert separates himself from Frederic, whose impotence manifests itself, among other things, by his inability to write, to become a writer. Far from suggesting the identification of the author with the character, it is certainly to register more clearly how far he is separating himself . . . that Flaubert indicates that Frederic undertakes to write a novel. (*Rules*, 25)

For Bourdieu, Flaubert's self-distantiation from Frederic, and also from the web of "social determinations" that entrap and defeat his character, partakes of a much larger historical project of constructing what he calls the "neutral place" of the field of cultural production. Frederic, alas, does not gain access to this place. But, as if to confirm the necessity of spatial metaphors that might otherwise seem to be post hoc fabulations, a version of this "neutral space" appears, as we have already seen in chapter 2, in remarkably literal form near the end of *The Princess Casamassima*. Ordered by his anarchist colleagues to assassinate a political figure, but unable now to betray the "beautiful" social order he has come to love, a morbidly conflicted Hyacinth finds himself "looking into a window" of a shop when "a vision rose before him of a quick flight. . . for an undefined purpose, to an undefined spot" (584). Though he manifestly fails to find this "neutral place," Hyacinth's failure becomes visible, from Bourdieu's perspective, as the negative image of James's own imaginary *success* in doing so. This "success" will in turn be conferred upon James by the critical tradition, justly criticized by Seltzer, that credits him with the production of a "pure" and "disinterested" aesthetic form of the novel.

What the "failed" *Princess* brings to the surface, however—perhaps precisely because of its failure—is the local structure of interest lodged at the foundation of this putatively asocial, unmaternal "neutral space." The same is true of another well-known space apart, the "republic of the spirit" in Edith Wharton's *The House of Mirth* (1905). These neutral spaces are reaction formations—imaginary negations, but also products—of the sort

of social struggle that appears on the first page of Stephen Crane's *Maggie:
A Girl of the Streets* (1893):

> A very little boy stood upon a heap of gravel for the honor of Rum Alley. He was
> throwing stones at howling urchins from Devil's Row, who were circling madly
> about the heap and pelting at him.
>
> His infantile countenance was livid with fury. His small body was writhing in
> the delivery of great, crimson oaths. . . . Over on the Island a worm of yellow
> convicts came from the shadow of a grey ominous building and crawled slowly
> along the river's bank.[12]

In moments like this one, I will argue, Crane's text turns itself inside out,
figuring the social production of an aesthetic discourse of the novel as an
emergence from the imprisoning womb of social space.[13] The very little
boy wants "honor," and he will both achieve and announce his status as a
"writhing" delivery of oaths. Much the same could be said of Stephen
Crane, whose sudden popularity upon the publication of *The Red Badge
of Courage* (1895) has tended to occlude his earlier self-construction as a
radical avant-gardiste willing to risk middle-class social failure in pursuit
of higher artistic honor. And yet, some of the equivocations of his emergence from the imprisoning womb are already visible in the passage above,
where that "worm" of convicts, momentarily free of the prison walls, continues to walk in the shadow of the house of shame.

Urban Ambitions: Crane, Wharton, O. Henry

One of the things that differentiates Stephen Crane's *Maggie: A Girl of the
Streets* from documentary texts to which it is obviously related, such as
Jacob Riis's *How the Other Half Lives* (1890), is the considerable attention
Crane pays in his novel to what his father had derisively called "popular
amusements," and which we have come more respectfully to call "popular
culture." Complicating, without negating, the oft-noted tendency of reformist journalism to constitute the poor as inert objects of a higher social
supervision, Crane's work, a fiction, portrays the consumption in the Bowery of another kind of fiction, theatrical melodrama, demonstrating how
this staged fiction is incorporated into the imaginative life of one of its
inhabitants:

> Maggie always departed with raised spirits from the showing places of the melo-
> drama. She rejoiced at the way in which the poor and virtuous eventually sur-
> mounted the wealthy and wicked. The theatre made her think. She wondered
> if the culture and refinement she had seen imitated, perhaps grotesquely, by the
> heroine on the stage, could be acquired by a girl who lived in a tenement house
> and worked in a shirt factory. (28)

Readers of *How the Other Half Lives* alone might not have known that
the inhabitants of the Bowery were capable of this thoughtful specular
longing and, even more importantly, of the *social ambition* this longing
inspires. Indeed, in Riis's account, the Bowery's pacification of ambitions
to social mobility—where, sinking "to the level of their surroundings," the
poor become "at last content to remain there"—produces some of its most
disturbing sociological effects.[14] Sapping its inhabitants of organized ambition, the Bowery might one day combust in anarchic anger, but it can
be reformed only from without, by agents acting on the poor's behalf.
Crane's novel, by contrast, remains interested in the effects of ambition
itself, and in the sentimental fantasies of class mobility Maggie consumes.
But what difference does his attention to fiction and ambition make?

Much like Riis, Crane is engaged in *Maggie* in an attempt to turn the
dim interior of the tenement inside out, exposing it to the light of public
conscience. In this discourse a crowded "dark bedroom, prolific of untold
depravities" (Riis, *Other Half*, 5), emblematizes the imprisonment and, in
a literal sense, de-moralization of the poor by their social environment.
Engaging with the market economy mainly at the level of production—in
Maggie's case it is the production of shirts—the poor are at the same time
steeped in an environment of "prolific" sexual reproduction, aided by the
single commodity they consume in excess, alcohol: the close quarters of
the tenement, crowding inebriated bodies together, reproduces an even
larger crowd. While Riis supplemented his journalistic documentation of
poverty with a remarkable series of photographs of Bowery life, Crane's
in its own way was a project of envisioning. Predicting Joseph Conrad's
1897 call for a literary impressionism—"Before all, to make you see!"—
Crane writes as though Conrad's dictum is as much a social as an aesthetic
imperative: "See how these people live!"

Some measure of the power of his and of Riis's projects of envisioning
derives, no doubt, from their resolute materialism. In these texts abstract
concepts like "social structure" are given a kind of pornographic embodiment by their literal representation as tenement houses—"social structures" in which the poor actually live. Indeed, nothing is more striking in
these texts than the way they virtually collapse the distinction between
buildings and people, as though Crane's oft-repeated assertion that "environment is a tremendous thing in the world and frequently shapes lives
regardless" could be pursued full circle, producing a personification of the
tenement itself.[15] The tenement "building quivered and creaked from the
weight of humanity stamping about in its bowels," writes Crane early on
in *Maggie*, as though this building is a massively and revoltingly pregnant
woman: "Eventually they entered into a dark region where, from a careening building, a dozen gruesome doorways gave up loads of babies to the

street and the gutter" (6). Later, at the novel's conclusion, he completes this personification when he describes how Maggie

> went into the blackness of the final block. The shutters of the tall buildings were closed like grim lips. The structures seemed to have eyes that looked over her, beyond her, at other things. Afar off the lights of the avenues glittered as if from an impossible distance. (53)

For Crane, as for Riis, the question of "how the other half lives" is to a considerable degree answered by describing *where* the other half lives, as though ultimately these buildings offer a more reliable, because more concrete, index of human behavior than human behavior itself.

Literalizing the idea of social structure, this architectonic materialism also literalizes the notion of "reform." To reform the Bowery social structure, it is suggested, one must actually alter the form of its structures, a process barely begun in 1869, Riis notes, with the "cutting of more than forty-six thousand windows in interior rooms" (13). The immediate intent of this "structural reform" was to provide these rooms with ventilation, but always in these texts it is assumed that "an atmosphere of actual darkness" produces a darkness "both moral and physical," which can be alleviated by the appearance of an equally multivalent "light." Though we will want to attend further to important differences between the two, we need first to join recent critics in emphasizing the degree to which this rhetoric of reformist journalism conditions Crane's impressionist aesthetics.

Indeed, the reach of the architectonic topoi of reformist documentary writing was by no means limited to the work of Crane. In O. Henry's short story "A Furnished Room" (1906), for instance, we are introduced to persons who do not so much occupy the spaces in which they live as haunt them, whose "vagrant" inhabitations are so brief as to already suggest their absence.[16] "Restless, shifting, fugacious as time" is this "vast bulk of the population" of lower Manhattan. "Homeless, they have a hundred homes. They flit from furnished room to furnished room, transients forever—transients in abode, transients in heart and mind" (98). Indeed, so "ghostly" are they that the telling of their stories must proceed not by tracking their movements, but by a "close reading" of the empty spaces they leave behind. This, literally, is what the "young man" protagonist must do as he searches for his lost love: "One by one, as the characters of a cryptograph become explicit, the little signs left by the furnished room's procession of guests developed a significance" (101). Not the least interesting of these little signs, it seems to me, are the "tiny fingerprints on the wall," which "spoke of little prisoners trying to feel their way to sun and air" (101). For here, discovering evidence not of transiency but of infantile entrapment—echoes of young Hyacinth's visit to his mother—the young man hits upon the fundamental ambiguity of this living space that speaks

so insistently, so literally, of *social mobility*: that the freedom of movement
exercised by this vagrant class is barely distinguishable from its imprisonment. Indeed, it merely seems that, in the cheating of what O. Henry calls
the "home instinct," our usual understanding of imprisonment as a confinement that removes one from public space has been reversed, and that
in this case locking in has become indistinguishable from locking out.

So too is Florence, the pretty trimmer of hats in O. Henry's "Brickdust
Row" (1906), in a sense imprisoned in the open. Living in a crowded
tenement, she has no parlor, so she must conduct her social life in public.
This ultimately discredits her as an object of desire in the blinkered vision
of Blinker, the rich man she meets on the ferry to Coney Island. Blinker is
blinkered because he does not see that his own social mobility—as the
story opens he is at the point of leaving the city for a vacation, but is kept
from doing so by his lawyer, who needs him to sign documents relating to
his ownership of real estate in New York—is the social inversion of the
mobility imposed upon his young love. This inversion works in the registers both of class and of gender, a sort of double double standard, as the
rich man becomes the mirror reversal of the poor woman. He does not see
that the legal papers he is so loath to sign are evidence of a profound
continuity between classes that appear, on the surface, to have nothing to
do with one another.

This, indeed, is what the unlikely coincidence we discover at the story's
conclusion—Blinker actually owns the building in which Florence lives—
serves to reinforce: that Blinker has always already been in relation to his
object of desire, and that he himself has already been the agent of her ruin.
This ontological intimacy between subject and object is what underwrites
Blinker's momentary ability to see the "shrieking, struggling, hurrying,
panting" proletariat in Coney Island not as his absolute other, but as
"brothers seeking the ideal" (87). And yet it is this same intimacy, as
Blinker finds his own shameful insouciance mirrored in the face of his
de-moralized object, which reproduces the class separation the story has
momentarily found a way to suspend.

But what is the ideal that these classes, rich and poor, might pursue as
one? In Coney Island it appears to be the "empty but shining casque of
Chivalry, the breath-catching though safe-guarded dip and flight of Ad-
venture, the magic carpet that transports you to the realms of fairyland"
(87). Alternatively, it might simply be that parlor, or reception room, that
Florence doesn't have. In her first published book, *The Decoration of
Houses* (1897), Edith Wharton had meditated upon the importance of
such an intermediate space, understood to enable the regulated interpenetration of the public and private realms. "In relation to the other rooms of
the house," she had written, this reception room "is like a public square."[17]
But it is a curiously private public square, a protected one. It is precisely

such an intermediate space that neither Florence nor, for that matter, Wharton's heroine, Lily Bart, can find. Indeed, in its own way, *The House of Mirth* seems as intent on examining the paradoxes of access and egress, freedom and enclosure, as does O. Henry's "A Furnished Room."

When, toward the end of *The House of Mirth*, the downward trajectory of Lily Bart's social "career" has carried her into a modest tenement room not unlike the ones described by Crane and O. Henry, we are given to understand that her inhabitation of this "narrow room, with its blotched wall-paper and shabby paint" bespeaks her imprisonment in debt.[18] She is now "obliged to work for a living." And yet, again and again in the earlier parts of the novel, we have been told that the luxurious spaces of the social elite in which Lily has featured as a conspicuous female "ornament" are themselves no less imprisoning. Thus, her sad end in a humble furnished room is a sign not only of entrapment, but of her asserted freedom in face of social conventions that would see her "placed," once and for all, in a socially advantageous marriage. To escape from these confines, however, is merely to find herself imprisoned on the outside with women like Maggie, as her "freedom" quickly becomes visible as the freedom to waste away. She might shrink "from observation and sympathy" by opting for the "privacy and independence" of a furnished room instead of living with her friend Gerty Farish, but this merely produces an "unwonted confinement" that pushes her into the shrieking "tumult of trams and wagons" in the street. She might avoid the public display required of her if she works in the showroom of Mme Regina's millinery establishment, but this merely exposes her to the amused scrutiny of her fellow proletarians in the back room:

> On and on it flowed, a current of meaningless sound, on which, startlingly enough, a familiar name now and then floated to the surface. It was the strangest part of Lily's strange experience, the hearing of these names, the seeing the fragmentary and distorted image of the world she had lived in reflected in the mirror of the working girl's minds. She had never before suspected the mixture of insatiable curiosity and contemptuous freedom with which she and her kind were discussed in this underworld of toilers. (285–86)

Here, in a revery reminiscent of the confused babble of odors and sounds that overwhelms the protagonist of "A Furnished Room," Lily suddenly understands the "strange" continuity, the distorted and fragmentary mirror relation, between her present class placement and her former one.

That O. Henry and Edith Wharton should, to such an uncanny degree, be seen to collaborate with Crane in the production of a shared response to the question of class placement in New York is, on the face of it, surprising. Indeed, one might think that the comparison of these writers would mostly yield evidence of contrast. O. Henry, born Will Porter, a former pharmacy

clerk, accountant, and convicted felon, rose to fame as the tribune of what
he called the "Four Million." This was a polemical inversion of the idea of
the Knickerbocker "Four Hundred," the term used to describe the restricted numbers allowed to circulate at the highest levels of New York
society. His short stories were published in mass circulation newspapers
and magazines such as the *New York World* and *McClure's*.[19] Edith Wharton, by contrast, was a child of the very Knickerbocker elite against which
O. Henry unleashed so much satiric irony. The wealth of her family derived
from what O. Henry in "Brickdust Row" calls "hereditaments"—from real
estate holdings in New York. Wharton was not only the first woman, but
the first person in her family in several generations to make money by her
own labor.[20] After a long period of apprenticeship, publishing occasionally
in *Scribner's Magazine*, the appearance of *The House of Mirth* in 1905
established her, in Elaine Showalter's phrase, as the "elegant scribe of
upper-class New York society, a novelist of manners and decor."[21]

And yet, a glance at Wharton's first major novel suggests how much
more complicated than this the situation of Wharton was. For if she established herself as an elegant scribe of upper-class New York in *The House
of Mirth*, she did so conspicuously by representing the "career" of a woman
who falls out of this class into the laboring class. I would argue that,
in doing so, Wharton recuperates the problem of downward mobility
as a figure for the opportunities of literary production. The representation
of urban poverty is thus a "pastoral" enterprise in the revised sense of
Empson discussed in the introduction to this book. In this view, the literary
discourse of Bowery pastoral is less plausibly invested in "controlling" or
"policing" the poor—as the plainly overstated Foucauldian account would
have it—than in performing a transitory identification with the poor that
enables a certain kind of success within the institutions of literature. Thus,
one might say, the "problem" of downward mobility appears in Wharton's
work not as a problem but as a solution to the problem of career: Wharton
was, after all, the only major American novelist for whom being a "successful novelist" might, as a version of being "in trade," have signified a drop
in social level.

This is what lends a certain allegorical quality to a scene in the millinery,
where Wharton could be taken to be asking herself about the status of her
own labor as a writer: "There were twenty of them in the work-room . . .
bowed in the harsh north light above the utensils of their art; for it was
something more than industry, surely, this creation of ever-varied settings
for the face of fortunate womanhood (282)." For what has Wharton done,
in this novel of downward mobility, but to create "ever-varied" settings
for Lily Bart? It is as though her identity can truly be seen only as an effect
of transition, of transiency. This is evident in the preference Lily shows for
working at the millinery shop rather than for the nouveau riche Miss

Hatch. The character Rosedale, referring to her previous employment as a social secretary to Miss Hatch, calls that job a "soft berth." But for Lily it was perhaps "too soft—one might have sunk in too deep" (290). Here it is as though to stay put in any one place, in any one class placement, is to lose one's identity entirely. Against this danger—the danger of Wharton's own constricted class placement—the novel obsessively presents what it calls the "value of contrast" (47), where, "relieved against the dull tints of the crowd," Lily becomes all the more "conspicuous" (4). Later on this idea appears again, as Rosedale looks at Lily over tea: "Against the dull chocolate-coloured background of the restaurant, the purity of her head stood out as it had never done in the most brightly-lit ballroom" (289–90).

For Wharton, then, contrast makes beauty visible, but it also makes *identity* visible, and it is the mobility enabled by the market economy that produces her as "her own person," a self-supporting writer. Indeed, for all the evident differences of their social milieux, Edith Wharton, Stephen Crane, and O. Henry found not an identical but a proximate relation in common space in the literary market, where all three, emerging from upper-, middle-, and working-class social backgrounds, eventually sold tremendous numbers of books. This must of course complicate our sense that these writers were in any simplistic sense opposed to the market economy; if all three seem to cast a jaundiced eye on the way cynical "market values" supersede human fellowship and love, all three understood that they were deeply implicated in this market as participants. That, no doubt, is part of what makes their absorption of the topoi of reformist documentary into their fiction at once so marked and so vexed.

And indeed, for all its similarities to reformist texts, Crane's fiction remains quite different from works like Riis's in its form, intent, and effect. To describe this in terms of the more or less obvious difference between the "literary" and the "nonliterary" text—the former producing, say, a heightened intensity of metaphor and imagery frequently attributed to literary discourse, the latter setting out after positive knowledge—would no doubt be accurate to a very limited degree. But it would leave the question of why and how this difference is produced unanswered, indeed unasked. So too would it run the risk of attributing to the "literary," and to the field of literary production in this period, a homogeneity that it did not by any means have. In the case of Crane this would be particularly unsatisfying because, as Christopher Benfey has noted, it is precisely an uncertain relation of literary and nonliterary elements—an uncertain relation between the "real" and the "imaginary"—that lends to Crane's work such unusual and uncanny force.[22] It was after all Crane who produced in *The Red Badge of Courage* a vivid evocation of the Civil War without ever having been near a battle, and it was Crane who thereafter was sometimes treated as though he were a veteran of that conflict. Thus Crane's fiction cannot adequately be explained, a priori, in terms of the difference between the literary and the nonliterary, or between the fictional and the nonfictional text. Rather, one wants to say that it is, in a sense, *about* the uncertain relation of the two, and never more so than when Crane represents Maggie as a consumer of melodramatic fiction. But neither can it be adequately explained without in turn mapping this discursive relation to struggles for symbolic capital in the field of literary production itself, as Crane makes clear in a fascinating 1894 letter to Lily Brandon Munroe:

> My career has been more of a battle than a journey. You know, when I left you, I renounced the clever school in literature. It seemed to me that there must be something more in life than to sit and cudgel one's brains for clever and witty expedients. So I developed all alone a little creed of art which I thought was a good one. Later I discovered that my creed was identical with the one of Howells and Garland and in this way I became involved in the beautiful war between those who say that art is man's substitute for nature and we are the most successful in art when we approach the nearest to nature and truth, and those who say—well, I don't know what they say . . . [but they] keep Garland and I out of the big magazines. Howells, of course, is too powerful for them.
>
> If I had kept to my clever, Rudyard-Kipling style, the road might have been shorter but, ah, it wouldn't be the true road. (*Letters*, 31–32)

This expresses with remarkable concision a process explored at length by Bourdieu, who argues that assertions of specific aesthetic positions in the field of literary production are typically, at the same time, investments in an economy of literary prestige. Looking ahead to *Red Badge of Courage*—indeed, already suggesting a way one might begin to read that novel—Crane describes the circumstances of his career as a "battle" and a "beautiful war." From Bourdieu's perspective, the delayed gratification to which Crane submits by taking the "true road" rather than the "clever road" is entirely typical of the social dynamics of a youthful and ambitious avant-garde. Emphasizing the fact that his artistic "creed" was first developed in Romantic isolation—figuring himself, in Bourdieu's terms, as an "uncreated creator"—and abjuring the immediate economic benefits to be gained by writing in a conventional commercial mode, Crane understands himself to be making a bid instead for the symbolic capital of artistic purity. Only after a period of honorable privation can this symbolic capital be converted into the economic benefits of consecration, recognition, and worldly success.

Seen in this context, one can see why Crane's novel might ally itself with morally serious reformist documentary against the merely "clever" or trivial fiction of the Kipling school: it does so in order to stake a powerful claim on "truth," which it understands to reside not in the middle-class parlor—nor indeed in the Syracuse fraternity house where *Maggie* was first drafted—but among the bodies struggling for survival in the slums. It is as though the intense gravitational pull of these bodies, as referents, can draw his rhetorical "art" closer to the surface of "nature" and "truth," and show up by contrast the falsity of the merely clever fiction he no longer writes. One way to understand this is as a literary version of the urban phenomenon of gentrification—a process that converts low- into high-cost housing even as the "gritty" energy of the slum environment is vampirically subsumed in the hipness of the adventurous urban middle class. But one can also see why this alliance cannot at any cost be allowed to collapse into an identity with the "nonliterary" reformist texts to which it is allied (and still less with the vulgar "natural" referent they share): this would imply his departure from the field of literary production altogether, his participation in a distinctly different game. This is, no doubt, the constitutive risk of the avant-garde text, and the balancing act that it must perform: to "bravely" reject literary conventions without, after all, making itself institutionally unrecognizable *as literature*.

One might therefore read Crane's novel in terms of its triangulated relation on the one hand to a reformist documentary that (in theory) effaces itself rhetorically before its vulgar social object, and on the other hand to a genteel literature whose relation to "truth" is mediated by an inauthentic "cleverness." This triangular relation, a complex of identifications and differentiations, structures Crane's Bowery pastoral in any number of ways. Indeed, I will argue that it is submerged in the very fabric of the novel, visible, in some cases, at the level of the single sentence. What I will emphasize here, and draw to the surface as an explanation of some of the uncanny effects produced by Crane's impressionist prose, is the extreme instability of this structure of identification and differentiation, which requires a constant shuttling on Crane's part between two contradictory and, for him, mutually uninhabitable positions. By turns allying himself with and repudiating these positions, playing one against the other, Crane produces the space of his own career—a gentrified tenement of his own—in and by means of his representation of the crowded social space of the Bowery.

Now, it is importantly the case that this shuttling between positions in the cultural field does not occur in an ordered fashion. It will however be useful to untangle this structure and to analyze its parts as though they did. This will allow us to see how, even as it seems to communicate directly with documentary narratives of social fact such as Riis's, from another point of view *Maggie* can be seen to engage in a dialogue with distinctly literary interlocutors, and with a relatively distinct novelistic tradition. Dating at least from Samuel Richardson's *Pamela, or Virtue Rewarded*, this tradition is far more fascinated by the problem of class mobility than the problem of class entrapment explored in Riis's *How the Other Half*

Lives. We have already noted how critics in the tradition of Ian Watt have
argued that the novel bears a fundamental relation to the problem of class
mobility, in particular to a newly emergent and upwardly mobile commercial middle class. Maggie's appreciation of how the "poor and virtuous"
in the melodrama she watches overcome the "wealthy and wicked" echoes,
even as it shifts its terms, the class politics of virtue that for Michael
McKeon is one of the novel's central ideological components. For instance,
McKeon reads Richardson's fiction as an assertion of the rights of middle
class moral virtue over and above the claims of aristocratic honor. Female
chastity, in this reading, becomes a figure for a virtuous middle class be-
sieged by the phallus of a corrupt aristocracy, "honorable" in name alone.

Like James's *The American*, then, Crane's *Maggie* can be seen to be
carrying remarkably large portions of the genre's original ideological baggage. By the 1890s, however, the commercial middle class—particularly
in the constitutively capitalist United States—has been successful enough
in asserting cultural, political, and economic hegemony that it can now be
rotated into the position of aristocratic "wickedness"—contrasted now
with a virtuous *working class*—against which the middle class had originally defined itself. And yet the weight of the novel's generic history still
presses on Crane's novel, distorting this terminological rotation: thus Maggie can seem, in her modest efforts to decorate her home, indeed in her
very aspirations to social mobility, curiously "middle class," while the middle classes themselves are often described by Crane as "aristocrats."

One way to explain the reappearance, or persistence, in *Maggie* of this
politics of virtue, then, would be to say that Crane's novel participates in
two genres at once: Maggie may be a product and victim of the urban
environment documented by Riis, and represented so memorably by Crane
himself, but she is also, in a sense, the product of a discursive tradition.
As early as Austen's *Northanger Abbey* (1818; completed in 1803) the
novel had become conscious enough of its own social presence to wonder
at the "real" social consequences—in particular for a female readership
understood to have an insecure grasp of reality—of fiction itself. Though,
importantly, she is not literally represented as a reader, Maggie seems as a
spectator of theatrical melodrama to fall into a long line of represented
female readership. She seems in many ways an updated, urbanized, and
proletarianized Emma Bovary.

Emma's problem, notoriously enough, was her inability to distinguish
between the romantic fiction she reads and the real life she lives, and these
bad reading habits are what set her on the path to perdition. Flaubert's
problem, notoriously enough, was how to distinguish his own novel from
these same popular romances. In his influential essay "Mass Culture as
Woman," Andreas Huyssen adds an important dimension to Bourdieu's
account of Flaubert, arguing that the gendering of the novel's readership

as female is gradually transposed onto the object, the "low" genre of the novel, itself. "Modernism," as it begins to appear in Flaubert, thus becomes for Huyssen a masculinist demystification of "female" mass cultural delusion.[23]

Similarly, Crane's novel, representing Maggie's consumption of fiction, raises the question of its own relation to the "popular amusements" whose consumption it describes. But it also, and perhaps more importantly, questions its relation to the deceptively "clever" Kipling fiction against which it defines itself. Allying itself with Riis's nonfiction narratives of class entrapment (and more or less ignoring the conceptual difficulties embedded in his own artistic creed), Crane critiques "clever" fiction as escapist fantasy that does not know how to separate this fantasy from fact.[24] Doing so he claims for his own novel the symbolic prize of truth. Maggie *c'est moi*— but not quite: no less than Frederic had done for Flaubert, or Hyacinth for James, Maggie serves, in her gradual debasement and eventual death, as the objectified, negative image of the "free spirit" of Crane himself. He will not, like Maggie, be fooled into "prostituting" himself—in his case to the immediate conditions of the literary market. Thus her ambitions to class mobility are legible as an echo of Crane's own ambitions to distinguish himself in the masculinized battlefield of literary production, and her ambitions must fail so that his might succeed.

But there is another half to this story, and to leave it untold would be to leave the complexity of Crane's novel only half appreciated: even as Crane engages in a relation with the "literary," he can also be seen to be taking issue with the moralizing rhetoric of social reform. And whereas the grounds of Crane's critique of clever fiction are its insufficient attention to *difference*—to the difference between fantasy and fact, class mobility and class entrapment—here Crane's critique is carried out in quite the reverse terms. Take, for instance, the "Other Half" of Riis's title, which excludes this "other half" from the domain of discourse even as it implicitly constitutes a literate "Same Half" as his work's audience.

If Riis preaches to this middle class audience, it is nonetheless clear that this preaching operates on a different basis, indeed in a different medium, than the moralizing that might be heard by the inhabitants of the Bowery themselves. This rhetorical structure has the inadvertent effect of reinforcing the social division it describes and decries. Crane's novel, by contrast, produces moments that seem nothing short of a dialectical critique of the closed social circuit of literate reformer and literate middle class audience Riis's text establishes. It does so by attending to the connections between this written form of preaching and the oral preaching directed at the poor:

> [Jimmie] clad his soul in armor by means of happening hilariously in at a mission church where a man composed his sermons of "yous." . . . [Once a philosopher

asked this man why he did not say "we" instead of "you." The man replied,
"What?"] Many of the sinners were impatient over the pictured depths of their
degradation. They were waiting for soup tickets.

A reader of the words of wind-demons might have been able to see the portions
of the dialogue pass to and fro between the exhorter and his hearers.

"You are damned," said the preacher. And the reader of sounds might have
seen the reply go forth from the ragged people: "Where's our soup?" (13
[1896 ed.])

Michael Fried has drawn our attention to Crane's remarkably pervasive
tendency to become fascinated, if not entirely distracted, by the actual or
potential visibility of language. In his account of literary impressionism,
Conrad's "Before all, to make you see" signifies a project of envisioning
intensified to such a degree that the impressionist begins to see what is
literally there "before all" when he writes: the surface of the page, the
inscription on this surface of ink.[25] Of a part, it seems, with the materialism
that imagines social structure as architecture, the rhetoric of impressionism generates what Fried calls a "thematics of writing" that often seems
to operate entirely independently of the "story" being told. In this case,
however, one senses that the problem of linguistic visibility may remain
tied to its immediate thematic context.

The ghostly figure of a "philosopher"—ghostly because his presence in
the scene is sociologically inexplicable—inserted between the preacher and
his audience in the 1896 edition of the novel mediates that exchange by
drawing attention to the divisive pronouns that differentiate speaker and
addressee. Imagining that this oral exchange can become visible as a kind
of writing, Crane supplements his critique of pronomial differentiation
with an imaginary identification of oral and written media, as though the
severe social differentiations implied by literate versus oral modes of
preaching could be overcome by reducing them to an equally material and
visible substrate. Without canceling the difference between writing and
orality—the metaphoricity of Crane's "wind-demons" remains clear—this
gesture nonetheless draws writing and orality into a single system of discourse where their difference is produced against a backdrop of structural
relation. Thus, while Riis's text asks its literate audience to care about the
poor, Crane's text could be said in a more aggressive way to *implicate* his
audience in the poverty of the poor: it does so by drawing attention to the
social inequalities that have produced the difference between literate and
oral culture—between Maggie as a "mere" spectator of melodrama and
Maggie as a potential reader of texts like *Maggie*.

Noting how a problematical grammatical opposition—"you" versus
"we"—can be conceived by Crane as a problematized opposition of textual
and oral media, we can then hypothesize a relation between these opposi-

tions and the opposition between fiction and nonfiction, so important in the career of Crane, noted above. We can propose that the separate discourses of pronomial grammar, written and oral media, and now "fictionality" and "reality" are three ways of getting at the overarching problem of social distinction itself. When he is engaging in his "beautiful war" with clever fiction, Crane critiques this school's insufficient differentiation of fantasy and fact. In order to critique moralizing reformist rhetoric, however, he is forced back into an alliance with the literary, from which point of view he now criticizes reformist rhetoric's insufficient attention to relation and identity: insisting on the importance of the imagination, he shows how social differences can be bridged, conceptually at least, by a shared structure of relation.

Thus, for instance, in the passage that personifies the Bowery building as an observer of the glittering city, quoted above, we can now see how important it may be that the "distance" between the tenement and the glittering city, though "impossible," is nonetheless already in a sense bridged by the specular relation through which this distance is measured. And we can furthermore link this specular longing on the part of the building to Maggie's own specular longing as she watches the theatrical melodrama. Maggie might not, after all, be able to acquire the "culture and refinement" she sees imitated by the actress on the stage, but her fantasy of doing so is possible only on the basis of a hypothesized continuity between her world and the world of aristocratic refinement the melodramatic representation mediates. Here again Crane's text is remarkable in that it locates this "continuity" in a concrete form, in this case in a single system of cultural distribution with uptown and downtown outlets:

> In the finale [the actress] fell into some of those grotesque attitudes which were at the time popular among the dancers in the theatres up-town, giving to the Bowery public the phantasies of the aristocratic theatre-going public, at reduced rates. (23)

However briefly this "aristocratic theatre-going public" appears in Crane's text, their presence makes clear the degree to which the "audience" of culture is both a single entity and a divided one, depending on one's point of view. I say this, it should be clear, not to credit Crane with a moral superiority that might be thought to follow from his ability to bridge the social difference between literate "we's" and illiterate "you's." This would be to accept one of the self-justifications of the "literary" at face value, without placing this "imaginary bridge" between subjectivities in the social and historical context in which it is erected. Indeed, as we shall see, the same structures of relation and identification that enable Crane's intensified sympathy with the poor are productive, at the same time, of considerable horror. Still less, however, is it necessary to understand Crane's "sympathy" merely as a kind of cynical sham. There is every reason to believe that his sympathy was as real as sympathy ever is. Instead what we are after is way of understanding the complex structure of identification and differentiation in which sympathy and self-interest, "true" art and a successful literary career, are produced at the same time.

The master-trope governing this complex of identification and differentiation is the figure of the mother, a figure who presides over Crane's work with remarkable persistence. This is evident even in the title of Crane's second Bowery novel, *George's Mother*, and extends to *The Red Badge of Courage*, where Henry Fleming's mother stands as a crucial point of departure for the accession to heroic manhood the rest of the novel will chart. It is, however, in Crane's first novel, *Maggie*, that the force of maternity as the governing trope of identity and difference is most startlingly evident. Consider a passage that has, since Michael Fried drew attention to it, been the subject of much discussion:

> Her mouth was set in the same lines of vindictive hatred that it had, perhaps, borne in the fight. . . . The urchin bended over his mother. He was fearful lest she should open her eyes, and the dread within him was so strong, that he could not forbear to stare, but hung as if fascinated over the woman's grim face.
>
> Suddenly her eyes opened. The urchin found himself looking straight into that expression, which, it would seem, had the power to change his blood to salt. (12)

We have already glimpsed this dreadful maternal figure in Crane's description of how "from a careening building, a dozen gruesome doorways gave up loads of babies to the street and the gutter"—which seems almost to literalize the title of one of Riis's later works, *Children of the Tenements* (1904). In Crane, where buildings do not stand upright but rather "careen"—a synonym, suggestively enough, for "career," as well as a homonym of "Crane"—the architectonic materialism of reformist documentary becomes an architectonic *maternalism* that softens the edges of buildings, blurring the strict geometrical organization of spaces traditionally associated with architecture. The term "volume-fluidity," appearing in Luce Irigaray's *Speculum of the Other Woman*, serves as an accurate description of the consequences of the thematic linking, in *Maggie*, of matter and maternity. This fluidity follows, as Irigaray has explained, from an understanding of "woman" as "neither open nor closed. She is indefinite, in-finite, form is never complete in her. . . . This incompleteness in her form, her morphology, allows her continually to become something else."[26] I don't know whether it is true, as Irigaray suggests, that an understanding of woman as "not-one"—as protean antiform—has governed Western subjectivity at all times. It is, however, deeply explanatory of a text like Crane's *Maggie*, where the careening "fluidity" of tenement spaces figures the problem of individuation as such. In Crane the "well-formed" subject is constantly threatened by the maternal-material substrate, or "other," from which it has arisen.

Michael Fried has taught us to see in the passage above, in which the urchin looks down upon his prostrate mother, an echo of the literal scene of writing, where the author looks down upon the "prostrate" page that he inscribes, producing by means of this inscription figures—characters— suspended between materiality and vivacity, death and life. For Fried this thematics of writing is produced as the uncanny aftereffect of a strictly formal imperative: the impressionist call for a literature of the visible. It seems possible, however, to build upon Fried's insights, opening the "thematics of writing" he uncovers in Crane to what might be called a "thematics of the writer's career," which reinforces and historicizes the continuity between "writing" as a physical action and "writing" as a distinct social occupation. This would amount to taking up a middle position between Fried's formalist reading of Crane's thematics of writing as saying something about the physicality of writing, and Mark Seltzer's assimilation of these moments, in *Bodies and Machines*, to the pervasive "logistics" of the "body-machine complex" whose imperial power makes it explicable only in its own "intrinsically and immanently intelligible" terms.[27] From this productively crass perspective—trading the negative theological force of Seltzer's "complex" for an account of specific social relations involved in writing—Henry Fleming's departure for battle becomes legible as Crane's entry into the "battle" of career, his participation in the "beautiful war" between clever and avant-garde fiction. Rotating the problem of subject formation in the direction of the production of discourse, Irigaray explains the complex relation of "form" to maternity/materiality in terms that seem useful for thinking about Crane's project, which wants to disengage itself from merely clever rhetoric in order to take hold of nature and truth:

> Everything [is] thrust aside wherever the "subject" seeks to escape from his emprisonment. But even as he struggles to fracture that specular matrix, the enveloping discursivity, that body of the text in which he has made himself a prisoner, it is Nature he finds, Nature who, unknown to him, has nourished his project, his production. It is Nature who now fuses for him with that glass enclosure, that spangled sepulchre, from which . . . she is unable to articulate her difference. (*Speculum*, 228)

For Irigaray, the disturbing power of maternity extends equally to the "body" of rhetoric, where it is experienced as the threat of an "enveloping discursivity," and to the putative outside of rhetoric, Nature, which in turn becomes a "glass enclosure." For Crane, as for Irigaray, "mother" is everywhere, "shaping lives regardless," posing an omnipresent threat of indentic obliteration.

I call this maternal figure the governing trope of identity and difference because it serves to figure *both* of the positions with which Crane must at once identify and disengage. This dispersal of maternity is already evident in the way Maggie's mother appears not simply in her own horrifying person, but in the maternal architecture in which Maggie is imprisoned, and sometimes in the effluvious air of the Bowery itself: "From above came an unceasing babble of tongues, over all of which rang the mother's derisive laughter" (48). Indeed, in *Maggie*, the pre-Oedipal "mother" appears in places where we might least expect her. Early in the novel, when Maggie is being courted by the young rake, Crane describes how

Pete, raking his brains for amusement, discovered the . . . Museum of Arts. . . .
While [Maggie] wandered in the vaulted rooms, Pete occupied himself in returning stony stare for stony stare, the appalling scrutiny of the watch-dogs of the treasures. . . . When he tired of this amusement he would go to the mummies and moralize over them. (26–27)

The "mummies" referred to are presumably the Egyptian sort, the prostrate bodies, wrapped in rags, put on display in museums. And yet, in Crane, an account of a cultural excursion cannot work its way entirely free of the architecture of maternity, or of the "specular matrix" that structures Crane's account of the urchin staring down upon his prostrate mother. This structure has merely been altered by a displacement of the urchin's stare into the castrating visage of his mother onto Pete's staring contest with the museum guards—representative, perhaps, of a paternal authority otherwise absent from the novel. It is difficult to say whether Pete, in this instance, figures Crane's own relation to the moralizing paternity of his own father, bible-wielding author of *Popular Amusements*, or whether, as he proceeds to moralize over mummies, he is himself a figure of this paternity. The point is that in formless maternal space the articulation of identity has become a radically unstable, sometimes incoherent, process, which in this instance becomes visible only by means of a symptomatic reading.

But if my reading of "mummy" as "mommy" seems a stretch, it will seem less so when juxtaposed with the figure of the Port Jervis gossip, who appears in one of Crane's letters of 1894:

I will not insult any dog by comparing this damned woman to it. There is a feminine mule up here who has roused all the bloodthirst in me and I don't know where it will end. She has no more brain than a pig and all she does is to sit in her kitchen and grunt. But every when she grunts something dies howling. It may be a girl's reputation or a political party or the Baptist Church but it stops in its tracks and dies. . . . No man is strong enough to attack this *mummy* because she is a nice woman. . . . If this woman lived in Hester Street some son or brother

. . . would go bulging up to her and say, "Ah, wot deh hell!" and she would have
no teeth any more, right there. . . . Now, my friend, there is a big joke in all this.
This lady in her righteousness is just the grave of a stale lust and every boy in
town knows it. No man has power to contradict her. We are all cowards. (*Letters*,
42–43, emphasis added)

Crane does not know when or how his bloodthirst for this "mummy" will
end. And indeed, this dreadful, pathetic, and yet all-powerful female figure
will reappear in Crane's *The Third Violet*, *The Monster*, and *The O'Ruddy*.
Crane's fantasy of revenge through the surrogate agency of a Bowery "son
or brother" he might otherwise show considerable contempt suggests some
of the chaos of alliances that structures Crane's career. The "lines of vindictive hatred" the urchin sees in the expression of his mother, above, become in this context difficult to distinguish from the lines of vindictive
hatred Crane himself writes, and that form the uncanny discursive underpinning of the "beautiful war" represented in, and by, Crane's impressionism. As Wilson Follett has observed, "Crane pilloried [this Port Jervis
woman] over and over again, where she fitted the story and where she did
not" (quoted in *Letters*, 42). That "lack of fit" between this dreadful female figure and the discursive "form" of Crane's fiction is precisely the
point. In this reading she figures the threat that the erected spaces of
Crane's fiction, and of his career, might collapse, or "deconstruct," upon
their own uncertain foundations. Thus, while his work seems to evince a
remarkable degree of self-obsession, it would be wrong to confuse this
self-obsession with self-expression in a conscious sense; rather, his work
internalizes a structure of *social production*, only one of whose components is the disposition of the individual writer, Stephen Crane. As *Maggie*
describes how the dreaded "rampant" mother *"stopped in a career* from
a seething stove to a pan-covered table" (7, emphasis added)—even the
short journey from one side of the kitchen to another can be seen to detach
itself from its thematic and syntactic context and to meditate upon a career
always at risk of being stopped in its tracks by external forces. This was
the career Crane had described as "more a battle than a journey."

    It would be unsatisfying, however, having noted the disorganizing power
of matter and maternity in Crane's text, to pronounce his novel "decon-
structed" and leave it at that. Rather one should go on to observe how the
"intense" rhetorical effects produced by these internalizations became, in
themselves, the very sign of avant-garde literariness for which Crane's
texts would eventually be celebrated. This was so even as the tremendous
commercial success of *The Red Badge of Courage* soon made him, in his
own short lifetime, one of the most popular American writers of his day.
One must observe, that is, how an encounter with a disabling figure of

maternity enables Crane's accession, as a compensation for his brave pursuit of artistic "truth," to a space above the fray, to a secure position in the aristocracy of letters:

> This winter fixes me firmly. We have proved too formidable for [the genteel literary crowd], confound them. They used to call me "that terrible, young radical," but now they are beginning to hem and haw and smile—those very old coons who used to adopt a condescending air toward me. There is an irony in the present situation, that I enjoy. (*Letters*, 32)

The young radical is "fixed." The outsider is now "situated" as an insider. After deconstruction comes the "irony" of establishment.

Transient Occupations: From Howells to Crane to Dos Passos

"I wish I was a skyscraper."
    —Dos Passos, *Manhattan Transfer*

But what, finally, does the "careerism" of Stephen Crane and the others tell us about the emergent forms of the modernist novel? What is the legacy, as the novel comes to be perceived as a bearer of cultural capital, of these transient occupations of the Bowery, these pastoral identifications with the poor? How is it that a provisional enactment of downward mobility—an "Experiment in Misery"—can coincide with the upward mobility of the novel itself?[28] Modernism is, in part, the continuing elaboration of the metaphysics and narrative mechanics of these "ironic" identifications, in which ontological risk is followed by artistic reward.

One can indeed trace the emergence of at least one signal feature of modernist narrative form in this way, beginning with the work of Crane's sponsor from the older generation, the self-described "theoretical socialist and practical aristocrat," William Dean Howells.[29] Howells's *A Hazard of New Fortunes* (1890) could hardly be more explicit in its development of a thematic of literary risk: the new fortune hazarded in the novel is used to start a literary journal in New York City, something "not so very different from the chances an author takes when he publishes a novel."[30] But if the fortune most literally hazarded in the novel is that of the nouveau riche social climber, Dryfoos, who has made his money in the natural gas fields of the Midwest, we gather that a risk of a deeper kind is taken by the novel's protagonist, Basil March. As the novel opens March has left his secure and well-paying job at a Boston insurance company—insurance heaped upon insurance—and, just as Howells himself had done when he

left the editorship of the *Atlantic Monthly* in 1881, moved to the comparative wilds of New York City.

The shift in the center of American culture from genteel Boston to booming, commercial New York has been much commented upon; what we want
to pay attention to here is how Howells's novel, with no serious aspirations
to formal innovation of its own, so clearly sets the stage for the appearance
of Crane's avant-garde *Maggie* some three years later. It happens that Basil
March and his wife, Isabel, "liked to play with the romantic, from the safe
vantage-ground of their real practicality, and to divine the poetry of the
commonplace" (22). Doing so, they are delineated by Howells as a certain
social type: upwardly mobile, socially liberal members of the professional-
managerial class, the kind of persons who feel their liberality and good
taste "reflect distinction on them" (23). In one of their long, amusing
searches for a dwelling in New York that will adequately and affordably
express themselves, they are driven "accidentally through one street"
where the "sidewalks and doorsteps swarmed with children" and "wom-
en's heads seemed to show at every window" (56).

Noting, as would Jacob Riis, the way this tenement environment saps
its inhabitants of ambition, the narrator describes a scene of "poverty as
hopeless as any in the world, transmitting itself from generation to generation and establishing conditions of permanency to which human life ad-
justs itself as it does to those of some incurable disease, like leprosy" (56).
These unfortunate and helpless people, "who wouldn't know what to do
with a bath" if they had one, will become the subject of a series of literary
impressions March will write for the new literary magazine. Later in the
novel we see him emerge as a kind of *flaneur*, an urban aesthete who travels
amidst the "shapeless, graceless, reckless picturesqueness of the Bowery,"
a place whose "prevailing hideousness" and "uproar to the eye" "always
amused him" (159).

It is easy to imagine Stephen Crane reading this novel and taking notes
for his own transient occupations. The crucial difference is that when we
get to Crane, an entire level of narrative mediation has been removed from
the story: Howells's true subject is, after all, not the Bowery itself, the
"Other Half," but the higher class that takes the Bowery as an object of
aesthetic and moral contemplation. *Maggie*, by contrast, would minimize
the distance between itself and the Bowery, borrowing its "uproar to the
eye" and reproducing it in Crane's excruciated impressionist prose. And
yet, even as Howells's elaborate realist-sociological analysis of "Bowery
discourse" is crushed flat in *Maggie*, the social distance to which it admits
still clings to the representation as a narrative grammar (third person) and
a tone: *irony*. In other words, Howells's full-blown sociological *theme* has
been condensed into one layer of Crane's famously ironic *form*.

And that, in at least one important sense, is "the modernist novel" itself:
a removal of "telling" narrative mediations, the discipline of the restricted
point of view. The process begun in Crane finds an urban terminus, of
sorts, in John Dos Passos's Joycean depiction of New York in *Manhattan
Transfer* (1925).[31] Dos Passos's generation, unlike Crane's, did not need
to imagine a "beautiful war" from whole cloth: for this generation the
battle of career could instead be launched from direct experiences of war.
If war was horrifying, it was not without its terrible beauty, and, especially
for educated Americans, not without its own promise of literary opportunity. Dos Passos's first use of his war experiences, *One Man's Initiation,
1917* (1920), is given an impressionist dedication to the "memory of those
with whom I saw rockets in the sky, on the road between Erize-la-Petite
and Erize-la-Grande, in that early August twilight in the summer of
1917."[32] And yet, though it here lays explicit claim, like so much war
writing, to an authorial legitimacy won by risky personal experience, this
novel seems deeply indebted to Crane's imaginary *Red Badge of Courage*,
for its chromatic impressionist effects if nothing else:

> Dawn in a wilderness of jagged stumps and ploughed earth; against the yellow
> sky, the yellow glare of guns that squat like toads in a tangle of wire and piles
> of brass shell-cases and split wooden boxes. . . . Torn camouflage fluttering
> greenish-grey against the ardent yellow sky, and twining among the fantastic
> black leafless trees, the greenish wraiths of gas. (88)

Reversing Crane's movement from the Bowery to the battlefield, Dos Passos's impressionism is transposed from his World War I texts into the many
rooming houses and tenements of the model modernist text, *Manhattan
Transfer*.

It is perhaps easiest to explain this "modernism" as an echo of Joyce's
Ulysses, another tale of the city, but one might also trace certain elements
of its narrative form back to Henry James. Especially is this true in *Manhattan Transfer*'s nearly absolutist use of what James called the "scenic
method," by which he simply meant the narrative dramatization, typically
with ample dialogue, of the novel's events. Adhering to the scenic method
so rigorously, texts like *Manhattan Transfer* make clear again what this
method was intended to occlude: the independent consciousness of an "intrusive," pedagogical narrator who might organize and explain the story
from a point of remove. Thus, somewhat like Crane, Dos Passos in *Manhattan Transfer* would minimize the distance between his own impressionist literary discourse, fashioned at Harvard and in Paris, and the demotic
throngs of New York. Indeed, this kaleidoscopic work can initially
produce, in its crowd of unannounced characters, something like the effect of walking down a busy street. Looking closely, however, one can
find amidst this throng a character who seems to speak for the young,

ambitious Dos Passos himself. This is Jimmy Herf, the sensitive young
newspaper reporter who, we take it, aspires to be a writer of a loftier kind:
"Jimmy kept walking nervously about the front room. His drunkenness
ebbed away leaving him icily sober. In the empty chamber of his brain a
doublefaced word clinked like a coin: Success Failure, Success Failure"
(303). Downward upward, inside out: braiding elevated discourses and
abject objects, high conceptions and low company, the modernist novel is
doublefaced.

Highbrows and Dumb Blondes

Literary Intellectuals and the Romance of Intelligence

"Be good, sweet maid, and let who would be clever."
—Charles Kingsley

One Civilized Reader Is Worth a Thousand Boneheads
—*Smart Set: A Magazine of Cleverness*

Playing Dumb with Anita Loos

"I wanted Lorelei to be a symbol of the lowest possible mentality of our nation," wrote Anita Loos of the heroine of her novel, *Gentlemen Prefer Blondes: The Illuminating Diary of a Professional Lady* (1925).[1] That, Loos explained, is why she is said to have been born and raised in Little Rock, a backwater city in the region her friend H. L. Mencken had cruelly dubbed the "Sahara of the Bozart." Surveying the culture of the South in the early-twentieth century, Mencken had found it "indeed, amazing to contemplate so vast a vacuity."[2] Once a center of American intellectual life, wholly possessed of the "vague thing that we call culture" (185), the South had after the "vast hemorrhage" of the Civil War been "drained of all its best blood." Now "half exterminated and wholly paralyzed," the graceful, leisured, and thoughtful Southern aristocracy of old has left the region to the "harsh mercies of . . . poor white trash" (188) even less attuned to the life of the mind than were the crassest capitalist Yankee.

Borrowing the cultural authority of Mencken in the construction of her character, Loos installed not only a Southern-regional, but also a lower-class backstory to Lorelei Lee's cosmopolitan tale of gold digging in New York, London, Paris, and points between. Lorelei emerges from Mencken's "region of worn-out farms, shoddy cities and paralyzed cerebrums" (184) to pursue luxury items and adornments whose purpose, among other things, is to announce her social ascent. But her upward mobility entails something more than the filching of diamonds from rich men. Her tale is also conspicuously, if satirically, about the acquisition of culture, an aesthetic education Lorelei refers to as "improving her mind." Only thus, we take it, can Lorelei consider herself truly "refined." In fact, the pursuit of intellectual improvement occupies Lorelei's recorded thoughts easily as much as diamonds do, and is meant to explain the existence of the diary we read. "Money [is] not everything," she will conclude, voicing a sentiment with which Mencken could only have agreed, "because after all, it is only brains that count" (148). The problem, of course, is that she is a moron.

But while it is true that Lorelei Lee seems, from a certain perspective, very dim indeed, her tale is somewhat complex, even uncanny, in its rhetorical effects. Partly this derives from the fact that despite the heavy symbolic burden of regional and national stupidity she is meant to carry, Lorelei is presented not as a dumb, in the sense of speechless, object of the text but as its author.[3] The sheer unlikelihood of authorship issuing from such a source is accounted for on the novel's first page:

> A gentleman friend and I were dining at the Ritz last evening and he said that if I took a pencil and a paper and put down all of my thoughts it would make a book. This almost made me smile as what it would really make would be a whole row of encyclopediacs. I mean I seem to be thinking practically all of the time. . . . So this gentleman said a girl with brains ought to do something else with them besides think . . . [and] he sent me a book. And so when my maid brought it to me, I said to her, "Well, Lulu, here is another book and we have not read half the ones we have got yet." But when I opened it and saw that it was all a blank I remembered what my gentleman acquaintance said, and so then I realized that it was a diary. So here I am writing a book instead of reading one. (19)

Filling that blank with her thoughts, Lorelei's hilariously breezy diary works, in another dimension, as a fairly rigorous narratological experiment in perspectival limitation. Since Lorelei's is the only account we have of the events she describes, and since she is not conscious of her own intellectual limitations, the contempt that motivated Loos's writing is present in her text only by implication. Lorelei's friend Dorothy, in many ways a projection of Loos herself, might easily have been used as an ironic observer-narrator in the manner of Fitzgerald's Nick Carraway in *The Great Gatsby* (1925). But her sarcastic commentary appears in the text only as reported by Lorelei, and intermittently at that. Mostly we remain trapped in the mind of an idiot, and can only draw inferences as to what the intelligent version of her story might be.

Lorelei's "unreliability," arising not from duplicity but stupidity, may be intended to place author and reader in a position of intellectual superiority to the story's narrator—as, for instance, when we encounter many uncorrected misspellings in the text such as "for instants." And yet this "pathos of distance" hovers remarkably close to a stream of discourse that continues to solicit the reader's identification and sympathy. After all it is Lorelei's simplicity, her innocent avarice and guileless guile, that seems to enable her triumph over the series of predatory males who patronize her. The entire effect, on Loos's part, is of a kind of misogynist feminism: the valence of her somewhat vicious satire of a dumb blonde woman is partially reversed as it becomes the vehicle for an even stronger satire of ridiculous men. Speaking not about but through a female moron, Loos's own authorial voice becomes subject to the rhetorical alterations, instabilities, and double entendres produced by what one might call its pastoral ventriloquism—a verbal form of what Lorelei calls, in another context, a "maskerade."

The casual complexity of Loos's novel might thus be seen as a product of its narratology, of the contrasting, indeed competing, mentalities made to mingle in its hybrid first-person voice. Another, complementary explanation for its appearance might be sought in the context in which it was written and first appeared. It was Mencken, sworn enemy of American stupidity, who encouraged Loos to publish the work she had begun to scribble after encountering a blonde woman whose obvious lack of "mental acumen" proved no barrier to her "being waited on, catered to and cajoled by the entire male assemblage"(*Gentlemen*, 11) of a train headed from New York to Los Angeles. The editor of the *Smart Set* and *American Mercury* was Loos's strongest link to a circle of literary intellectuals relatively distinct from the "elite of cinema" to which Loos, a successful screenwriter, by her own account belonged. "Why did that girl so far outdistance me in feminine allure?" Loos asked herself. "Could her strength possibly be rooted . . . in her hair?" (12). As Lorelei's diary is written at the behest of a man, so too did Loos's novel become a quasi-private message to a man, Mencken himself.

What began, that is, as a self-assessment of her relative merits as an object of male attention became, as Loos completed the manuscript, a manifestation of the gender politics operating in the relationship between two prominent persons: Mencken's fulminations against the idiocy of the American "booboisie" were contradicted, in Loos's view, by his notoriously fervid enjoyment of vapid pretty girls. At the same time the novel served as a communication between the distinct cultural elites, connected by the train from New York to Los Angeles, that Mencken and Loos could be said to have represented. Both of these groups are present in the novel along with various aristocrats, spies, politicians, and plutocrats. Part of the complexity of Lorelei's voice, as Susan Hegeman has suggested, might be attributed to Loos's desire, from the standpoint of Hollywood, both to identify with and to spoof the intellectual pretensions of the New York literati.[4] Indeed, *Gentlemen Prefer Blondes* could be said to embed in Lorelei's ramblings a simplified geography of early-twentieth-century cultural hierarchies: Shadowed less and less by the prestige of Europe, weighted by the heavy density of the South, barely pausing in Chicago, and perplexed to find Mencken living in Baltimore, American national culture begins in this period to cross back and forth between the centers, respectively, of print and of mass-visual media.

First published as a serial in *Harper's Bazaar*—Mencken " 'had just left *Smart Set*,' " we are told, " 'and didn't think it was right for *The American Mercury*' " (14)—*Gentlemen* was soon issued as a book by Boni and Liveright. This publisher's list that year included Hemingway's *In Our Time* (which manuscript had itself passed through the hands of Mencken on its way into print) and Sherwood Anderson's successful *Dark Laughter*. Thus situated, the novel quickly exploded the highbrow institutional aura of Liveright and became a massive best-seller, running to several editions and making for Loos more than a million dollars in royalties. This process of massification would be completed decades later upon the appearance of Howard Hawks's 1953 film, starring Marilyn Monroe, which has succeeded in virtually displacing its literary source as the definitive version of the story.[5] This could be said already to have been predicted by the novel itself, however, as Lorelei's story takes her from the circle of "literary gentlemen" who ply her with editions of Joseph Conrad, through the vestigially bejeweled world of postwar European nobility, and ultimately to Hollywood. At the conclusion of *Gentlemen* she and her fussy society fiancé have landed in the film business along with seemingly everyone else. Much as it would prove to do for many American novelists in the decades to come, Hollywood seems to have been hovering in the background of Lorelei's tale all along, exerting a strong gravitational force on the cultural and social elites with whom she consorts. "From what I had seen of society women trying to break into the films," says Lorelei of her ultimate decision to become a film actress, "I did not believe that it would be so declasee if one of them really landed. . . . So after that came my wedding and all of the Society people in New York and Philadelphia came to my wedding and they were all so sweet to me, because practically every one of them has written a scenario" (154–55).

Entertaining the threat of widespread social indistinction, where the institutions of mass culture seem to act as a solvent of class difference, *Gentlemen Prefer Blondes* takes its place as one of several texts examined in this study that seem preoccupied, if here only satirically, by the problem of social indistinction and cultural leveling. Indeed, tracing the history of the text's production and reception, one might argue that it exemplifies this leveling. But as it does so it lays bare certain forms of distinction developed for use in precisely this imagined context of diffuse, triumphant, and tyrannical stupidity, where even morons like Lorelei Lee are encouraged to write books and even the Philadelphia social elite try their hand at film scenarios.

A "hundred thousand second-hand Coronas rattle and jingle in ten thousand remote and lonely towns," complained Mencken of the "army" of "gassy young gals" who sent him fiction in the hope of seeing it published. But what one gets is "simply the same dull, obvious, shoddy stuff. . . . They all seem to write alike, as, indeed, they all seem to think alike." (*Chrestomathy*, 463–64). He longed instead for novels of distinction. An earlier editor of the *Smart Set*, Willard Huntington Wright, had been equally bothered by what Mencken called the "disparity between aspiration and equipment" in the American novelist, but he saw hopeful signs that things were beginning to change. Wright complained in 1916 that writing fiction "has seemed so natural an occupation that thousands who are without any genuine aesthetic equipment have adopted it as a life work." Now, however, he saw signs that the novel was in the process of defining itself "*as an art*," a "difficult and subjectively solid" enterprise in "literary architecture." Under these conditions, Wright hoped, one might be able at last to "distinguish the true literary artist" from the profusion of dimwitted pretenders whose success in the literary market was no proof of their talent.[6]

Primary among the qualifications of the emergent art-novelist, he suggests, will be his "intellect." His "generating intelligence," allied with "pure sensitivity," will distinguish him from the "ignorant and unrefined" (288) and feminized masses with whom he competes. Written by a screenwriter with no evident aspirations to distinguish herself as a novelist, *Gentlemen* appears as a curiously distorted echo of these concerns, at once reinforcing and, in several senses, disregarding the distinctions demanded by Mencken and Wright. Diffidently describing herself as not a "real novelist such as Sherwood Anderson, Dreiser, Faulkner or Hemingway" (13)— precisely the kind of ambitious male novelists whose careers Mencken was so instrumental in promoting—Loos nonetheless absorbs and manifests, in the highlight of spoof, some of the most basic preoccupations underlying the emergent forms of the modernist novel in the United States.

The exemplary quality of the *Gentlemen* was first noted by Wyndham Lewis.[7] Comparing it to Gertrude Stein's avant-garde text *Three Lives*, Lewis criticized Loos's use in *Gentlemen* of what he called the "naif-motif," seeing it as a symptom of the "affected naivety" of an American literary "child-cult" that he eloquently abhorred. Emphasizing the simple urge to identify with the simpleton suggested by the naif-motif, Lewis underestimated the complexity of the phenomenon he perceived, paying too little heed to the way the "affected naivety" of modernist pastoral identification served to throw the actual cultural sophistication of the art-novelist into relief. Indeed, in the texts of modernist narrative, as in Loos's *Gentlemen*, the contrastive interaction of intelligence and stupidity would prove crucial to determining not only the forms that these narratives would take, but also to determining the social group—the Smart Set—these forms would work to define.

In this chapter the dialectic of intellectual superiority will be traced and gradually specified as we see it working in two parallel discourses, distinct but tightly braided both with each other and with modernist fiction. These are the discourses of education, including moral education, and of "native" intelligence, including its counterpart, native stupidity. Doing so we will see how, in modernism, the idea of innate intelligence appeared as a ro-mantic-essentialist alternative to the various "conventionalities" that had come to be associated with schooling, and how this intelligent sensibility was instead institutionalized in a culture of "smart" magazines. Modern-ism's antipedagogical bias is reflected formally, in an occlusion of the teacher-narrator in the text; thematically, in its pastoral attraction to per-sons understood to be "too stupid" to be "ruined" by education; and con-textually, in its reliance on a market culture of magazines as a medium of group identification. This stage in the emergence of modernist pastoral discourse will be seen to culminate in another tale told by a Southern idiot, the Benjy section of Faulkner's *The Sound and the Fury* (1929). In what I will argue was an entirely symptomatic contrast of represented object and rhetorical intent, Faulkner's intense narrative identification with the simple mind of the idiot produces perhaps the most technically sophisti-cated, notoriously difficult, and prestigiously "Joycean" stretch of prose in American literature. This alchemy of simplicity and sophistication seems to me to be one of the deepest and most enduring puzzlements of the mod-ernist art-novel, one well worth the effort of untangling some of the morass of elements, ideologies, and institutions that made it so.

Bad Students and Smart Sets

Who reads *Ulysses* today? Who reads *The Sound and the Fury*? Students do, students and also teachers, and almost no one else. Insofar as these canonical modernist novels, and others like them, continue to have a read-ership, this readership is in school. Indeed it seems fair to say that the primary cultural function of a text like *The Sound and the Fury* in our time is to serve as a college textbook, a richly ambiguous and difficult object, a fine occasion for pedagogy. Presented with such a text, the litera-ture student is invited, through the painful process of ascesis, to convert his or her confusion into lasting riches of cultural capital. Meanwhile, the teacher who offers this invitation has an obvious role to play. Standing at the receiving end of over a century of radical experimentation with narra-tive form, the teacher finds that a generous amount of room has been made for him or her in the modernist text itself. A certain kind of narrator famil-iar from earlier or less experimental fiction—an impresario, a moralist, a pedagogue, in any case a "know-it-all"—has left the scene. But where has he gone? One answer to this question was given in chapter 3, where we noted how Stephen Crane radically compresses the sociologist-narrator of realism into the tight space of tonal irony. Yet another answer might be: He is now standing in the classroom making sense of the text that once contained him. In the nineteenth century, as we saw in chapter 2, it had been common to understand the novel *as* a kind of school. By contrast the difficult modernist novel, left to its own devices, teaches almost nothing. Rather, it humiliates. It can be understood only *in* school.

Of course I sketch this case for the institutionalization of modernism in somewhat simplified and exaggerated terms. There no doubt remains for a writer like Faulkner a vestigial extracurricular readership. And it is not as though earlier periods in the novel, especially insofar as they have come to seem dated or otherwise inoperative in the pursuit of pure leisure, leave nothing for the teacher to do with them. Indeed it is true that even the most popular text or film, submitted to one or another form of scholarly analysis, can be converted into a sophisticated textbook, and in turn into a relatively exclusive form of cultural capital. Still, it is worth emphasizing the remarkable dependence, in our time, of the early-twentieth-century modernist text on the early-twenty-first-century university, if only to emphasize how dramatic a reversal has occurred. For it is the case that the modernist project in America had defined itself not merely outside of, but in stark opposition to, the university. As Alfred Kazin attests,

> When I was in college in the 'thirties, it was still well understood that scholars were one class and writers quite another. They did not belong to the same order of mind, they seemed quite antithetical in purpose and temperament. . . . You can no more imagine Hemingway or Fitzgerald in a university than you can picture one of the new critics out of it.[8]

Writing of the strong post–World War II alliance between modernist writers and the university as though it had always been so, Thomas Strychacz removes all traces of this opposition from his otherwise indispensable account of modernist professionalism.[9] In his view, the difficult modernist text should be seen as one of many forms of professional discourse emergent in the late-nineteenth century and intertwined with the rise of the university as an accrediting institution. Particularly as a description of modernism since the war, this model of modernism is persuasive. And yet, despite Strychacz's careful articulation of the obvious differences between the modernist text and the technical jargon used by lawyers, doctors, and professors, his model distorts, or rather blurs, the literary history of the early-twentieth century, removing an entire turn of the dialectic that eventually puts modernism (its theories and its works) at the center of the university literature department. In this sense, at least, Strychacz is a bad storyteller: compressing a complex historical sequence of opposition and incorporation into one century-long moment, his account narrates the relation between modernism and the university as one thick word.

The effect of this compression is to induce a kind of intellectual claustrophobia; in the tight, dark space enclosed by Strychacz's modernism, the literary scholar can see no relevant difference between him- or herself and his or her modernist object. Speaking of modernism as though it were always already cozy with the literature professors, and of academic literary critics as though they never had to teach undergraduates, Strychacz's modernism has from the outset been stripped of the impulse to oppose the university that, however partially, and however ironically, was one of its driving forces. At the same time the university, deprived of its intimate other, is deprived of the knowledge of its own victory-by-incorporation of the modernist movement that initially tended to despise it. While this victory surely signified a diminution of modernism's oppositional energies that one might romantically regret, and while universities are hardly yet to be seen as places of unrestricted social access, this incorporation surely also entailed what one might timidly venture to call the democratization of modernism: a partial reversal of valence that converts antipedagogical modernist texts into occasions for mass pedagogy in the explosive expansion of the postwar university.[10]

Speaking for an older generation, Henry Adams's account in *The Education of Henry Adams* (1906) of his own college days at Harvard remained apposite when it was finally published for a broader audience in 1918: "The chief wonder of education is that it does not ruin everybody concerned in it, teachers and taught."[11] A similar sentiment is spoken by George Prewitt in Carl Van Vechten's *Blind Bow-Boy* (1923): "Understand then, young man, that I myself am the victim of a college education. I went to college . . . and learned nothing. I left the doors of the university without the slightest preparation for the life to come . . . I had been much better off had I never seen a campus."[12] " 'Well, I started to tell you of my education, didn't I?' " asks Maury in Fitzgerald's *The Beautiful and Damned* (1922). " 'But I learned nothing, you see, very little even about myself.' "[13]

There are of course many ironies attached to the antipedagogical statements that litter the writing of this period, and yet it is the case that, until after the second World War, few major American novelists—Thomas Wolfe is one exception—had a significant relation to the university after leaving school to pursue their careers as writers. The institutionalization of experimental fiction that would produce the familiar "writer in residence" had not yet occurred. Some—for example, Hemingway—never went to college, preferring the rigors of "real" experience to the classroom. Some, like Gertrude Stein, had proved themselves promising students but were soon moved to drop out. Faulkner would find an honorary position in the university after the Second World War, but this serves mainly, in retrospect, to throw into relief the strikingly extracurricular nature of his intellectual formation, in which Professor Faulkner had only glancingly sampled the university education available in his own backyard in Oxford, Mississippi. Neither, with the important exception of the Fugitives at Vanderbilt, were many of the major contemporary critics of modernism—Mencken, T. S. Eliot, Van Wyck Brooks, Edmund Wilson, Malcolm Cowley, et alia—consistently attached to a university.[14] Symptomatically, even a figure as "professorial" as Eliot would decide, having written his thesis on F. H. Bradley, that he would rather work at a bank than join further in the enterprise of higher education. Rather, these critics tended to define themselves in opposition to the university professors. Mencken's war with the professors was exaggerated but representative. In the pages of the *Smart Set* he had asked them not "to sit in judgment upon" contemporary literature,

> for that job requires, above all things, an eager intellectual curiosity, a quick hospitality to ideas, a delight in novelty and heresy—and these are the very qualities which, if he had them, would get a professor cashiered in ten days. He is hired by the God-fearing and excessively solvent old gentlemen who sit on college boards, not to go scouting for what is new in the world, but to concentrate his mind upon the defense of what is old and safe.[15]

Associated either with a dry and mechanical philology or with a pious, conservative humanism, and tending to look upon contemporary experimental literature with great suspicion, the university in the early-twentieth century was considered no place for the modernist artist or critic.[16]

And yet, while the extracurricular origins of modernism can be explained, at least in part, by a widespread hostility to the perceived intellectual conservatism of the university, its hostility to educational institutions extended farther down the chain than this. As we have already seen in chapter 2, mass secondary education came under particular scrutiny in this period as well. In the aftermath of compulsory school-attendance laws passed in the late-nineteenth century, the secondary school system was expanding as rapidly in the United States as it had been in England after the passage of the Education Acts. Public high schools quickly overwhelmed the declining private academy as the dominant institution of secondary education, and this was met in some quarters with alarm. As in England, these schools were conceived as instruments of nation building, the means whereby citizens were incorporated into the broader Republic and made fit for an increasingly urbanized and industrialized economy.[17] Observing these phenomena, Wyndham Lewis would describe this expansion of mass education in proto-Foucauldian terms as the rise of the "Democratic Educationalist State." In his account, mass education becomes synonymous with capitalist social indoctrination:

> Education consists, of course, of a decade of soaking in certain beliefs and conventions. . . . [It] is of course the soul, and not knowledge, that education signifies. It is character-stimulus, and actually the reverse of mind stimulus, that popular education sets out to provide.[18]

Passing through this course of social indoctrination, the "contemporary European or American is a part of a broadcasting set, a necessary part of [the capitalist] machinery" (105) who has been prepared to produce the illusion of informed consent to the status quo.

Note how in Lewis's account of the Educationalist State a critique of the *institutions* of mass education produces an elision whereby the notion of education *as such* is brought under suspicion. If education is merely indoctrination, and indoctrination, in turn, is the reverse of "mind-stimulus," then education can oddly enough be said to make the student stupider. This lends an element of self-serving irony to claims such as Henry Adams's, usefully condensed by Leon Wieseltier, about his ineducability:

> Adams's education was more an unlearning than a learning. And its most significant feature was its foundering. He is almost tiresome in his insistence on the point: "all the education in the world would have helped nothing," "he had wholly lost his way," "all that had gone before was useless, and some of it was worse," "education, systematic or accidental, had done its worst," "religion, politics, statistics, travel had thus far led to nothing. . . . One might as well try to educate a gravel-pit," "never had the proportions of his ignorance looked so appalling," and so on. (intro. to *Education* xv)

It is obvious that Adams—a highly educated person by any conceivable standard—is only ironically declaring himself a "gravel-pit." To remain "unschooled," from this point of view, is a way of protecting one's intelligence from the stupefying forces of incorporation, and indeed of declaring one's individual authenticity in the face of pedagogical mechanisms of social standardization and assimilation. It also suggests a curious affiliation between the independent intellectual who rises above mere education and the person one might consider his or her polar opposite, the literally ignorant person, the "peasant" or "primitive" who has remained below the reach of mass education altogether.

But while "staying ignorant" or "unschooled" could, from a certain perspective, suggest a noble resistance to assimilation by social institutions, it was not the case that intellectuals were left without the means and desire to participate in other forms of group identification. Not yet absorbed by the university, literary intellectuals were required to seek institutional support and self-definition within the culture market itself. They did so mainly by organizing themselves in and around the magazines, typically of highly restricted circulation, that they edited and in which their work appeared. These included Harriet Monroe's *Poetry* and Margaret Anderson's *Little Review*, tiny publications that owed their existence as much to patronage as to profit. Mencken's the *Smart Set: A Magazine of Cleverness*, with a circulation that at times approached 100,000, was considerably larger, and was run, in theory at least, as a profit-making entity. It has the virtue for us of laying bare, in its very title, the way a magazine could function as an extracurricular mechanism of group definition and distinction. To read the *Smart Set* was to be *of* the smart set, and not one of the masses of "boneheads"—say, the 5 million or so readers of the pious *Saturday Evening Post*—against which this set defined itself.

S. N. Behrman recounts how, while he was still at Harvard, the *Smart Set* seemed to him and his friends an inviting enterprise, superior in cultural sophistication even to the exclusive educational institution they still attended:

> Among its other appeals *The Smart Set* seemed to us electrifyingly avant-garde. With a Nietzschean expansion Beyond Good and Evil, a fellow-member of English 47 picked to dramatize from "The Aristocrat of the Magazines" a story about a dying wife whose husband has an affair with the nurse attending her. Professor Baker was not as advanced as we and *The Smart Set* were . . . [and] was sorry he had chosen a story in which the hero is such an unmitigated cad. Dear Professor Baker! How canny he was to die before the *nouvelle vague*; how much has been spared him![19]

In the hands first of Willard Wright, and then, for a much longer period, of H. L. Mencken and George Jean Nathan, the *Smart Set* had sought to establish itself as the primary organ of a new American cultural sophistication that could equal that of Europe, and could match its raffish disregard of bourgeois moral uplift. Taking over the magazine in 1913, Wright announced that it is "not altogether true that America is incapable of producing literature such as is being brought from overseas every season. I believe that only an outlet is needed to prove that American writers are capable of meeting European writers on an equal footing" (quoted in Dolmetsch, *Smart Set*, 35). Thus defined in terms of its cultural and artistic sophistication, the *Smart Set* was in fact redefining itself: it had begun its career in 1879 as *Town Topics: A Journal of Society*, a scandal sheet and organ of "society news" of the wealthy Gilded Age Four Hundred. Purchased in 1885 by William D'Alton Mann, and retitled the *Smart Set* in 1900, its "foremost aim" in this early period, according to Carl Dolmetsch, had been to "attract to the new magazine readable stories and verse from socialite

amateurs whose lustrous surnames would sell the magazine quite regardless of its literary merits" (5).

When it was taken over by Wright, its title could be said to have shifted
its meaning: a "smart set" defined in terms of socialite style would now be
understood as a group of people with brains. Social would become intellectual distinction. And yet, importantly, the valence of this shift in meaning
remained reversible, suggesting that persons of intelligence might be considered "aristocrats" even if they had not exactly been to the manor born.
The idea was to produce a virtual social medium in which "the natural
aristocrat of taste could join with the aristocrats of privilege and money to
defend the Temple of Art and Culture against the onslaughts of parvenu,
Philistine and dangerous democrat" (6). Now "wealth and position were
to be wedded to intellect" (7). Forming a short-lived publication of similar
intent, the editors of *Mlle New York* had announced their "ambition" to
"disintegrate some small portion of her public into its original component
parts—the aristocracies of birth, wit, learning and art and the joyously
vulgar mob" (6). The suggestion here is that the public addressed by publications like the *Saturday Evening Post* has become indistinct enough,
under the sway of mass education and mass marketing, that it needs to be
"disintegrated" again into hierarchical groups.

In the case of publications like the *Smart Set* and its imitators—one of
these was Sherwood Anderson's New Orleans–based the *Double Dealer,*
which first published William Faulkner—these distinctions would be
forged not at the very margins of the market, as in the case of *Poetry* and
the *Little Review,* but within the mass market itself. Thus the cultural
distinctions enacted by the *Smart Set* operate upon a basis of economic
continuity with the institutions and artifacts of mass culture. Indeed, the
Smart Set would eventually owe its very existence to what Mencken called
"louse magazines": when, in 1916, *Smart Set* began to run into economic
difficulties, Mencken and Nathan began to repackage whatever literary
chaff they had on hand in cheap covers and send it out under profitable
titles such as *Snappy Stories,* which frequently sold well in excess of their
legitimate parent publication. They performed the same feat in 1920 when
they started *Black Mask,* a detective magazine that quickly rose to over a
quarter million in circulation. Designed as an economic mechanism to
keep high culture afloat, *Black Mask* would become central to the development of modern American detective fiction in the twenties and thirties,
discovering and promoting Dashiell Hammett. Hammett, as I will discuss
in my final chapter, would become painfully conscious of the taunting editorial proximity—which could also seem like a great divide—between the
oily precincts of the "louses" and the lofty station of the "smart set." Meanwhile Willard Wright, the scourge of talentless popular novelists and au-

thor of his own "advanced" novel, *The Man of Promise* (1916), would, having fallen on hard times, be forced to reinvent himself as the hugely popular detective fiction writer, "S. S. Van Dine." Wright's first attempt at an autobiography, written in deep shame at how far he had fallen and how fabulously rich he had become, would be titled *I Used to Be a High-brow, but Look at Me Now*.[20] The institutional interdependence of high and mass culture, culture smart and culture stupid, that one sees in the relation of the *Smart Set* to *Black Mask* could, in other words, also become a mechanism of intellectual self-definition: one did not have to matriculate to be a member of a "school of thought." The literary intellectual in the early-twentieth century was formed not apart from the stupid masses, in the ivory towers of academe, but in their very midst.

Morons and Moralizers: The Eugenic Romance

Anybody can sit in a classroom. Intelligence is something else, a gift of nature. To modernist writers this idea was appealing, but not without problems. The difficulty derived, in the first case, from an ambiguity surrounding the very nature of intelligence: what is it, exactly?

This ambiguity was understandable, given that the specifically modern conception of intelligence that informed early-twentieth-century writing had barely existed even ten years earlier. Differences in intellectual abilities, talents, and skills had of course been noticed before this time. What was original to the period was the idea that intelligence could be understood as a single, quantifiable entity lying behind various behavioral and mental competencies—a "general" intelligence, often represented in the specialist literature as "g." As it took shape after the seminal work of Francis Galton and Alfred Binet, "g" came to be understood as a genetically determined quantum of "intellectual force" that could be measured, and thus placed on a hierarchical scale, by means of what came to be called IQ tests. With the invention of the IQ the individual was assigned (though not necessarily apprised of) a single numerical representation of his or her total inborn intellectual capacity. Applied to social groups, IQ made available a technology of social distinction quite different, in effect, from traditional conceptions of the cultural "backwardness" or untutored simplicity of the lower orders: to call these persons unintelligent was to suggest that this cultural division could not be remedied by education.

Indeed, the immediate use of IQ, in the work of Alfred Binet, had been to define the limits of educability, weeding out students who could not be expected to stay afloat in the mainstream of an expanding French public education system. Available for various kinds of ideological deployment, IQ would soon become a cipher of the complexities and competing impulses underlying the idea of a liberal "meritocracy"—government by the fittest. In the hands of progressive reformers IQ would become a means of identifying and promoting lower-class "natural aristocrats" into social and cultural elites. In other hands it would become a means both of justifying the rule of certain social groups as natural and of asserting the futility of various forms of affirmative action. While the theorization of IQ had begun in Europe, the United States quickly proved to be fertile ground for the theory, practice, and politics of intelligence testing, which it continues to be to this day. Indeed, despite periodic exposures of the disingenuousness, and sometimes outright fraudulence, of its champions, this relatively novel theoretical construction has become so deeply embedded in American culture that its existence typically remains unquestioned even as debate rages around its precise nature, social implications, and techniques of measurement.[21] In the earlier days of IQ, its scientific standing was uncertain enough that, looking back in 1920 on its first few decades as a concept, one of the major theoreticians of intelligence, Charles Spearman, was forced to concur with the observation that while "the teacher tried to cultivate intelligence, and the psychologist tried to measure intelligence, nobody seemed to know precisely what intelligence is."[22] And yet the case of IQ suggests that the vagueness of a concept is not always an impediment to its success.

Some of this uncertainty is present in John Erskine's essay "The Moral Obligation To Be Intelligent," which I had occasion to examine briefly in chapter 1.[23] Here, as Erskine makes his case for intelligence over traditional moral virtue, the problem is not so much its precise nature or quantifiability but rather, as his title suggests, its relation to morality. For writers working outside the specialist enclaves of experimental psychology, this relation would soon prove to be of paramount importance. A writer might gladly accept the notion that some people are simply smarter than others, and might just as gladly believe, or at least hope, that he or she rests near the top of the heap. It was, however, a particular understanding of the relation between intelligence and moral convention that would differentiate the modernist intellectual from more conventional mindworkers of the period.

Should intelligence, as Erskine first suggests, be considered an *aspect* of morality, that part of moral virtue that will allow it to be realized as fact in the modern social world? Or should it rather be considered a virtue apart, an intrinsic good with no necessary relation to conventional moral practice? The latter view emerges when Erskine momentarily drops his mantle of progressive expertise and addresses his audience as "lovers of literature" who must also, if they are to be discriminating in their tastes, become "lovers of intelligence." Here Erskine confesses that none of the reasons here suggested will quite explain the true worship of intelligence, whether we worship it as the scientific spirit, or as scholarship, or as any other reliance upon the mind. We really seek intelligence not for the answers it may suggest to the problems of life, but because we believe it is life,—not for aid in making the will of God prevail, but because we believe it is the will of God. We love it, as we love virtue, for its own sake. (26–27)

One hears an echo of Henry James's famous rejoinder to H. G. Wells in this passage—"It is art that *makes* life, makes interest, makes importance"—and indeed it was this aestheticized, "smarts-for-smarts'-sake" view that was adopted by the majority of literary intellectuals in the Jamesian modernist tradition. Further radicalized by Nietzsche—both Mencken and Willard Wright were to write book-length accounts of his thought—literary intellectuals of the period tended to conceive intelligence not as the mental capacity to act morally, but as a force of "aristocratic" resistance to the "slave morality" of the "bewildered" American herd. Thinking beyond good and evil, as conventionally defined, these intellectuals would redress what Mencken called the "capital defect in the culture of These States"—their "lack of a civilized aristocracy, secure in its position, animated by an intelligent curiosity, skeptical of all facile generalizations, superior to the sentimentality of the mob, and delighting in the battle of ideas for its own sake" (Mencken, *Chrestomathy*, 178). They would also, more simply, identify themselves as a certain kind of intellectual, a member of the smart set. The alternative position, that conventional morality and intelligence are one thing, was left to eugenicists, social reformers, and others still wedded to bourgeois proprieties and mores. And yet, at least at this early moment of their development, one can still discern some shared premises underlying the differences between these two positions in the intellectual field.

Consider the case of Henry Herbert Goddard, one of the leading American popularizers of eugenics and certainly the period's most alarmist observer of the encroachment of "feeblemindedness" into American life. For Goddard there could be no such thing as an intelligent criminal, a brainy drunkard, or a savvy prostitute, since these behaviors constituted prima facie evidence that a person was, at best, a "high grade moron." Persons of normal intelligence, it was assumed, would know better than to engage in such immoral behavior. "Morons," it is true, were not to be confused with "imbeciles," the term used to describe those who could not be taught to write, nor yet with "idiots," who could not be taught even to speak properly. Indeed, "moron" was a neologism Goddard devised to describe mental defectives closest in appearance and behavior to "normal" members of society. As Stephen Jay Gould has recounted, the moron quickly became the primary object of Goddard's concern, since this liminal figure embodied a boundary between normality and defect that needed rigorously to be policed. For Goddard the low-grade idiot, while "loathsome," is "not our greatest problem" because he typically "does not continue the race with a line of children like himself." It is "the moron type that makes for our great problem," because he is so often allowed to procreate, adding soldiers to the "large army" of morons already besieging American society.[24] If, in dealing with this dilemma, Goddard favored "segregation and colonization" rather than systematic sterilization or extermination of the moron, this was only because he believed it would be easier to sell this idea to a public too squeamish to act in its own best interest.

Goddard's thorough imbrication of conventional morality and intelligence sets him apart from the literary intellectuals who were his contemporaries. Nonetheless, it is striking how much of the gap between the institutions of experimental psychology and the writing of fiction appears to be bridged by Goddard's effort to sell a wider public on the necessity of strong eugenic remedies. His most popular and influential work, *The Kallikak Family* (1914), deploys many of the techniques and tropes of the novel for the explicit purposes of effective propaganda. "The present study of the Kallikak family is a genuine story of real people" (xiii), he writes in the preface to a work that, at least in its representation of the idea of a family curse, recalls Hawthorne's *The House of the Seven Gables*. The difference is that Goddard's curse is a specifically genetic, and purportedly scientific one, the biological aftermath of the introduction of an "evil" strain of feeblemindedness into a prominent American family in the time of the Revolution. In those years a young scion of the family committed an "indiscretion" with a "nameless feeble-minded" barmaid that resulted in an unacknowledged child; later he married a woman of "good family" and procreated again. *The Kallikak Family* purports to trace the parallel development of these two sides of the pseudonymous family—"Kallikak" combines the ancient Greek for "good" and "bad"—one presenting a lineage of good citizenship and high social standing, the other a sorry record of crime and illegitimacy. Disavowing the "delusion" that these differences might be attributed to social and environmental factors—that is, the social costs of inherited illegitimacy and poverty paid by one side of the family and not the other—Goddard rather insists that the innate feeblemindedness of the bad half emanates outward and produces its own environment. "The career of Martin Kallikak Sr. is a powerful sermon against sowing wild oats," he concludes, and so "let it be impressed upon our young men of good family that they dare not step aside for even a moment" (102–3).

While *The Kallikak Family* shows a certain resemblance to a family saga novel, it also mobilizes many of the tropes of the tenement pastoral such as they were seen operating twenty years earlier in texts like Crane's *Maggie*. It begins by introducing us at some length to a character, an illegitimate young woman called Deborah, who has been confined in Goddard's Vineland Training School for Feeble-Minded Girls and Boys since she was a child. Presenting what seems to be fairly inconclusive evidence of her feeblemindedness—"She is quick and observing, has a good memory, writes fairly," but she is a "poor reader and poor at numbers" and also forgetful (7–8)—Deborah is nonetheless described as

> a typical illustration of the mentality of the high-grade feeble-minded person, the moron, the delinquent, the kind of girl or woman that fills our reformatories. They are wayward, they get into all sort of trouble and difficulties, sexual and otherwise. (11)

She also marks the limits of the transformative power of education, since she is an example

> of the same type of girl in the public school. Rather good-looking, bright in appearance, with many attractive ways, the teacher clings to the hope, indeed insists, that such a girl will come out all right. Our work with Deborah convinces us that such hopes are delusions. (11–12)

Rewriting Crane's *Maggie: A Girl of the Streets* as, let us say, *Deborah: A Girl of the Mental Institution*, Goddard's book necessarily forecloses on what might otherwise have been a lurid tale of Deborah's tragic decline at the hands of unscrupulous men like her ancestor Martin Kallikak. While Crane had exposed Maggie to her "terrible" Bowery environment and derived his narrative from this fatal interaction, Goddard's eugenic narrative leaves Deborah in her institutionalized safety and doubles back, for the remainder of the study, to trace the unfortunate lineage that has produced her. Asserting that the educability of the moron is a "delusion," Goddard in effect redefines the nature of the "training school" he runs as an institution of perpetual confinement and quarantine. Similarly, while his book may be an instructive sermon to potentially wayward young men, there is literally nothing to be learned from it, on Goddard's logic, by the morons into whose hands it might have been imagined to fall. These bearers of "bad stock," while they may be taught to read, cannot be expected to learn.

Set in this context, Anita Loos's tale of a blonde moron can now be seen as a kind of crossing of Crane and Goddard, releasing a feebleminded woman "with many attractive ways" into a world of predatory males. We can also register the full force of the irony Loos applies to the notion that these males want, as they claim, to "educate" her, or that Lorelei might be taken seriously in her efforts to "improve her mind." Her stupidity, no less than Deborah's, leaves her beyond the reach of true education, and it is only by virtue of this serendipitous dimness that she does not become conscious of the misery of her life. Indeed the difference, in Loos's own prefatory account, is simply one of tone:

In fact, if one examines the plot of *Gentlemen Prefer Blondes*, it is almost as gloomy as a novel by Dostoievsky. . . . It concerns early rape of its idiot heroine, an attempt by her to commit murder . . . , the heroine's being cast adrift in the gangster-infested New York of Prohibition days, her relentless pursuit by predatory males . . . , her renunciation of the only man who ever stirred her inner soul of a woman, her nauseous connection with a male who is repulsive to her physically, mentally and emotionally. (12–13)

Considered as an object of the narrative, rather than its author, Lorelei might appear of a piece with Maggie or Deborah, a tragic young woman whose body will become the contested terrain of patriarchal power, a war zone of virtue and vice. And yet her author will not let her suffer at the hands of unscrupulous men. Indeed, Lorelei is supplied with her own internal Goddard, a voice of bourgeois morality and virtue. She is also provided, in her fiancé Henry Spoffard, with a companion whose main interest in life is in "senshuring" movies. At the outset of the sequel to *Gentlemen, But Gentlemen Marry Brunettes* (1927), Lorelei decides to become a literary "authoress" in New York, "where all the Art and Literature is."[25] Planning her new career, she asserts that she will not be "the kind of an authoress who leaves the world no better off than it was in the first place, by being destructive, but I would always try to teach some lesson, that would make it even better" (23). Lorelei, in other words, would be a moral educator, not a modernist.

In figuring both as a moron and as a moralizer, Lorelei combines two figures to which literary intellectuals would oppose themselves. Like Goddard, Mencken was preoccupied by the genetics of stupidity and the pervasiveness of the American moron; quite unlike Goddard, he saw the prudish Comstockery of the likes of Goddard and Lorelei as evidence of the moralizer's own thoughtless and benighted conventionality. Indeed, the contempt of literary intellectuals for the latter would produce some remarkably powerful ironies and reversals in the series of alliances by which their own position was forged. This is part of what has made it so difficult to piece through what the pastoral impulses of the modernist project actually signified. What emerged was a tripartite structure in which moron, bourgeois moralizer, and modernist intellectual revolve in a shifting set of ideological dependencies, with elements both of identificatory and of contrastive self-definition.

For literary modernism, by far the most important of these ironic affiliations would be with the "immoral moron" him- or herself. This seems to me one of the most powerful, if by no means the only, valences of modernist primitivism: the libidinous "primitive" character—frequently, though not exclusively, figured as a black person—was seen to embody an ironically "intelligent" critique of Victorian conventionalities. Doing so, literary modernism produced one of its signal genres: culturally sophisticated representations of primitive urges. By far the dominant gesture in period discussions of modern fiction, we must always recall, was either to defend or to decry its sexual immorality: novels like *Ulysses* or James Branch Cabell's *Jurgen* were banned not for their rebarbative difficulty, after all, but for their purported obscenity. What was needed, in this context, was a mode of identification with the libidinous primitive that would leave no doubt about the actual elevation of the intellectual's intellect.

Smart White Blacks: Mencken, Stein, and Race

While H. L. Mencken must be distinguished, on any number of levels, from his contemporary H. H. Goddard, still he shared Goddard's interest in biological determinants of culture not susceptible to being altered by education. In Mencken's hands a notional aristocracy of the intellect, superior to the sentimentality of the mob, would become a virtually racial designation, an ironic afterimage, or ghost, of its polar opposite—a deeply embodied, untutored blackness. "What is needed down there," he says in his account of Lorelei's home region, "The Sahara of the Bozart,"

> is a survey of the population by competent ethnologists and anthropologists. The immigrants of the North have been studied at great length, and anyone who is interested may now apply to the Bureau of Ethnology for elaborate data as to their racial strains, their stature and cranial indices, their relative capacity for education, and the changes that they undergo under American *Kultur*. But the older stocks of the South, and particularly the emancipated and dominant poor white trash, have never been investigated scientifically. (189)

Never one to slow the rush of his own opinions, Mencken did not allow this lack of scientific data to impede his speculations on the causes of the South's loss of its "capacity to produce ideas." Like Goddard disavowing economic, environmental, or educational explanations of the phenomenon, he had really meant it when he had argued, earlier in the essay, that the "South has simply been drained of all its best blood" (188). Indeed, he believed it "highly probable that some of the worst blood of western Europe flows in the veins of the Southern poor whites"—mainly the "Celtic strain"—and that this certainly explained the unfortunate "mental traits" of the region (190). For Mencken, that is, the transformative discourse of social class—where the "poor white" necessarily becomes something else when he or she acquires money and education—is rather conceived as an unalterable genetic inheritance, an inborn disposition to worthlessness. Recapitulating the ideology of romance, which believes it will always recognize the aristocrat hidden in the rags of the foundling, Mencken has no patience for the "delusion that class distinctions are merely economic and

conventional, and not congenital and genuine." Those "extraordinary ple-
beians" who do occasionally emerge from the lower classes are evidence,
for Mencken, not of the vast reserves of mute inglorious talent that remain
untapped in uncultured environments, but of the covert presence there of
a few wayward drops of aristocratic blood.

Thus what Mencken calls "class distinctions" function in precisely the
manner that the terminology of "class," as it had emerged in early-nine-
teenth-century British utilitarianism, and later in European Marxism, had
been intended to negate. For utilitarianism—associated, like the novel itself, with a newly assertive middle class politics—it had been crucial to
assert the (mere) conventionality of social hierarchy as well as the importance of environment and education in shaping the individual. In this climate of thought, even as prodigious a figure as J. S. Mill would insist that
he owed his achievements not to inborn ability but to training alone.[26] For
Mencken, by contrast, class is what might more commonly be thought of
as caste—a biological determination of group identity and hierarchical
social placement virtually identical, in its identitarian logic, to period conceptions of racial identity.[27] Recasting class as caste, Mencken could in fact
be said to intensify the racism of racial theory of the period, since the
constitutively hierarchical notion of "caste" was not subject to the solvent
of a "cultural pluralism" that, in this period, began to redefine racial difference as relativist cultural equality. To be different, in Mencken's
scheme, was to be either worse or better.

This had also been the implication of the work of those "ethnographers
and anthropologists" on Northern immigrants to whom Mencken respectfully refers. John Erskine, figuring the love of stupidity in American culture
as an Anglo-Saxon inheritance, was a rarity in arguing that the life of the
mind in America had been improved by the recent influx of non-English
immigrants. "Our land assimilates all races," he observed, and if "some
of us do not greatly err, these newcomers are chiefly driving to the wall
our inherited criticism of the intellect" (*Moral Obligation*, 22). A few years
later, after the war, his point of view would be turned on its head by the
diverse group of ethnographers, anthropologists, and experimental psy-
chologists committed to eugenic science. As these sciences became intertwined with a nativist politics that defined whiteness as a necessary component of American-ness, and in turn sought to redefine whiteness in more
restrictive terms, immigration came to be perceived not as a source of intellectual betterment, but as the primary threat to the American intellect:

> American intelligence is declining, and will proceed with an accelerating rate as
> the racial admixture becomes more and more extensive. The decline in American
> intelligence will be more rapid than the decline of the intelligence of European
> national groups, owing to the presence of the negro.[28]

These are the "plain, if somewhat ugly, facts" uncovered in Carl Brigham's *A Study of American Intelligence* (1923).

Brigham derived these "facts" from an analysis of the results of intelligence tests administered to army recruits during the recent war—the first time intelligence testing had ever been conducted on a massive scale. Organizing his data in terms of the national origin and years of U.S. residence of his subjects, Brigham had "discovered" that recruits of "Nordic" extraction were by far the smartest. The other large racial groups who had comprised the majority of recent immigrants, "Alpine" and "Mediterranean," could be placed in a downward array that finally arrived at the lowly "Negro." Recasting Goddard's warning against the admixture of "good" and "bad" stock in specifically racial terms, Brigham's book helped promote the absurd idea that the average "mental age" of the adult American now stood at fourteen.[29] Offered as testimony in debates surrounding immigration restriction, the book played no small part in the passage of the Johnson Immigration Act of 1924.

The importance of nativist politics and of race theory in general to the emergence of the modernist aesthetic has been examined elsewhere.[30] Here I would emphasize that aspect of this project likely to draw the attention of persons identifying themselves as "intellectuals"—as those who think. Without insisting too much on what, left alone, would amount to an impoverished account of the intellectual in this period, one can easily imagine the fascination with which a writer like Mencken might greet a study such as Brigham's. The surprising thing is that in his own ethnographic account of the South, Mencken places Southern blacks—for whose intellect he shows no particular respect—higher on the scale of mental acumen than their "white trash" neighbors.

Indeed, for Mencken, the history of Southern race relations, in some ways advantageous to blacks, explains the evident feeblemindedness of white Southerners like Lorelei Lee. "In the great days of the South," he writes, "the line between the gentry and the poor whites was very sharply drawn. There was absolutely no intermarriage" and "the men of the upper classes sought their mistresses among the blacks" (191). Thus deprived of infusions of better blood from above, poor whites in the South naturally went into relative decline with respect to their black neighbors. Indeed, after "a few generations there was so much white blood in the black women that they were considerably more attractive than the unhealthy and bedraggled women of the poor whites" (191)—and smarter, too.

In Mencken's formulation, Southern black women are more attractive than poor white women because they are, in a sense, *whiter* than these poor white women. The unhealth and bedraggledness of the poor white becomes, for Mencken, the stigmata not of poverty but of a kind of white-trash "blackness"—a genetically encoded inferiority that had historically

been reserved for "real" blacks. Meanwhile, at least in the relatively iso-
lated context of the South, blackness has become the visible mark of relative racial superiority, since it is assumed not only that white blood flows
copiously in black veins, but that this "is not the blood of poor whites but
that of the old gentry" (192).[31]

Tracing Mencken's argument, one sees how his unquestioned assumption of the racial inferiority of "homo noir" could coincide with the idea
that actual black people, inasmuch as they are white aristocrats in racial
disguise, represent an elevation in culture and intelligence over their benighted white trash neighbors. Pushed further, the "black" person of
"mixed blood" might become a figure of the warring impulses of reason
and urge fundamental to the divided psychoanalytic subject, the human
being, as a whole. Pushed further still, and socially specified, the person
of mixed blood could be seen as a inverted figure of the modernist intellectual him- or herself. This "mixed" figure of intelligent immorality would
signify the intellectual's inborn capacity to resist the stupefying forces of
moral training and formal education. And indeed, as early as Gertrude
Stein's "Melanctha" (1905)—whose use of the "naif-motif" Wyndham
Lewis would link to Loos's *Gentlemen*—one finds a text plainly preoccupied by questions of racial admixture, intelligence, and education that
might be read in this way.

Although the story is sometimes described as an attempt by a white
American writer to enter deeply into the experience of a black woman,
Stein's character Melanctha is in fact somewhat more complicatedly described in the text as a "subtle, intelligent, attractive, half white girl"—a
"graceful, pale yellow, intelligent, attractive negress" who was "half made
with real white blood."[32] For all its formal innovations, Stein's text participates in the long tradition of literary interraciality recently documented
by Werner Sollors; indeed, it might be read as a variation on the theme of
the tragic mulatto, a figure brought to ground by the contradictory racial
impulses warring in her veins.[33] As the story progresses, the racially "complex" Melanctha engages in a series of relationships with figures who are
equally, indeed almost systematically, taxonomized in terms of their place
along a scale that runs from "real" whiteness to "real" blackness, which
poles represent a very familiar opposition between higher intellect and
sensuous embodiment. As Melanctha approaches these characters in
search of "wisdom," she finds that she must redefine what "education"
means. The worldly Jane Harden "was a negress, but she was so white that
hardly any one could guess it" (103). Jane "had much white blood and
that made her see clear, she liked drinking and that made her reckless.
Her white blood was strong in her" (104) and she had "a good deal of
education" (103). The abstemious Dr. Jeff Campbell is a slightly darker
"young mulatto . . . good and strong and very intellectual" but ultimately

susceptible to the urge for "excitement" he criticizes in Melanctha. The conventional Rose Johnson, in turn, "was a real black, tall, well built, sullen, stupid, childlike, good looking negress." She may have been "brought up by white folks," but this "white training had only made for habits not for nature" (85–86).

In "Melanctha," we see, an intraracial color politics is unevenly mapped to an independent set of class distinctions measured by varying degrees of "roughness" and bourgeois moral training. Rose may be, with Jeff Campbell, the most socially elevated character in the story, possessed of a "strong . . . sense for proper conduct" (200), but we are assured that this is merely a patina on her natural identity as a "sullen ordinary black . . . unmoral promiscuous shiftless" woman (210). Thus, while it accurately predicts intelligence, and in fact a tendency to excessive thinking, the "white blood" flowing in Stein's "negro world" cannot be said to predict either the goodness or the propriety of its bearers. Mixed with blackness, it rather produces the complexity of divided beings and competing desires.[34] If a half-white person "naturally" desires to be good, in the manner of Goddard's intelligent moralists, then for Stein she is also, by virtue of her incomplete blackness, attracted even more strongly than "real" blacks to the "hot passion" associated with this blackness: "she did not care much now to know white men of the, for her, very better classes. It was now something realler that Melanctha wanted, something that would move her very deeply" (108). And so she begins to "wander" with black men. Soon to be awoken to his own hot passion, Jeff Campbell echoes Stein's account of Melanctha's divided racial identity when he says to her that "sometimes you seem like one kind of a girl to me, and sometimes you are like a girl that is all different to me, and the two kinds of girls is certainly very different to each other, and I can't see any way they have much to do, to be together in you" (138). He might have said something similar of the strangely hybrid voice of Lorelei/Loos in *Gentlemen*.

Melanctha is at once moral and immoral, black and white, two persons in one, complex; she is also, correspondingly, subject to two contrasting notions of "education" that define themselves across the divide between moral reasoning and carnal knowledge. We are told, on the one hand, that Melanctha "went on with her school learning; she went to school rather longer than do most of the colored children." She knows how to "use her learning with a father"—he is described as a "hard handed, black angry negro"—"who knew nothing" (92). Like the white-skinned Jane Harden, Melanctha "has a good mind" and is able to ask "intelligent questions" of the pious Jeff Campbell. And yet her relative capacity for formal education is mirrored, and then wholly overcome, by a competing desire for "education" of a different sort. Though Jane Harden had a "good deal of education," had been to college, and had "once taught in a colored school" (105), Melanctha looks to her for a kind of knowledge different from that offered in the classroom: "Jane Harden was not afraid to understand. Melanctha who had strong the sense for real experience, knew that here was a woman who had learned to understand" (103–4). An eager student of real experience, Melanctha becomes, as she "wanders" in search of "wisdom," a bad student of conventional social mores. "I done my best always to be telling it to you Melanctha Herbert," Rose Johnson will tell her, "but don't never do no good to tell nobody how to act right; they certainly *never can learn* when they ain't go no sense right to know it" (233, emphasis added). An intelligent woman but a bad student, the hybrid Melanctha is a modernist manqué. She is also a pivotal figure in the production of the pastoral discourse of modernist narrative.

Pastoral Intellection

We saw, in chapter 2, how in the late novels of Henry James one encounters characters whose remarkable capacity for intellection becomes visible against a background of flat-minded "fools" who serve as foils to the operations of higher and more complex consciousness than their own. Refracted through and blended with the consciousness a third-person narrator hard to differentiate from the author himself, this intelligence is made manifest in a particularly smart and sensitive character who stands as a rebuke to the general thoughtlessness, stupidity, and indistinction that surrounds her. Thus the novels of James must be understood not, or not merely, as representations of thinking, or of consciousness, but as a means of distinguishing the smart from the stupid.

And yet it was also seen how this pathos of intellectual distance was dependent on the stupid mass, the stupid matter, from which it was understood to arise and upon which it was understood to operate. I suggested that this dialectic of superiority and dependence might be read as symptom of the strategized relation of James's fiction to mass culture, a hostile relation, true, but also one of thorough intimacy with the forms, figures, and institutions of the mass market that provided the immediate context of the emergent art-novel.

Granting that James must be considered a crucial figure in this emergence, one is nonetheless presented with something of a mystery: if James is so crucial a figure, why does so much of the fiction that follows in his wake take such a radically different form from his own? While one can see a further elaboration of the "psychological" novel in the turn to "stream of consciousness" narration in texts such as Joyce's *Ulysses* and Faulkner's *The Sound and the Fury*, other experimental texts are more difficult to assimilate to the Jamesian project of representing consciousness.

One way of explaining this would simply be to say that James was by no means the only influence on the novelists who followed him, and that would be quite true. One might, in particular, point to the naturalist discourse with which James himself stages an encounter in *The Princess Casamassima*. If only in its characteristic fascination with the "lower orders"—persons removed from the domain of literary culture in which the naturalist text itself participates—one can see how the naturalist project is continued well into the so-called modernist period. In Stein's delineation of the "negro world" of Bridgepoint in "Melanctha"; Sherwood Anderson's depiction of the relatively unsophisticated world of the Midwestern village in *Winesburg, Ohio* (1919); Hemingway's attention to taciturn men in natural or combative settings that seem wholly opposed the effete world of letters; Faulkner's treatment of a Southern world beyond the pale of sophisticated culture; through to the oceanographic naturalism of a writer like John Steinbeck, one has to grant that the naturalist project, inflected by its particular contexts, shows considerable staying power in the twentieth century.

This will seem even more powerfully true if one emphasizes the continuity between literary naturalism—fiction that would, among other things, plumb the primitive Darwinian essence of human civilization—and "primitivism" itself. This crucial phase of modernism's pastoral enterprise—seizing, for instance, upon the simple complexities of the African mask—often inflected naturalist themes with the question of race, but not always. The primitivism that links James Frazer's *The Golden Bough* and Gertrude Stein's "Melanctha" is not uniformly but intermittently fascinated by racial difference. Indeed, if one looks at Stein's collection, *Three Lives*, as a whole, one immediately sees that its attraction to Flaubertian "simple hearts" begins with a racially neutral conception of this simplicity that encompasses the stories of Lena and Anna. Only as the story "Melanctha" begins to dominate our sense of the collection does the question of race overtake (for modernism and for its latter-day critics) a more general concern for simple hearts and simple minds.

And yet, supposing one takes the systematic importance of the "simple minds" dwelling at the margins of James's fiction seriously, there is at least one compelling way to understand the continuity between his depiction of immensely thoughtful, typically wealthy characters and the work of his "naturalist" inheritors in the tradition of the art-novel. This would be to say that what happens, in a text like Stein's "Melanctha," is that the simpletons who remained at the relative periphery of James's fiction, throwing the operations of his higher minds into relief, have now been rotated from that periphery to the center of the narrative. Thus situated, they begin to generate the complexity not of a thoughtful protagonist embodied in the fictive world of the novel, but of the entire fictional utterance. As an adherent of probabalistic realism, James had felt that he needed an alibi for his own endlessly thoughtful sophistication as an author and narrator. That is why he constantly adverts to the remarkable intelligence of the central characters he will contrast with the fools. Stein begins a process that eventually dispenses with the "smart character" alibi and produces sophistication in an unmediated encounter between high-art discourse and its relatively simple object. Taken as a general claim about modernist narrative, this begins to account for the fact that a modernist fiction frequently characterized by a notorious "difficulty," as compared to nineteenth-century realist fiction, in fact founds itself in meditation on various kinds of simplicity. Addressing the question of "the meaning of simplicity in art," Willard Wright, not yet exiled to the world of popular detective fiction, was quick to counter the notion of the "simplicity of great art," the idea that "the great minds are the simple minds, that art should come within the comprehension of all" (*Creative Will*, 161). Great art, according to Wright, is "complexity itself." Though it might seem simple to the uninitiated, this is "a seeming, not an actual, simplicity" (162).

It is arguably a seeming, not an actual, simplicity that one encounters in a work like Stein's "Melanctha". What Wyndham Lewis noted as the "childishness" of her prose, its singsong rhythm, restricted vocabulary, and striking repetitiveness, might alternatively be understood not as an *instance* of simplicity, but as a complex demonstration of the emergence of mental and discursive complexity from its unformed, simple state. In this Stein can be seen to share one of the central preoccupations of anthropology of the early-twentieth century, the uncertain relation of the primitive or "savage" mind to the "superior mental functions" of the civilized (white) man.[35] Stein's repetitive "technique," Michael North has observed, "has the curious power to complicate even as it reiterates."[36] Thus the hypnotic repetitiveness of her prose, while it might, in the manner of Lewis, be read simply as stupid discourse, might also be understood to reveal, indeed to foreground, the operations of the mind that gives form and language to matter: in this view each word, phrase, or statement one encounters in a text like "Melanctha" is taken not as a unique sign of something in the world, as in a naive realist account of language, but as a linguistic variation on a generative cognitive form. Stein's repetitions are always, as she herself always insisted, repetitions-with-a-difference.[37] If only as a function of appearing at different places in the text, but more often actually marked by a variation in phrasing or vocabulary, the phrasal refrains that punctuate her text seem to participate in a formal-discursive system that evolves as it moves through narrative time.

In "Melanctha" this looks like a series of waves of verb forms whose meaning, as they are repeated, become not clearer but more obscure: A repetitive density of the word "learning" in one segment of prose gives way to "teaching" and to "talking" and in turn to "saying" and "meaning" and "thinking" and "loving" in subsequent sections. In this way Stein gradually produces an abstract vocabulary of mind and discourse whose "real" relation to the thought and speech of the "simple folk" of whom she writes is uncertain at best. Indeed, I suggested above that the "divided" character Melanctha, while she might figure the pathos of mixed race in the tragic mulatto, might also stand as a figure of Stein's pastoral discourse itself, which founds an ambitiously experimental linguistic enterprise upon simple objects.

Loos's *Gentlemen Prefer Blondes* evinces this structure in another way, reminiscent, in some ways, of Stephen Crane. Loos does not present us with a figure of doubleness like Melanctha, since Lorelei remains a resolutely simple and depthless character. Rather, this diary supposed to have been written by a Southern simpleton is suffused with an alien, ironic consciousness at the invisible source of discourse itself. This is the irony of Anita Loos, the author of the author, who looks by contrast to her Lorelei very intelligent indeed. Looking back to William Empson's expanded notion of pastoral as a process of "putting the complex into the simple," Loos's novel becomes visible as an instance of pastoral intellection. An effect, in this case, of first-person narration, the braiding of simplicity and complexity is executed at the level of first-person cognition, or consciousness, itself.

This phenomenon, attached much more faithfully to a rhetoric of Southern regionalism than it is in *Gentlemen*, would reappear four years later in the work of a writer Empson would identify, with Gertrude Stein, as the preeminent American operator of "pastoral machinery." The first section of Faulkner's *The Sound and the Fury* (1929) is surely a preeminent example of what I am calling pastoral intellection. Here it is the retarded Benjy's simplicity, his cognitive disability, his seeming inability to make relevant distinctions or to live in chronological time that makes this section of the novel so difficult to comprehend. Like James, Faulkner occults the presence of a pedagogical narrator in this section, but takes this technique to a much farther extreme than James ever did, producing what John T. Matthews has called the "paradox of silent speech."[38] Though we can assume that an author/narrator must be present in Benjy's first-person narrative—how else have the illiterate Benjy's thoughts come to exist as writing?—Faulkner leaves the reader without a strong mediating presence who will do the work of translation. Absent some explanatory apparatus, nothing could prepare the reader to understand the prose he or she encounters on the first page of this novel: "Through the fence, between the curling flower spaces, I could see them hitting. They were coming toward where the flag was and I went along the fence. Luster was hunting in the grass by the flower tree. They took the flag out, and they were hitting" (3). None of these sentences produces any particular grammatical difficulty; Noel Polk has aptly described them as the "direct linguistic counterpart to a primitive painter's technique."[39] But for lack of the crucial referent "golf"—or, indeed, even an internal cue that one is in fact reading the first-person narrative of an idiot, and must not expect to be provided with such crucial referents—they remain mysterious in their import and significance.

This problem will be compounded when, without warning, Benjy makes an associative link from April 1928 back to a cold day in 1902, and so on to other time periods, and back, and forth, proceeding in the construction of his fractured account of the circumstances surrounding Caddy Compson's loss of virtue, which registers in Benjy's consciousness as her no longer smelling like trees. As with Crane's Maggie, Goddard's Deborah, Stein's Melanctha, and Loos's Lorelei, the question of intelligence in *The Sound and the Fury* sits hard by the questionable virtue of a young woman. Indeed, it seems as though the corruption of female virtue—once the job of the aristocratic rake—is a necessary component, or complement, to the art-novel's production of a discourse of intellectual virtue.

In chapter 5 I will take up the question of Faulkner's pastoral modernism at some length, tracking the curious inversion by which a region understood as being woefully bereft of cultural sophistication becomes the privileged site in American literature of precisely this sophistication. In conclusion here we need only note how Faulkner's pastoral intellection has the effect of dividing potential readers of the text into the intellectually weak and strong. Fascinatingly, as Polk has suggested, the weak reader of the text becomes the virtual double of Benjy, as confused (and perhaps even as emotionally distraught) as he is, if not more so.[40] Meanwhile, the strong reader, patiently (and usually with help) reconstructing the chronology and sense of the section, performs an intellectual operation precisely opposed to the confusions, if not to the thinking, of Benjy himself. Simultaneously "smart" and "stupid," the strong reader engages in his or her own pastoral intellection.

This process is echoed in the construction of the entire novel, as the tale of the idiot Benjy gives way to the first-person narrative of the young intellectual at Harvard, Quentin Compson. As the Benjy section, in its very difficulty, makes itself available for the production of exclusive cultural capital, the Quentin section could be said to double this process at the level of plot, as Quentin leaves the South in order to be educated in the North. The third, Jason section of the novel, in turn, could be said to situate the production of cultural capital—indeed, the production of the art-novel in the early twentieth century—in the context of the market and of economic capital: for who is the greedy Jason if not a symbol of commerce, of the moralizing cruelty of the conventional commercial mind?

In the final section of the novel, written from the perspective of a sense-making third-person narrator of a more traditional kind, the reader who has lasted that long encounters a form of narration that attempts to incorporate the elements of idiocy and intellect that we have seen to be warring in modernist discourse all along.

Faulkner's Ambit

Modernism, Regionalism, and the Location of Cultural Capital

> A certain notable spaciousness was in the Southern scheme
> of things.
> —H. L. Mencken, "The Sahara of the Bozart"

> "You cant understand it. You would have to be born there."
> —*Absalom, Absalom!*

Racinations: A Deeper South

It was Cleanth Brooks who, in the early 1960s, worked hardest to present William Faulkner as a Southern "nature poet," a provincial critic of what Brooks called the "prevailing commercial and urban culture" blowing in from cities to the north.[1] But from the outset there had been a tendency to attribute to Faulkner a virtuous marginality, an aversion to the mobilities of modern life: "He has roots in this soil as surely and inevitably as has a tree," wrote Phil Stone in his introduction to his friend's first book, a slim volume of verse published in Boston, *The Marble Faun* (1924).[2] "The author of these poems is a man steeped in the soil of his native land," Stone vouches, while the poems themselves are "drenched in sunlight and color as is the land in which they were written, the land which gave birth and sustenance to their author." Indeed, so efficient is this literary ecosystem, where land produces man produces poems about the land, that it allows no compass for what Stone calls "evasion or self-consciousness." Instead these are "the poems of a mind that reacts directly to sunlight and trees and skies and blue hills" (6–7)—a mind too simple even for the internal excursions of vanity.

But where exactly was Faulkner's land? Stone might have followed the lead of publications such as the *New Republic*, to which he had successfully submitted one of Faulkner's poems in 1919, insisting that his land was American land. In articles such as John Dos Passos's youthful salvo "Against American Literature" (1916), he would have seen American writing criticized as the "rootless product" of a people without "spiritual kinship to the corn and wheat," without that "unconscious intimacy with nature—the deeper, the less reflective it is—that has always lain at the soul of great writings."[3] Faulkner might have been promoted as an American who had learned, without too much reflecting upon, what Dos Passos called the "lesson of the soil." Instead Stone begins with Faulkner's sectional and regional affiliations, circumscribing his protégé in a shrinking series of concentric spaces, each more local than the last. Stone introduces Faulkner as a "Southerner by every instinct, and, more than that, a Mississippian," delineating a state within the region. But then, looking closer still, he suggests that it is in fact the "sunlight and mocking-birds and blue hills of North Mississippi"—far removed from the plantations of the Delta—that should be said to be "part of this young man's very being" (7). At any rate, he claims—skipping silently over the geographical unit that would prove so important to Faulkner, Lafayette County—once the alien "traces of apprenticeship" so evident in the poetry are removed, he will surely "bring forth a flower that could have grown in no garden but his own" (8).

Some two decades later, in his well-known introduction to *The Portable Faulkner* (1946), Malcolm Cowley would find no youthful charm in these mostly "worthless" poems of the indigenous north Mississippi faun.[4] But Cowley, too, orchestrating the rebirth of Faulkner's reputation, would promote an image of Faulkner as a writer with a privileged relation to his native land, the South, or, more specifically, the "Deep South."[5] "No other American writer takes such delight in the weather," he notes, recalling the mind that reacts directly to sunlight. Faulkner "has a brooding love for the land where he was born and reared and where, unlike other writers of his generation, he has chosen to spend his life" (xxv). This writer has not been "lost," that is, has not been "exiled" to Paris or even to the suburbs of Connecticut. He has thus been exempted from an early-twentieth-century youth Cowley describes in *Exile's Return* (1934/51) as a "long process of deracination," where a college education such as his own at Harvard seemed to be "directed toward destroying whatever roots we had in the soil, toward eradicating our local and regional peculiarities, toward making us homeless citizens of the world."[6]

Faulkner's notoriously intermittent and ineffectual scholarly efforts, though the campus of the University of Mississippi was for a time literally his backyard, might thus have been taken as further evidence of his willingness to stay home, undistracted, in this case, by alienating pursuits of knowledge. The potential virtue of Southern simplicity, if not of Southern ignorance, had been established by Allen Tate in his contribution to the Fugitive-Agrarian manifesto *I'll Take My Stand*, where Tate explained that the traditional "Southern mind was single, not top-heavy with learning it had no need of, unintellectual, and composed."[7] This "simple-minded" capacity to stay intellectually composed, and thus to stay put, finds a counterpart for Cowley, no less than for Phil Stone, in a remarkable lack of self-consciousness on Faulkner's part. Whereas Stone had contrasted Faulkner with poets like "Amy Lowell and her gang" who have "one eye on the ball and one eye on the grandstand" (intro, *Marble Faun*, 8), Cowley described him as holding "a curious attitude toward the public that appears to be lofty indifference . . . but really comes closer to be being a mixture of skittery distrust and pure unconsciousness that the public exists." Faulkner, in his early writing especially, is "not so much composing stories for the public as telling them to himself—like a lonely child in his imaginary world, but also like a writer of genius" (*Portable Faulkner*, xi).

Given the confinements imposed by even as laudatory a view as this one, it is perhaps no wonder that Faulkner was so unreliable a participant in his own pastoral immobilization. As has been cogently detailed by Michael Grimwood, Faulkner's work at this early moment of his career is suffused rather with metaphors both of immobility *and* escape and appears, on close inspection, to be anything but unselfconscious.[8] Indeed, Cowley's claims notwithstanding, nearly the first piece of business conducted by the speaker of *The Marble Faun*, back in 1924, had been to convene an imaginary audience: "And clouds glide down the western sky / to watch this sun-drenched revery" (11). Having done so the speaker, the faun himself, complicating the pastoral account of Faulkner even further, establishes and emphasizes his own self-consciousness by contrasting it to some unconscious poplars "Dreaming not of winter snows / That soon will shake their maiden rows." This faun understands that he exists in time, and also, perhaps even more importantly, that he dwells in a certain place. And yet, the immobility given such positive inflection by critics from Stone through Brooks appears here as the faun's central existential problem:

> Why am I sad? I?
> Why am I not content? The sky
> Warms me and yet I cannot break
> My marble bonds. That quick keen snake
> Is free to come and go, while I
> Am prisoner to dream and sigh
> For things I know, yet cannot know,
> 'Twixt sky above and earth below.
>
> . . . .
> The whole world breathes and calls to me
> Who marble-bound must ever be.
>
> (12)

This faun sounds a lot like a young man who wants to leave town. The things he "know[s], yet cannot know" sound like things he's heard or read about—a mediated knowing—but cannot see or experience for himself.

And indeed, in a letter of 1919, the same year the poems of *A Marble Faun* were first drafted, Faulkner can be found declaring to a friend in New Haven that he has "had enough of his 'God forsaken' home town to last him the rest of his life," a home town to which he fears he might be returned even from Hell.[9] He can't leave, he explains, because his sick mother (eventual dedicatee of *A Marble Faun*) does not want him to. Recently critics like Grimwood have begun to take an interest in Faulkner's youth in Oxford, Mississippi, where he was widely ridiculed as a shiftless, affected dandy, a quasi-aristocrat draping himself in various forms of painfully self-conscious artifice, extending even to the spelling of his name.[10] Like Hathorne, who became Hawthorne, Faulkner had been born Falkner, and in each case the extra letter would enable the long, open "awe" of upper-class pronunciation. Seen in this light these poems, whose diction Joseph Blotner describes as "closer to England than to Mississippi" (*Biography*, 70), begin to suggest an almost programmatic aspiration to mobility, the very opposite, it would seem, of simple Southern racination. Against the virtual automatization of Faulkner's discourse—visible in Cowley's claim that Faulkner "writes not what he wants to, but what he just has to write whether he wants to or not" (*Portable Faulkner*, xxiv)— this view of his authorship suggests a literary career produced not by nature but as the result of considerable ambition—an ambition no less salient or interesting for being artificial and ultimately social in origin.

Thus while it is true, as Carolyn Porter has noted, that Faulkner "grew up in a world on which his family's history was visibly inscribed," the monuments to that history could be said to incorporate, much like the marble faun himself, an urge to be elsewhere.[11] One can see this even in Faulkner's fictionalized description of the statue of his great-grandfather, W. C. Falkner, in his first Yoknapatawpha novel, *Sartoris* (1929):

> He stood on a stone pedestal, in his frock coat and bareheaded, one leg slightly advanced and one hand resting lightly in that gesture of haughty pride which repeated itself generation after generation with a fateful fidelity, his back to the world and his carven eyes gazing out across the valley where his railroad ran and to the blue changeless hills beyond, and beyond that, the ramparts of infinity itself.[12]

The "world" here is ambiguous, legible perhaps as the small town of Ripley, Mississippi, where the monument actually stands; the railroad, however, is clearly headed out and away, perhaps even to infinity. This aspiration to *transport* is one the minor railroad baron, Falkner, could also be said to have expressed in his other career as author of the best-selling novel *White Rose of Memphis* (1881)—a title taken from the name of a riverboat—and even more tellingly, for our purposes, *Rapid Ramblings in Europe* (1884). William Faulkner's own first, unfinished attempt at a novel, *Elmer*, would go ahead and narrate the escape of a young artist from the South for some rapid ramblings in Europe. Faulkner wasted no time, in the autobiographical sketch he provided to the publishers of *The Marble Faun*, claiming his relation to this illustrious local demigod of aesthetic and corporeal transport, whose interests he shared. "We have, in America, an inexhaustible fund of dramatic material," wrote Faulkner in a short essay published in the *Mississippian* in 1922. "Two sources occur to anyone: the old Mississippi river days, and the romantic growth of the railroads."[13]

That this young Southern writer, just learning to opine in public, should have chosen these subjects for American drama, each so important to the history of interstate commerce, is surprising only when seen in light of the ultimate value he is so often understood to have placed on provincial isolation and stasis. Throughout his career, however, the theme of transportation would remain a constant, if complex, theme in his work. Faulkner always had an eye well attuned to the significance of the road trip, as the bohemian excursion novel, *Mosquitoes* (1927); the automobile-versus-carriage novel, *Sartoris*; the airplane-racing novel, *Pylon* (1935); and of course the peripatetic novels, *As I Lay Dying* (1930) and *Light in August* (1932), make clear. This was true even to the very end, where Faulkner played his variation on Kerouac's *On the Road* (1955) in his own automobile novel, *The Reivers* (1962).

And yet, as the strictly regional, rather than national, parameters of his last road novel already suggest, it is true that Faulkner early on found ways to participate in his own racination, staking a claim by these means to his Southern distinction. " 'At home I always found myself remembering apple trees or green lanes or the color of the sea in other places,' " writes Horace Benbow in a letter toward the end of *Flags in the Dust*, " 'and I'd be sad that I couldn't be everywhere at once, or that all spring couldn't be concentrated in one place. . . . But now I seem to be unified and projected upon one single and very definite object" ' (397). Faulkner's own means of projecting himself upon a unified "object" was his production, beginning with *Flags* (originally published under the title *Sartoris*) itself, of the fictional county of Yoknapatawpha.[14] This county, its history, and its inhabitants, figuring as an ideal entity to which each of the printed novels and stories would stand merely as part-objects, would be called by Cowley a "living pattern," and would be proclaimed "Faulkner's real achievement." Invested at once in inhabitation and in motion, Faulkner imagines a kind of circular movement over this ground, where excursions always seem to return to their point of origin, if they can ever truly be said to have left this point at all. This ambivalent, or perhaps canny, admixture of staying and going is most strikingly, because most compactly, described in *Light in August* in the static motion of Lena Grove. Her progress along the road is "advanced in identical and anonymous and deliberate wagons as through a succession of crackwheeled and limpeared avatars, like something moving forever and without progress across an urn."[15] Thus the vehicle in which she rides "does not seem to progress." Rather it "seems to hang suspended in the middle distance forever and forever" (5), and it is unclear, though we know the roads eventually lead to non-Southern locales, whether she could ever travel the truly "fur piece" beyond the boundaries of the Southern states she names, Alabama, Mississippi, and Tennessee. At the same time, in what will become a characteristic preoccupation of Faulkner and his critics, it seems to become unclear whether the *meaning* of Lena's story—though it is literally published in New York— can be transported outside the South. Will it rather become something like the sound of the wagon, which "as though out of some trivial and unimportant region beyond even distance," seems "to come slow and terrific and without meaning, as though it were a ghost travelling a half mile ahead of its own shape" (6)? In a poem from the twenties published in the collection *A Green Bough*, Faulkner, however sick he may be of his home town, already seems to have discovered the necessity of Cowley's "exile's return":

> But I shall sleep, for where is any death
> While in these blue hills slumbrous overhead
> I'm rooted like a tree? Though I be dead
> This soil that holds me fast will find me breath.[16]

Here, much as the romantic advance of the railroads was understood to provide an inexhaustible source of dramatic material, Faulkner's native ground, somewhere in the natural South, figures as an inexhaustible source of respiration as well as artistic inspiration, what he would eventually call a "gold mine of other peoples."[17]

In this manner, at various points over the course of almost seventy years, sometimes with his active help, sometimes without, Faulkner has served as perhaps the premier sign in the American canon of regional cultural difference—of a specifically Southern resistance to the "standardization" of American life that is the purported consequence of the emergence of mass markets. Faulkner, the undisputed "giant of Southern literature," has been and no doubt remains foundational to the idea of a Southern literary culture in the twentieth century, a figure without whom the entire institutional apparatus of Southern literature and Southern studies— courses, conferences, journals, academic positions, and the like—is barely thinkable.[18] Lacking an equivalent figure—and also, of course, a relevant set of historical determinations—the idea of "Northern literature" is indeed unthinkable, as unthinkable as the idea of a "literature of white men" that announces itself as such. This tired analogy from the canon debates is instructive, suggesting the degree to which Faulkner's discourse, for all its tremendous prestige—indeed contributing significantly to this prestige—has been constructed as a white minority discourse. Southern culture, meanwhile, has been understood, as W. J. Cash notes with approval in *The Mind of the South*, as "another land, sharply differentiated from the rest of the American nation and exhibiting within itself a remarkable homogeneity."[19] It has thus been designated as a site of something akin to what F. R. Leavis called, in 1930, the "minority culture" to which falls the task of maintaining "distinction[s] of spirit" threatened by the "mass-production and standardisation" of information and entertainment in the American mass media.[20]

Encountering the sublimated militarism of even as recent an essay as Floyd Watkins's "What Stand Did Faulkner Take?" (1981)—which sees "enemies of true reading" in "theorists who march in named platoons of criticism," making "sociological" claims about Faulkner's South—one might be tempted to understand the construction of this minority culture as the self-construction of holdout Southern nationalists.[21] But this is not so. In a 1929 review of Faulkner's *Sartoris* for the *Nashville Tennessean*, for example, one can already find the most polemical of the Fugitive-Agrarians, Donald Davidson, proposing that Faulkner's first Yoknapatawpha novel, "bringing back a sense of style that almost vanished in the experimentalism of the post-war period," may in fact be "more American than [its] predecessors in being nearer to an old native tradition" of popular romance.[22] Enfolding Faulkner's Southern difference in the larger discourse of American nativism—just as Faulkner's "Southern novels" were without exception enfolded in a larger, national structure of publishing, marketing, and distribution—Davidson establishes that regional difference as a form of currency whose nationwide circulation is anything but impeded by its imaginary grounding in a specific bit of Mississippi soil.[23] This extended a long tradition, dating back to the 1830s, of intersectional cooperation in the construction and celebration of the idea of the natural South, the gentlemanly Southerner, and various other aspects of what William R. Taylor has called the "Southern legend."[24] Logically entailed in the very notion of a "South"—the antipode which can exist only relative to a North—this cooperative project was only briefly (and even then ambiguously) interrupted by the Civil War, as one can see in the idealization of the Southerner in such postbellum novels as Henry Adams's *Democracy* (1880) or Henry James's *The Bostonians* (1886).

Faulkner's oft-quoted answer to the question of what caused him, after the novels *Soldier's Pay* (1926) and *Mosquitoes* (1927), to begin to set his novels in and around a fictionalized version of Oxford, expresses this dialectic of circulation and circumscription, nationalism and regionalism, with useful and powerful brevity: "Beginning with *Sartoris* I discovered that my own little postage stamp of native soil was worth writing about and that I would never live long enough to exhaust it" he said (*Lion*, 255). The key here is the postal metaphor, which suggests a "native soil" that already circulates as a sign in a national (and eventually international) communications network. The operation of this national network is enabled, and to a degree embodied, by the medium of the railway described in *Sartoris/Flags*, which is not "complete" until it has become part of a system of national extent:

> John Sartoris had sat so on this veranda and watched his two trains emerge from the hills and traverse the valley into the hills again, with lights and smoke and bells and a noisy simulation of speed. But now this railway belonged to a syndicate and there were more than two trains on it, and they ran from Chicago to the Gulf, completing his dream. (*Flags*, 44)

This train can carry Quentin Compson, in *The Sound and the Fury* (1929), all the way to Harvard; it can also, as we see in *Absalom, Absalom!* (1936), act as a vehicle for the "the odor, the scent," of the South, which "Mr Compson's letter would carry up from Mississippi and over the long iron New England snow and into Quentin's sitting room at Harvard."[25] So, too, Faulkner's own representation of native value, circulating in this network, will be legible even to a Northern suburban Harvard graduate like Malcolm Cowley. In its very title Cowley's edition *The Portable Faulkner*—said to have brought Faulkner to the attention of the Nobel Prize committee—states the case with remarkable and only somewhat inadvertent precision. Cowley's assessment of the relation of his generation of writers to the publishing industry of the time, in his 1951 revision of the prologue of *Exile's Return*, suggests the context of William Faulkner's particular role in the twentieth-century American literary canon:

> Publishing, like finance and the theater, was becoming centralized after 1900. Regional traditions were dying out; all regions were being transformed into a great unified market for motorcars and Ivory soap and ready-to-wear clothes. The process continued during the childhood of the new generation of writers. Whether they grew up in New England, the Midwest, the Southwest or on the Pacific Coast, their environment was almost the same; it was a little different in the Old South, which had kept some of its local manners but was losing them. The childhood of these writers was less affected by geography than it was by the financial situation of their parents, yet even that was fairly uniform[ly middle class]. . . . Since their playmates were also middle-class they had the illusion of belonging to a great classless society. (4–5)

In Cowley's account mass marketing appears as a kind of steamroller, paving over and abolishing differences both of region and—or so it could seem—of social class. Thus what he is describing, though from a different historical and ideological angle of vision, seems quite similar to the culture previously projected and critiqued by Henry James in the first of his "American Letters," and later bemoaned by Leavis as a "sinister . . . process of levelling-down." This is the culture of the "total swarm," of the great classless "homogenous" mass in which all distinctions are lost: mass culture.

According to Cowley the South, unlike New England or the Midwest, has resisted the homogenization of mass culture, retaining some of its "local manners." But equally interesting, for our purposes, is his assertion that it is inevitably "losing" these manners. The regional resistance to national mass culture begins to seem in this way a new Lost Cause, a cause whose romantic attraction will not be compromised but increased by its futility. If the advent of "ready-to-wear clothes" has, for Cowley, begun to make everyone look the same—a sartorial night in which all cats are grey—then Faulkner's "Sartoris" clan will serve almost as a literal embodiment of distinctive tailoring, just as the novel in which the clan first appears was seen to bring back, for Davidson, a "sense of style" lost elsewhere in American writing.

Cowley thus makes clear two things that often remain only implicit in the recruitment of Faulkner's work to a general critique of "modern" or "industrial" or "mechanical" or "mass" civilization: first, that one of the targets of this critique is national cultural standardization *as such*, irrespective of the question of whether Ivory or any other national brand is a good and functional product or not; second, that at least as strong as any racial or ethnic homogeneity it might be imagined to have—in contrast, for instance, to the immigrant swirl of the Northern city—the appeal of the South as a region has always been its presentation of "aristocratic" images of traditional class distinctions and social hierarchy.[26] Thus, as we shall see, precisely that feature of Faulkner that will appeal to the Marxist critic Myra Jehlen—his "recognition of class . . . nearly unique in the American canon," his creation of characters "made of the stuff of class distinctions"—is also the trace of an important presence in Faulkner of class fantasies more readily associated with popular romance than with his own fiction.[27] In the American literary construction of "Southern culture," a rhetoric of cultural difference is reinforced by, and braided with, a rhetoric of class distinction.

In this enterprise—the maintenance of social distinctions within a putatively homogenous American mass culture—the central contribution of Faulkner's fiction has been epistemological. For a sense or image of Southern "style" and manners the literary and cinematic plantation romance—and even the early, antebellum moments of the megapopular drama of Southern industrialization, *Gone with the Wind* (1936)—has more than sufficed. It is to William Faulkner, in particular, that certain readers have

turned when they have wanted to believe that the South is uniquely difficult to understand. Faulkner's discourse has thus been made to suggest
the existence—alongside and against the absolutely absorbable prose of
Margaret Mitchell—of an authentic regional discourse incapable of ultimate assimilation to American national discourse. Of Faulkner it could be
said, as Mr. Compson puts it in *Absalom, Absalom!*, "It's just incredible.
It just does not explain. Or perhaps that's it: they dont explain and we are
not supposed to know" (80). The threat of a mass market that distributes
the same soap to every citizen is also the threat of a mass media (the
centralized publishing industry in Cowley's description is only one tentacle
of this octopus) that (in theory) distributes the same information, the same
novels and movies, and thus the same "culture," to everyone. Thus Mitchell and Faulkner could be said to play opposed, but complementary, roles
in the literary construction of Southern difference.

Already in 1929, Donald Davidson approves of the fact that though it
is "so distinctly Southern in flavor as to tempt one to apply the term 'regional,' " Faulkner's fiction does "not betray the weakness of the 'regional'
or 'local color' school, which is, as I see it, to write of negroes, poor whites
and 'colonels' in the terms best appreciated by Northern audiences" (*Reviews*, 27). Avoiding Southern stereotypes, Faulkner has resisted at least
one form of easy comprehension that violates a more complex local reality.
This notion will be further developed, thirty years later, by Cleanth Brooks,
who objects to what he calls the "gross oversimplification" involved in the
"well-established stereotype" of poor whites in the South, which

> like other oversimplifications . . . has proved perennially attractive and has been
> kept alive by much popular fiction and drama right down to the present day.
> Some of the sustaining fiction has been very popular indeed, as witness Erskine
> Caldwell's *Tobacco Road* and *God's Little Acre* and similar tales sold in paper-
> back volumes in drugstores throughout the land. (11)

Reading this, one is surprised to discover that Caldwell was respected by
Faulkner as a literary "coeval" despite his popularity (Blotner, *Biography*,
480), and that after the war Faulkner, too, was sold in paperback editions
(complete with hilariously lurid covers) sold in national drugstore chains.
The implication of Brooks's "paperbacks" sold "throughout the land" is
nonetheless quite clear in invoking a mass culture of national extent, a
circulating stock of stereotyped images and descriptions that the complexity of Faulkner's fiction, and of Faulkner's South, should naturally resist.
Indeed, so complex is it that, according to Floyd Watkins, even many "sophisticated students of literature" get it wrong, writing with "positive cer-
tainty" of a South about which "they know little more . . . than they know
of the lost Atlantis" ("Stand," 46–47). Here, associating lost causes with
lost islands, Watkins figures the South as an immobile, absent object of

knowledge, not susceptible to scrutiny from afar. That is no doubt why, according to Watkins, those "who have read Faulkner correctly are usually Southern or rural" or at least "extraordinarily empathetic" (49) in their point of view.[28] A graver error even than thinking they understand the South, however, is the one these strangers make in assuming that they can make conclusive statements about the fiction of its supreme native genius: "No one may summarize fully and well the aesthetic, philosophical, and cultural views of a man of profound mind. Faulkner and all of his critics cannot codify his fiction and its meaning"(51).

In Faulkner, that is, the Deep South meets deep thought. And indeed, the Benjy section of *The Sound and the Fury*, making the thoughts of a "simpleminded" Southerner an occasion for the highest literary difficulty, might stand as a figure for this encounter. The only problem with this claim, however, is that Faulkner's fiction might on these very grounds be seen to betray its affiliation to the discourse of international modernism and the Symbolist tradition of literary difficulty represented by James Joyce. This was a thoroughly worldly, thoroughly portable discourse difficult to assimilate to the image of an unselfconscious North Mississippi faun.[29]

The "Joycean influence" on Faulkner had been noticed as early as 1929, in Evelyn Scott's promotional pamphlet in support of *The Sound and the Fury*. Written at the behest of Faulkner's (and Scott's own) publishers, Jonathan Cape and Harrison Smith, and apparently sent along with the novel to all its initial reviewers, this relatively neglected text of Faulkner criticism was arguably among the few most consequential and crucial statements ever made on Faulkner's behalf. In this pamphlet, Scott, wishing to "save the worthy artist from a careless allotment, before the public, with those whose object in writing is a purely commercial one," sanctions the evident difficulty of the novel as an effect of a "greatness," a "tragic force," which could have been expressed only by these innovative formal means.[30] The effect of this act of consecration, whose reverberations can immediately be perceived in the reviews of the novel—"Mr. Faulkner's work has been magnificently praised by Evelyn Scott and other critics for whose opinions one must have respect" (*Reviews*, 38), wrote Clifton Fadiman in his own hostile review—was to provide the provincial nature poet with an important, if only very ambivalently displayed, set of modernist credentials. So provided, Faulkner might have felt himself praised even in his damnation by such as Winfield Scott, who objected that this "tiresome" novel was more concerned with "method" than with "plot," and, like the work of Joyce, Cummings, and Stein, did not "communicate" anything. "[T]he chief indictment against the modernists," he continues, "is their utmost complete lack of communication. Under this indictment young Mr. Faulkner must fall. His novel tells us nothing. . . . It is so much sound and fury—signifying nothing" (*Reviews*, 38).

The only difficulty presented by such an "indictment," for a writer of Faulkner's ambitions, was that his specific position in the field of cultural production also required that he maintain a claim to provincial, pastoral simplicity and authenticity that the self-consciously sophisticated, elitist tradition of the Great Artificer might be seen to undermine.[31] This is the realization that Malcolm Cowley seems to have come to by the time he added an afterword to his introduction to *The Portable Faulkner* in 1966, where he qualifies his earlier assertions about Faulkner's rootedness. Here he suggests that "there was a . . . sense in which he too was uprooted; in which he lived as a foreigner among his neighbors . . . an 'internal emigre.' For of course he lived almost from boyhood by another system of values— shared by many writers of his time—as well as by the local one; I mean the values of the artist in the Symbolist tradition."[32]

In *Exile's Return* Cowley states the organizing principle of this alienating, "aristocratic" system of values, which is nothing less than a principle of necessary alienation itself: *"Art is separate from life; the artist is independent of the world and superior to the lifelings"* (144; italics in original). For William Faulkner, however, this ideal of artistic independence would be quite difficult to realize: "I cannot and will not go on like this," we find a frustrated, haughty artist-aristocrat writing to his agent in 1935, worrying about his mounting bills. "I believe I have got enough fair literature in me yet to deserve reasonable freedom from bourgeoise material petty impediments and compulsion."[33] It is doubtful whether Faulkner, before the 1950s, ever attained a degree of freedom from bourgeois material, petty impediments that he would have considered reasonable. In his encounter with the problem of economic necessity, however, he had certainly found his great subject. This, I will argue, was the problem to which his creation of fictional property—indeed an entire fictional county, Yoknapatawpha—would be both a real and an imaginary solution.

Relations: Modernism and Mules

> "But it always shocks me to learn that art also depends on population, on the herd instinct just as much as manufacturing automobiles or stockings does—"
>   —*Mosquitoes*

> But then, so had vanity conceived that house . . . and built it.
>   —*Absalom, Absalom!*

The relation between *Absalom, Absalom!* (1936) and *The Unvanquished* (1938) has figured in Faulkner criticism as something of an embarrassment. How could the writing of the first, a complex and difficult masterpiece, for some readers the pinnacle of Faulkner's, if not of America's, achievement in the novel, have virtually coincided with the production of the second, a humdrum series of romantic tales of the Old South during the Civil War and Reconstruction? As a rule setting herself in opposition to the main line of Faulkner criticism, Myra Jehlen could nonetheless be speaking for many when she notes the drastic "difference in literary quality" (*Class and Character*, 16) between the two books, one "uncharacteristically clear, moderate" but for that reason "bland" (51), the other brilliantly "extravagant," elaborately "tooled to the demands of a complex and divided social vision" (53). For Carolyn Porter, similarly, to compare the two is to see that "Faulkner was playing for much higher stakes in *Absalom, Absalom!*" (*Seeing and Being*, 219) than he was in the simple romantic entertainments of *The Unvanquished*.

One way of accounting for this difference in quality, Jehlen suggests, is as evidence of Faulkner's arrival in the midthirties at a "point of exacerbated, polarized indecision" (*Class and Character*, 47) about which of two "ideological approaches" to take in his representation of Southern history, the first "deeply subversive," the second merely "conventional" and "redemptive." So, too, she proposes, it may have been the result of the exhaustion attendant to producing so "complete" a work as *Absalom, Absalom!*: hacking its way back to the "historical origin" of Southern mythology as through a dense wilderness, Faulkner might have found "periodic respite" (49) from this grueling literary labor in telling "the affirmative stories" of *The Unvanquished*. A somewhat more active role for the nostalgic tales is imagined by Carolyn Porter, for whom "it almost seems as if *The Unvanquished* helped him to write *Absalom, Absalom!* by siphoning off his own romantic attachment to the cavalier legends passed down in his own family, enabling him to face . . . the more brutal history obscured by those legends" (*Seeing and Being*, 219). Thus, though they prefer the "subversive" to the "redemptive" representation of history, and the "extravagant" modernist text to the "bland" entertaining one, both Jehlen and Porter allow that the bad novel fulfills an important function in the psychic economy that also produces the great novel, whether as a "respite" from hard work or a "siphoning" of romantic attachments. And yet, a brief examination of Faulkner's situation in the thirties suggests that the relation between the two works might have been economic in quite another, more plainly material, but no less intimate sense. Indeed, it is the intimacy of this link between texts that accounts both for their systematic differentiation as *kinds* of texts, and for the fact that it requires so little interpretive pressure to see the deep contextual continuity these stylistic differences have tended to remove from view.

In the 1930s Faulkner wrote for two fairly distinct audiences. The first was a sometimes devoted but highly restricted readership of such novels

as *The Sound and the Fury* and *Absalom, Absalom!*, works that, while met
with serious discussion in the national literary press and in the book pages
of major newspapers, managed each to sell only several thousand copies
in the first year of its publication. Faulkner's second audience might be
seen as being comprised both of the large number of purchasers of his only
best-selling novel, *Sanctuary* (1931), and of the several million potential
readers of his short fiction, which appeared throughout the decade in mass
publications such as *Scribner's, Cosmopolitan,* and most importantly the
Saturday Evening Post. This fiction was twice collected into volumes of
stories and in one case, *The Unvanquished,* was threaded together to form
what Faulkner would call an "approximate novel."

The antagonistic relation of these elite and mass audiences, or at least
of the literary values they were understood to represent, can be glimpsed
in Paul Bixler's militantly middlebrow review of *Sanctuary*:

> The little group of intellectuals who had faithfully followed him since the publi-
> cation of *Soldier's Pay* in 1926 came to believe that he was their own possession;
> that they would never have to share him. It has perhaps shattered their self-
> esteem, always in need of bolstering, that *Sanctuary* has been, and is continuing
> to be, a popular success. Its popularity, they explain somewhat regretfully, has
> occurred because the book is easier to read than any of its five brother novels.
> (*Reviews*, 53)

What can look like simple antagonism in the sphere of consumption, however, evidently becomes more complicated when viewed in the sphere of
production. Indeed, combining them with the money he was making as a
screenwriter in Hollywood at roughly the same time, Faulkner used his
proceeds from the sale of the stories that eventually made up *The Unvanquished*—five were initially published by the *Saturday Evening Post*—to
pay his household expenses during the two years in which he wrote *Absalom, Absalom!* This required him, when he was not laboring for the studios,
to alternate between the production of stories and the production of the
novel. That in Faulkner's mind the two texts were thus engaged in a literally economic relation, an economy not only of money but of time, is made
clear in a 1934 letter to his agent, Morton Goldman, where he wonders
what he will do after he finishes the film script he is working on:

> I may write the other stories [in *The Unvanquished* series] or I may go back to
> the novel [*Absalom, Absalom!*]; it all depends on how much or badly I need
> money at the time. That is, I would like to keep the Post hot for a while longer,
> so if, when I finish the script, I need more cash I can write the other stories. But
> I would not like to promise to do so, since I have had to put off the novel too
> much already. (*Letters*, 83)

Faulkner called his writing of the story series "orthodox prostitution" (85) or "boiling the pot"—the production of "trash" for "the best price I can get" (84). Hardly a "respite" from the difficult labor of writing *Absalom, Absalom!*, as Jehlen would have it, the story series appears here as the periodic labor that Faulkner performs in order to finance his work on the largely unremunerative project called at this point *Dark House*. While this puts the novel in a position of artistic privilege over the commercial stories, we should not miss the degree to which this relation was in fact one of reciprocal benefit: conceived in explicitly "high cultural" terms, the novel would suggest that, at least potentially, the business of fiction writing, Faulkner's business, could be something more than a "merely" commercial enterprise.

Though it would continually suggest a potential clash between international and native discourses in his work, Faulkner's adoption of the "values of the artist in the Symbolist tradition," hostile to the mass market, dovetailed perfectly with the (putatively) anticommercial "plantation" or "Cavalier values" he so often represented in their demise at the hands the crassly commercial class of Snopeses.[34] The high cultural ambitions Faulkner held for his novel, as well as the context of economic necessity by which they were conditioned, can be seen in a letter to his publisher, Harrison Smith, where Faulkner describes the novel that will become *Absalom, Absalom!* as

> the more or less violent breakup of a household or family from 1860 to about 1910. . . . Quentin Compson, of the Sound & Fury, tells it, or ties it together; he is the protagonist so that it is not complete apocrypha. I use him because it is just before he is to commit suicide because of his sister, and I use his bitterness which he has projected on the South in the form of hatred of it and its people to get more out of the story itself than a historical novel would be. To keep the hoop skirts and plug hats out, you might say. I believe I can promise it for fall.
>
> Now hold your hat. I have two stories out which should sell, but have not yet. I will have to draw some more money; I want $1,500.00. I have a $600.00 odd insurance due March 4, and income [tax] due the 15th. (*Letters*, 78–79)

Used as a framing device, Quentin Compson's hatred of the South—though apparently it is only a projection of his bitterness at his sister's loss of purity—will keep the story of Thomas Sutpen, parvenu homebuilder and homeowner, free of the "hoop skirts and plug hats" that might otherwise infiltrate it. Thus Faulkner would establish his distance from popular romance, as well as his own high modernist credentials, by framing his tale as the ironic story of its own telling: " 'So he just wanted a grandson,' " the outsider-character Shreve says. " 'That was all he was after. Jesus, the South is fine, isn't it. It's better than the theatre, isn't it. It's better than

Ben Hur, isn't it. No wonder you have to come away now and then, isn't it' " (176).

In this manner, the novel would be kept free of the taint of commercial historical romance, trading the representation of genteel Southern respectability for a certain kind of high *literary* respectability measured in terms inherited from the Symbolists. These terms require, above all, a rejection of the commercial motive for producing literature. In other words, Faulkner's own respectability as an artist would come, at least in part, by way of his critique of a certain image of "Southern respectability"—of the trappings of the romanticized plantation of popular literature.

It would also come, however, simply by inhabiting these trappings. Although it has not gone unnoticed, far too little has been made of the striking echoes between Thomas Sutpen and William Faulkner as ambitious men of property.[35] This similarity extends beyond that which links Sutpen's "design which I had in my mind" for Sutpen's Hundred to Faulkner's discovery, as he would say to Jean Stein vanden Heuvel, "not only [that] each book had to have a design but the whole output or sum of an artist's work had to have a design" (*Lion*, 256). It was for the text of *Absalom, Absalom!* that Faulkner first drew a map, and claimed ownership of his apocryphal county, Yoknapatawpha. But beyond this there was the old Bailey place. This old house, which Faulkner purchased in 1930 and renamed "Rowanoak" (alternatively "Rowan Oak"), was, according to his daughter Jill, "the symbol in Pappy's life of being somebody." Everybody in town "remembered that Pappy's father [merely] ran a livery stable," and this "nice old house [that] had a certain substance and standing to it" was "a way of thumbing his nose at Oxford" (Blotner, *Biography*, 261). Visiting Faulkner at Rowanoak to interview him in 1932—by which time Faulkner had had time to complete some much-needed renovations of the decrepit structure—Henry Nash Smith found a man "much interested in the new draperies which Mrs. Faulkner is planning for the living room of their very fine old house." Indeed, to Smith, the author of *The Sound and the Fury, As I Lay Dying*, and *Light in August* "seemed prouder of the hand-hammered locks on the doors than of anything he had written" (*Lion*, 32). The irony of this no doubt ironic "preference," accounts such as Grimwood's suggest, is that most of residents of Oxford would surely have agreed that ownership of the Bailey house represented Faulkner's most substantial claim to their respect.

Though he would devote a good deal of time and money to the restoration, renovation, and upkeep of this structure, it is only natural that this local project of Faulkner's should not figure as one of his more important works. For one thing, by contrast to the portable fiction, this property was immobile and irreproducible; but for the name "Rowanoak" itself, which

Faulkner had engraved in Gothic script on his stationery, the house could be viewed only by the few nonresidents worshipful enough in these early years to make the pilgrimage to Oxford, Mississippi. For another thing, it was merely a house; Faulkner, like Sutpen, had not even been the architect. And yet it is worth keeping this "fine old house" in mind—an expensive bid for gentlemanly social establishment, a fixed symbol of "being somebody," an occasion for renovation as well as restoration—as one thinks about *Absalom, Absalom!* The parvenu Thomas Sutpen, himself (according to the character Miss Rosa) in search of "respectability," would thus always function both as the *object* of Faulkner's critique and as his *double* in the creation of a noncommercial "design." As Faulkner does not write just for money, neither, it is assumed, would Sutpen "voluntarily undertake the hardship and privation of clearing virgin land and establishing a plantation in a new country just for money" (11).

Neither of these forms of respectability, architectural or literary, was available to the formally self-effacing tales submitted to the editors of the *Post*. And yet these stories were able both to underwrite Faulkner's ambition to produce a self-reflexive novel about the "breakup of a household" and to pay the expenses of his own nonfictional household. This household was itself always on the point of breaking up—not as a result of war or fratricide or fire, however, but for simple lack of funds. "[I]f I don't get some money somehow soon, I will be in danger of having some one put me in bankruptcy and I will then lose my house and insurance and all" (*Letters*, 92), we find Faulkner writing in a tone entirely characteristic of the period of composition of *Absalom* and *The Unvanquished*.

Indeed, as we read Faulkner's correspondence from this time, it is difficult to shake the sense that his fiction, a commodity produced to stave off the creditor, is also a series of meditations on or managements of the anxieties of the author-as-homeowner. For instance, in the story "Riposte in Tertio," which originally appeared in the *Saturday Evening Post* in 1936 under the eventual title of the entire volume, "The Unvanquished," one finds a remarkable scene in which the relation between representation and the restoration of property is made fairly explicit. Here the loyal ex-slave Ringo and the narrator, young Bayard Sartoris, are approached by some Northern soldiers near the charred ruins of the Sartoris plantation house that Ringo is drawing from memory:

> "Hah," [the soldier] said again, then he said, "What's that?"
>
> "A house," Ringo said. . . . "Look at it."
>
> The lieutenant looked at me and said "Hah" again behind his teeth. . . . He looked at Ringo's picture. Then he looked up the grove to where the chimneys rose out of the pile of rubble and ashes. Grass and weeds had come up out of the ashes now and unless you knew better, all you saw was the four chimneys.

Some of the golden rod was still in bloom. "Oh," the officer said. "I see. You're drawing it like it used to be."

"Co-rect," Ringo said. "What I wanter draw hit like hit is now for? I can walk down here ten times a day and look at hit like hit is now."[36]

This remarkably direct critique of representational realism—of drawing it "like it is"—where the *Post* stories seem already to be defending themselves from critiques such as Jehlen's, would be complicated when Faulkner wrote the seventh and concluding tale of the *Unvanquished* series, "An Odor of Verbena." This story was explicitly intended to tie the preceding tales together as a novel. It might thus seem a symptomatic, impulsive bid for modernist novelistic respectability, and a revision of Ringo's romanticism when, kissing his cousin Drusilla, Bayard "realised then the immitigable chasm between all life and all print—that those who can, do, those who cannot and suffer enough because they cant, write about it" (228). At any rate, the direct economic relation between *Absalom, Absalom!* and *The Unvanquished* is missed in the psychologized accounts of Jehlen and Porter.

While they both claim an affiliation to Marxism, these accounts seem curiously idealistic (or perhaps just Adornian) in championing the "high" over the "low" without any reference to the historical and institutional contexts that enabled and gave significance to these relatively different levels of discourse. To this degree, critics hostile to such "New Historicist" approaches to Faulkner as Jehlen's and Porter's, complaining that they display a thuggish preference for social "content" over artistic "form," happen upon a valid point: even a critic as laudatory of Faulkner's narrative complexity as Jehlen will claim that this complexity is simply transparent to a complex Southern *reality*—as though Faulkner's high style really were indigenous to the South.[37] This is what Jehlen means when she claims that Faulkner's "extravagant" prose has an "organic" link to the society in which it was written (*Class and Character*, 15), and also what allows us to see the extent to which Jehlen's Marxist account is still working over ground cleared by Cleanth Brooks.

To bring the economic relationship between the two novels to the foreground, however, is not merely to uncover the family relation—the miscegenation, as it were—of a pure masterpiece and commercial trash, a (purported) critique of romance financed by romance. It is also to draw attention to the texts themselves, where one finds two works that not only exemplify, to a degree, different kinds of discourse, high and low, but that are also preoccupied by their own discursive status, and by the differentiating mechanisms of the literary market that determine this status. Faulkner's fiction is everywhere marked by a concern not only for the Southern class system, as Jehlen has helpfully insisted, but also for class system of the literary market, absorbing into its representations the cultural-hierar-chical class antagonisms at play in Bixler's review of *Sanctuary*.

For all its sarcastic philistinism, indeed no doubt *because* of this philis-tinism, Bixler's review—gleefully wresting possession of the novelist Wil-liam Faulkner from the pathetic "little group of intellectuals" who have had him to themselves—is fairly direct in its grasp of one of the primary laws of cultural capital that I would argue is crucial to an understanding of the "sole owner and proprietor" of the fictional county of Yoknapataw-pha: the way knowledge—in this case of a certain difficult writer or text—can function as a form of relatively exclusive property that distinguishes its possessor from the mass. To reverse Bixler's perspective, and to look at the circulation of cultural capital from the point of view of one of its pro-ducers, is to see a writer no less concerned to take possession of a certain kind of fictional property than his elite intellectual audience was to take possession of him.

This is abundantly clear in the novel *Mosquitoes*, which if it is a sendup of the "charming futility" of the bohemian artistic circle surrounding Sher-wood Anderson in New Orleans—amidst which Faulkner lived for several months—is also a series of claims on Faulkner's part to be *in the know*, despite his provincial origins and his lack of certification by any school.[38] For instance, an adequate paraphrase of the sentence that appears early in the novel, "Spring and the cruellest months were gone, the cruel months, the wantons that break the fat hybernatant dullness and comfort of Time" (10), might be "I, too, have read T. S. Eliot," while a description of a dock as a "formal rectangle without perspective," "[f]lat as cardboard" suggests a familiarity with modern abstract art.[39] The awkwardness and repetitive-ness of such gestures on the part of north Mississippi's native genius is no doubt one reason so many critics have seen fit to call this Faulkner's worst novel of all. One might then imagine that Faulkner's next novel, *Flags in the Dust*, in which he first lays fictional claim to his "postage stamp of native soil," would be less concerned than *Mosquitoes* to demonstrate Faulkner's avant-garde credentials. And indeed, in the criticism one senses a sigh of relief that, with *Flags*, Faulkner has finally left behind this period of urban bohemian embarrassment, drawing now upon knowledge he pos-sesses not by painful acquisition but as a kind of birthright.

And yet, looking closely, it might seem that the concern for cultural capital so evident in *Mosquitoes* is merely sublimated in the subsequent work: indeed, rarely does one happen upon a novel that takes such rigor-ous and constant inventory of what its characters are reading. " 'I never knew you read so much' " (283), says the educated Horace Benbow—himself a lover "of printed words, [of] the dwelling-places of books"—to his sister Narcissa, who likes to "submerge" her "consciousness," to "surrender wholly" to the pages of a book. But Horace could be speaking to many characters in the novel. Old Bayard Sartoris's office, for instance, is "lined with book-cases containing rows of heavy legal tomes bound in dun calf and . . . and a miscellany of fiction of the historical-romantic school." All of "Dumas was there," we are told, "and the steady progression of the volumes now constituted Bayard Sartoris's entire reading, and one volume lay always on the night-table beside his bed" (35). Meanwhile, Miss Jenny reads "the daily Memphis newspaper. She enjoyed humanity in its more colorful mutations, preferring lively romance to the most impeccable of dun fact, so she took in the more lurid afternoon paper even though it was yesterday's when it reached her" (41). Dr Peabody lies asleep beside "a stack of lurid paper-covered nickel novels. This was Dr Peabody's library, and on this sofa he passed his office hours, reading them over and over. Other books there were none" (106).

Here, noting the various kinds of narrative his characters consume, Faulkner suggests in every case a preference for the lurid or romantic representation of the past—in Miss Jenny's case it is only one day past—over the "dun fact" of the present. And yet, almost more important than this specific observation of the penchant of his characters for romance over realism is a more basic one: the mere fact that certain residents of Jefferson are seen to read, and thus must be considered not only as objects but also as consumers and producers of representation. Faulkner's characters, that is, are as intensely related to mass culture as they are to Southern nature, linked in a system of narrative disbursements that establishes every reader as a way station on the information network that connects Jefferson to places as far as Memphis or New Orleans or even Chicago. It thus comes as no surprise that it is hard to tell where these stories come from, difficult to judge to whom and at what times it is proper for them to be told:

> Miss Jenny travelled very little, and in Pullman smokerooms not at all, and people wondered where she got her stories; who had told them to her. And she repeated them anywhere and at any time, choosing the wrong moment and the wrong audience with a cold and cheerful audacity. (29–30)

The same concern with the origin and circulation of stories is present throughout the story series, *The Unvanquished*. "I want $1500.00," Faulkner had told Harrison Smith, needing to pay his household expenses, and in the story, "Riposte in Tertio," too, fifteen hundred dollars is the relevant sum; it is what Granny Rosa Millard will make if she takes the advice of Ab Snopes, acting here as a kind of literary agent, and sells four horses she has managed to embezzle from the occupying Yankee army:

> [S]oon Father would return home to his ruined plantation and most of his slaves vanished; . . . how [nice] it would be if, when he came home and looked about

at his desolate future, she could take fifteen hundred dollars in cash out of her pocket and say, "Here. Start over with this"—fifteen hundred dollars more than she had hoped to have. He would take one of the mares for his commission and he would guarantee her fifteen hundred dollars for the other three. (151)

If Ab Snopes appears here as a sort of fictional Morton Goldman, then he will seem even more so when we remember that the scam Granny has been running has been fundamentally a matter of producing representations for an audience of Yankees: when Ringo (inexplicably) gets hold of a hundred sheets of official letterhead stamped "*United States Forces. Department of Tennessee*," he and Granny use them to forge requisition orders for mules the U.S. Army has itself expropriated from the Southern plantations it has been burning to the ground. Acquiring these mules, Granny then sells those that have not been branded "U.S." back to the same army, only to requisition them again with a new forgery under a different name. It is possible to read in this scam an allegory of the national market for regional fiction, founded on a strange but I think compelling affinity between Faulkner's herd of short stories and Granny's herd of mules. Here, in the rapid circulation of forgeries, false representations, and mobile commodities—transactions meticulously accounted in Granny's and in Faulkner's own ledger books—it becomes unclear whose property is actually being sold, who is stealing what from whom: as though to write a romantic commercial short story is to steal time from the serious novel; as though to sell a simple story to the *Post* is to sell back to the national audience a Southern "stereotype" that is already, in a sense, U.S. property.

It is at any rate clear that what it means to be "unvanquished" in this story, and in *The Unvanquished* as a whole, is to convert the *field of battle* into a *literary field*, to trade arms for wits, matter for mind:

> "Yessum, you got my respect. John Sartoris himself cant tech you. He hells all over the country day and night with a hundred armed men, and it's all he can do to keep them in crowbait to ride on. And you set here in this cabin, without nothing but handful of durn printed letterheads, and you got to build a bigger pen to hold the stock you aint got no market yet to sell." (122–23)

The South of Rosa Millard is a South smart enough to understand its place in a national economy of images, and to bring its own "regional difference" to market. In this respect, at least, *The Unvanquished* is reminiscent of *Gone with the Wind*, in which we see Southern nature turned into profitable lumber. The limit to that similarity is reached somewhere behind that hazy veil where Granny's "literary labor" manages to distinguish itself from Scarlet O'Hara's brutal skills in factory management.

Another version of this transaction is the one that stands as one of the governing motifs of *The Sound and the Fury*, where some lamented Southern land is converted into immaterial educational capital: "Going to Harvard. We have sold Benjy's *He lay on the ground under the window, bellowing. We have sold Benjy's pasture so that Quentin may go to Harvard.*"[40] It is important to remember, tracing this motif through *The Sound and the Fury*, that it had been during Phil Stone's year at Yale that he had acquired the central texts of the international literary avant-garde that he would bring home in a trunk to Mississippi, where they would in turn be read by his young protégé Faulkner. In this sense, at least, *The Sound and the Fury* is always explaining its own origin as a high literary text as a conversion of "native land" into intellectual capital. Sliding from the entrepreneurial Miss Rosa of *The Unvanquished* to the literary Miss Rosa of *Absalom, Absalom!* becomes very easy at this point. Miss Rosa, "who even in his (Quentin's) father's youth had already established (even if not affirmed) herself as the town's and the county's poetess laureate" (6) makes this clear:

> "[Y]ou are going away to attend the college at Harvard they tell me," she said. "So I dont imagine you will ever come back here and settle down as a country lawyer in a little town like Jefferson since Northern people have already seen to it that there is little left to do in the South for a young man. So maybe you will enter the literary profession as so many Southern gentlemen and gentlewomen too are doing now and maybe someday you will remember this and write about it. You will be married then I expect and perhaps your wife will want a new gown or a new chair for the house and you can write this and submit it to the magazines." (5)

Substituting Mrs. Faulkner's new draperies in the Rowanoak living room for that new chair, one seems to encounter here a mode of authorial self-allegorization in some ways simpler and more direct than that found in *The Unvanquished*. And indeed, as the novel goes on to propose different motivations for telling of the tale of Sutpen and different reasons for the willingness of God to let the South lose the war—the "ungentlemanly" nature of ambitious men like Sutpen, the deep shame of slavery—none of these is a distinct alternative to the economic motive of the "gentlemanly career" in letters that Miss Rosa first proposes. Thus we could say that the most interesting claim that *Absalom, Absalom!* makes about the history of race relations in the South is somewhat more limited than recent historicist critics might lead one to believe. This claim is twofold, condensing Faulkner's sense of both the opportunities and pitfalls of Southern regionalist discourse: it is because of slavery that the Southern writer is condemned to produce regional fiction; it is because of slavery that the Southern writer has something "different," and thus interesting, to write about.

   "Beginning with *Sartoris* I discovered that my own little postage stamp of native soil was worth writing about" he would say in his *Paris Review* interview in 1955,

> and that I would never live long enough to exhaust it, and by sublimating the
> actual into the apocryphal I would have complete liberty to use whatever talent
> I might have to its absolute top. It opened up a gold mine of other peoples, so I
> created a cosmos of my own. (*Lion*, 255)

In this, perhaps the most interesting non-fictional utterance he left on
record, Faulkner imagines his entire output as a novelist in terms of his
production of imaginary property, the county of Yoknapatawpha, and of
himself as its "sole owner and proprietor." This was, in a sense, simply to
scale his ambitions up from the architectural to the geographical, from
being owner of a house to being the owner of a real/fictional landscape.
That he conceives of the people who inhabit this landscape as a "gold
mine"—deeply installed in the earth, but retrievable as negotiable
currency—suggests that they will circulate in a kind of imaginary slave
trade, a pale echo of the nonfictional past. For Faulkner, no doubt the
greatest virtue of this kind of property that he calls "apocryphal," and that
might also be called "intellectual," was that it could be alienated—sold
elsewhere in the South, up North, anywhere in the world—without ever
being relinquished.

Making "Literature" of It

Dashiell Hammett and the Mysteries of High Culture

> What is the thing in itself? We shall not reach the thing in itself until our thinking has first reached the thing as a thing.
> —Martin Heidegger, "The Thing"

> The thing in itself folded itself up inside itself like you might fold a thing up to be another thing which is that thing inside in that thing.
> —Gertrude Stein, "Portraits and Repetition"

> Then you think the dingus is worth two million?
> —Dashiell Hammett, *The Maltese Falcon*

God, Mammon, and Willard Wright

Nowhere is the dialectic of modernism and mass culture more tightly braided than in the genre of detective fiction inaugurated, it is said, by Edgar Allan Poe. Poe was of course deeply embedded in the burgeoning mass print culture of the mid-nineteenth-century United States, a literary tradesman through and through, and yet it is no accident that this would-be Southern gentleman became the guiding spirit of French Symbolism, a literary movement whose apparent hostility to unholy mass culture is so striking.[1] Indeed, reflecting some of the doubleness of Poe himself, the genre to which he gave a modern form has functioned as a privileged site in the domain of modern fiction for the negotiation of the "high" and the "low." There are many reasons for this, not least of which is that detective fiction has, with crucial exceptions, traditionally been marked both as a *masculine* and as an *intellectualist* genre, indeed as a gentlemanly exercise of reason. Presenting itself as an occasion for pleasurable mental labor, and standing at some remove from sticky swamps of "feminine" sentiment, it could be said always to have carried a latent potential for the high-literary prestige recently conferred upon it by John Irwin in *The Mystery to a Solution* (see chapter 1). Already in the early-twentieth century detective fiction was the popular genre of choice in the odd hours of any number of major modernist figures, the likes of T. S. Eliot, Gertrude Stein, William Faulkner, and even Ludwig Wittgenstein.

The double-faced quality of detective fiction is powerfully exemplified in the careers of the two most popular American detective fiction writers of the early twentieth century, the long-forgotten S. S. Van Dine and his successor, the increasingly canonical initiator of the "hard-boiled" version of the genre, Dashiell Hammett. "S. S. Van Dine," who published fifteen in the "Philo Vance" series of detective novels between 1926 and 1939, was the pseudonym of Willard Huntington Wright, formerly editor in chief of the fashionably intellectual *Smart Set*, author of a book on the philosophy of Nietzsche and of a treatise on aesthetics, *The Creative Will* (1916). Wright's case will be a particularly instructive setup for a longer discussion of Hammett, for it makes clear both how strong were the taboos against crossing the "Great Divide" between high and mass culture in the early-twentieth century and how predictably they were violated.

In 1909 Wright himself had opined, with the absolutism of youth, that "when an author has been so unfortunate as to write a popular novel, it is a difficult thing to live down the reputation. Personally I have no sympathy with such a person, for there are few punishments too severe for a popular novel writer."[2] Staying perhaps too true to these beliefs, his debut as a novelist, *A Man of Promise* (1916), was a dead flop. What is interesting is how complete an alibi for its own failure the novel provides in advance. Part of a thriving genre of the period—the fictionalized auto-biographical bildungsroman best exemplified by Joyce's *Portrait of the Artist*—this novel tells the story of young male "promise" stunted by the philistinism of the American herd and by the subtle entrapments of those "great conservatives, unconscious and unknowing": women.[3] Absent the impressive presence of Catholicism in Joyce's *Portrait*, which lends the heroism to Stephen's rebellion as an artist, Wright's book comes off as a somewhat noxious brew of narcissistic self-pity and megalomaniacal fantasy-nightmare.

It is, however, a model fantasy-nightmare of the modernist career in the United States, and thus a useful map to at least one imaginary point in the "space of positions" in the literary field of the period. Leaving his conventional home, Wright's young "intellectual aristocrat" (113), Stanford West, undergoes what amounts to a series of spiritual trials. First he must resist "feminization" at the hands of the "reactionary" university in Cambridge, Massachusetts, searching instead for the "masculine . . . freedom and aggressiveness" of the "modern" world (67). Recovering from his prissy Harvard education, he then bravely embraces the "squalor of intemperate living," undergoing a "complete submission to the grosser dictates of the body" from which he can "profit . . . intellectually" (85). Later, shutting himself away in acceptance of the fact that culture "can never be a property of the masses" (113), he writes an epic "poetic drama" intended to win the "battle against the tawdriness of modern literary thought." Presenting a bold "new ideal" in a pathetic "world of democratic compromises," this poetic drama voices instead "the culture of aristocracy" (109). Suffering the public neglect that is the fate of true superiority, but needing money to support his suffocatingly stupid wife, Stanford West lowers himself to the writing of a mere novel:

> His book sold well. It was not a large commercial success, however. It was too careful and able a piece of work ever to have succeeded greatly from a purely popular appeal. But there were few people interested in popular literature who did not know of him and the book, and who did not respect him and believe in his greatness. (259)

Alas, even this modest compromise of his principles, though it wins some recognition of his greatness, sets Stanford on an inexorable downward path from intellectual aristocracy to bourgeois conventionality. The novel ends with a statement of the "unutterable and tragic irony" (351) of Stanford's life as an ordinary married man.

Failing to win even the small commercial success that torments Stanford West, Willard Wright was eventually moved to "sell out" to a degree he never imagined for his tragic character. Desperate for money to support himself and a wife and daughter, Wright plotted three detective novels featuring the detective Philo Vance—whose own name, we are told by his intimate friend and narrator "S. S. Van Dine," is an alias. Taking pity on his acquaintance, Max Perkins accepted and published the novels with Scribner's. In the aftermath of their tremendous commercial success, both as novels and as film properties, Wright could now luxuriate in his embarrassment of fabulous riches: the autobiographical essay *I Used to Be a Highbrow but Look at Me Now* (1929) was intended in part, his biographer speculates, to let his old friends at the *Smart Set* know that he had not lost his lofty aesthetic values on the way to the mass market.[4] Deeply resenting the humiliating terms—not only as a novelist, but as a *detective* novelist—upon which he had been forced to make his upward ascent into the dog-breeding set, Wright, we see, never paused to consider the "high art" potential of the detective fiction he wrote. And yet the Philo Vance novels, beginning with *The Benson Murder Case* (1926), barely sublimate their disappointed longings for a spiritual habitation in the aristocratic realm of high art. Indeed, they present as thematic content what, as we shall see, Dashiell Hammett will try to enact at the level of literary form.

Picking up on and exaggerating the fin de siècle dandyism of Conan Doyle's Sherlock Holmes, the narrator-author Van Dine admits that his friend Philo Vance is what many would call a dilettante. But the designation does him injustice. He was a man of unusual culture and brilliance. An aristocrat by birth and instinct, he held himself severely aloof from the common world of men. In his manner there was an indefinable contempt for inferiority of all kinds. . . . Yet there was in his condescension and disdain no trace of spuriousness. His snobbishness was intellectual as well as social.[5]

Combining elements of Edith Wharton and Gertrude Stein, Vance is an independently wealthy Knickerbocker who has studied psychology at Harvard with Hugo Munsterberg and William James. Now, demonstrating his advanced taste, he collects the paintings of Cézanne. Though he had high art aspirations of his own, Dashiell Hammett would construct his detectives in direct opposition to Van Dine's smarmy gentleman-amateur, Philo Vance. Vance is indeed a hysterical, but to all appearances unintentional, burlesque of the "intellectual aristocrat" that Wright, in his promising youth as philosopher-editor of the *Smart Set*, might have imagined himself to be. That Vance was so popular a fictional character is something to ponder, suggesting how little modernism's claims to intellectual or social superiority actually mattered to the mass audience: indeed, in the creation of Philo Vance, this "superiority" is *itself* served up as mass cultural entertainment.

What one must note in particular, however, is the sliding between intellectual and social snobberies in the character of Philo Vance. As we saw in chapter 4, this sliding could be said to have been embedded in the *Smart Set*'s origins as a Knickerbocker gossip sheet *Town Topics* (just as its reliance on mass culture is apparent in its economic reliance on "louse magazines" like the detective rag *Black Mask*). These paired snobberies, evidence of the increasing recognition of the value of intellection, feature importantly in the plot of the second Philo Vance novel, *The "Canary" Murder Case* (1927), whose victim is a famously beautiful showgirl of the New York demimonde, Margaret Odell. Here the sharp blade of Vance's "witty" sarcasm comes to the aid of the ever-bumbling public servant, District Attorney F. X. Markham. While he must be brought to justice, the murderer, Spotswoode, is deeply admired by Vance for the "artistry" of his crime. Indeed, for Vance, art and crime are one and the same thing, expressions of the creative (or in this case destructive) will.[6] Spotswoode is thus an artist of sorts, and yet he is equally admired for coming from "Old Puritan stock. . . . All Yankee forebears—no intermixture." "As a matter of fact," Markham assures Vance, "Spotswoode represents the oldest and hardiest of the New England aristocracy" (160).

No wonder, then, that he must murder his illicit lover, the lower-class Canary: " 'This woman, Mr. Markham, had demanded the impossible of me. Not content with bleeding me financially, she demanded legal protection, position, social prestige—such things as only my name would give her' " (336). Spotswoode's murder in defense of a good name is, we see, a defense against precisely the kind of social leveling that the novel itself was enacting in the career of Willard Wright/S. S. Van Dine. We hear a distinct echo of the situation of Wright when, after reading out loud a passage from Oscar Wilde's *De Profundis*—"I had become tired of dwelling on the heights—and descended by my own will into the depths" (338)—Spotswoode is given leave to shoot himself like the gentleman he is.

For Willard Wright, then, detective fiction was commercial trash that, while it could wistfully *represent*, could not *exemplify* the lofty intellectual aspirations of art. Others of the period, less reflexive in their snobbery than Wright, saw it in more complicated and productive terms. It was a popular genre, and yet it was also a meeting place of "high" and "low," especially as these terms were seen to mark an opposition between high intellectual theology and civic commercialism, as they did for Van Wyck Brooks. Brooks's essay " 'Highbrow' and 'Lowbrow' " (1915), in which the analysis of this peculiarly American form of the high/low opposition makes its first sustained appearance, argues that the cultural divide these terms signify has been an unfortunate feature of American life since its very beginnings.[7] Unable to merge the "steep, icy and pinnacled" (6) theology of Jonathan Edwards with the civic commercialism of Ben Franklin, "human nature itself in America" has ever since existed "on two irreconcilable planes, the plane of stark intellectuality and the plane of stark business" (15). Detective fiction, however, operated between these two planes. To the degree that the genre is defined by its engagement with *policing*, this line of reasoning suggests, it partakes of the larger discursive project of realist narrative of making individuals accountable to social norms and to the law, as D. A. Miller has shown.[8] This view is, however, perfectly reversed by Gertrude Stein, who in the essay "What Are Master-pieces and Why Are There So Few of Them" (1936) speaks of the asocial masterpiece and the detective story in virtually the same breath:

> In real life people are interested in the crime more than they are in detection . . .
> but in the story it is the detection that holds the interest . . . , it is another function
> that has very little to do with human nature that makes the detection interesting.
> And so always it is true that the master-piece has nothing to do with human
> nature or with identity, it has to do with the human mind and the entity that is
> with a thing in itself and not in relation. The moment it is in relation it is common
> knowledge and anybody can feel and know it and it is not a master-piece.[9]

This version of the detective story, turning the genre inward, rather than to the outward production of "common knowledge," runs directly counter to policing, or what Stein calls "governing," which "has completely to do with identity but it has nothing to do with master-pieces" (153). For Stein, ignoring the obvious commercial appeal of the genre, the philosophical purity of detective fiction means that it serves "God," not "Mammon." Indeed, her account can be seen to link detective fiction to the long tradition of the religious *mystery*, which addresses the unbridgeable distance of God from "human nature." Lying everywhere latent in the Father Brown stories of G. K. Chesterton, this connection is made explicit by Waldo Frank in his own high-art mystery novel, *Chalk Face* (1924). In the dedication to his father, with whom he shares "a hankering after good mystery stories," Frank admits that the novel "may seem to you at least as much a Parable as a mystery story. But what indeed is the difference between them? . . . What event is so great a mystery as life itself?"[10]

The detective genre thus could be said to inhabit the very breach between the high and low, the "theological" and the "commercial" described by Van Wyck Brooks. And if for Brooks the problem with "poetry" in his divided nation is that it is "hidden away, too inaccessible, too intangible, too unreal in fact ever to be brought into the open" (15), Poe's purloined letter, as we saw in chapter 1, responds rather precisely to this problem of intangibility and invisibility. Turned inside out and "hidden" in plain view, Poe's letter admits, indeed asserts, its presence as a physical object in social space. At the same time it suggests that a text's "higher" truth is not available on its surface as common knowledge. In this way Poe's text offers a model of the social relations of a certain kind of modernist text. By contrast to the emergent discourse of the "middlebrow"—one response to the bifurcations decried by Brooks—which operates by a logic of *averaging* (halfway intellectual, halfway entertaining books for the "average intelligent reader"), this modernism operates by means of a dialectical *alternation* between dimensions dominated respectively by matter and mind.[11] Advertising both its physical availability and its spiritual-intellectual difficulty, this text seeks to serve "God and Mammon" at once.

This search, however, does not necessarily succeed, as we shall see in Dashiell Hammett's *The Maltese Falcon* (1930). This novel recalls "The Purloined Letter" in proposing what Irwin identifies as a characteristically Symbolist analogy between an object in the novel and the object that is the novel itself.[12] This recursive gesture, enfolding a version of the text in the social world it imagines, enables, among other things, the text's interrogation of its own social function. As a result of this ekphrastic self-interrogation, Hammett ultimately recognizes his failure to merge the high and low in the detective novel, and this sense of failure is, as we shall see, important.

Hammett's deep involvement with these problems is confirmed, however, not only by the ambiguous nature of his chosen genre, but also by his peculiar status with respect to early-twentieth-century literary institutions, the complexity of which has not, I think, been adequately addressed.

For while Hammett's career begins in the pulp serials, most notably *Black Mask*, it takes him rather quickly into the literary institutions of the "smart set," where his work functions not so much to exemplify the "low" as to represent the mechanisms of distinction that generate this abject category in the first place. Admired by such as Andre Gide, Andre Malraux, and Stein, Hammett's fiction echoes the more obviously elite modernism whose central texts he appreciated and discussed even as he continued to sell his work to the pulp audience. A sort of Willard Wright in reverse, his work shows us both what modernism looks like to mass culture and what mass culture looks like to modernism, without canceling the relative autonomy of these two discourses.

Hammett's own sense of the doubleness of his position, and also his frank aspiration to produce high art, emerges in a letter he wrote to Blanche Knopf upon being taken up by this highly respected publisher in 1928, after six years of publishing in the pulps:

> I'm one of the few . . . people moderately literate who take the detective story seriously. I don't mean that I take my own or anybody else's seriously—but the detective story as a form. Someday somebody is going to make "literature" of it . . . and I'm selfish enough to have my own hopes, however slight the evident justification might be.[13]

To be published by Knopf was, for Hammett, a badge of distinction, a sign that his work had somewhat departed the grubby milieu of the serials where his sleuth, as he once put it, had "degenerated into a meal ticket" (quoted in Johnson, *Hammett*, 53). An internal memo at Knopf would warn that it "is a great mistake to think of Hammett as a mere popular fiction writer. We can sell him as that but let's not kid ourselves."[14] Here at Knopf the fragments he published in pulp would be bound together and presented whole by a publisher as famous for the beauty and high production values of its books as for its importation of serious European modernism into America. "I liked the look of those . . . books," Willa Cather would write, explaining why she began to publish with Knopf. "Every publisher nowadays tries to make his books look interesting (jacket, cover, type, make-up), but . . . it was Alfred Knopf who set the fashion."[15] This fashion became widespread enough so that historians of the publishing industry now refer to the late-twenties and thirties as a "golden age" of the American book. Hammett's well-bound fictions would now rub shoulders with the likes of Gide, whose novel *Les Faux-Monnayeurs* (1925) Knopf had published in 1927 as *The Counterfeiters*. For his part Gide would claim, much to Hammett's satisfaction, that the greatest American writers of the time were Faulkner and Hammett (Johnson, *Hammett*, 12). Indeed, by 1934, with the publication of *The Thin Man*, one critic would hail him, with uncanny exactitude to his stated aspirations of six years earlier, as a writer who has "made literature out of detective fiction." Another would describe him as the "darling of brows both high and low."[16]

Hammett's statement of high purpose to Blanche Knopf, however, suggests the inadequacy of the idea either that Hammett's fiction, any more than S. S. Van Dine's, unambiguously sips from the sacred fount of "literature" or that, in the manner of more recent postmodernist populisms, Hammett simply saw through the insidious "Great Divide." For Hammett the distinction between high and low retains an obvious force, where the relation of his actual work to an ideal "form" of the detective story is managed in the affective register of "seriousness." My contention here, pressing this idea further, will be that the problem of Hammett's ambiguous place in early-twentieth-century cultural hierarchies, which he hoped to overcome by taking his genre seriously, reveals itself in his habitual lack of seriousness, paradoxically, with respect to the ontological status of his own representations. In this he echoes the critique of stable, or popular, symbolism by the rigorously hermetic Symbolists, and by their self-conscious heirs such as Eliot.

Hammett's problem with representation becomes explicit at the very end of his career. In the penultimate paragraph of the unfinished novel "Tulip," the Hammett-like narrator looks back to the time when he was still a productive professional writer and observes that

> representations seemed to me—at least they seem now, and I suppose I must have had some inkling of the same opinion then—devices of the old and tired, or older and more tired, to ease up, like conscious symbolism, or graven images. If you are tired you ought to rest, I think, and not try to fool yourself or your customers with colored bubbles.[17]

Thus Hammett attributes the sudden collapse of his productivity after *The Thin Man* (1933) to a fundamental, indeed theological, disappointment with his craft. He is disappointed with its inability to transcend the fallen forms of Representation—its failure simply to *be* rather than to *mean*. This critique of representation takes the form of a kind of ritual murder in the early novels, where what are murdered are not so much persons as representations of persons. The murder of these representations expresses, for one thing, a deep uneasiness with what most saw as the popular novel's fundamental appeal. In her critique of the debased "best-seller," *Fiction and the Reading Public* (1930), Q. D. Leavis disdains the naive mass reader precisely for his "confusion of fiction with life," and for his "co-operat[ing] to persuade himself that he is in contact with 'real people' " who might be his friends.[18]

Hammett's "murder" of his own representations enables him to negotiate the relation of high to low, at once distancing himself from his popular work and figuring an image of "literature" and its "timeless" spiritual value as its unrealized aspiration. Through an examination of Hammett's *The Dain Curse* (1929), I will show the operation of this ritual murder, a project perhaps most fully realized in *The Maltese Falcon*. In the context of *The Dain Curse*, we can see that the grail-like statuette revealed at the end of Hammett's third novel to be an enameled fake—that is, a species of "colored bubble" or counterfeit coin—is a figure for the failed aspiration to the status of "literature," or, more precisely, the failed aspiration to the dialectical unity of matter and spirit, of commerce and theology, that "literature" had come for Hammett to represent.[19]

Murdering Representation

Dashiell Hammett liked the word "dingus." In his writings of the period from 1924 to 1952, "dingus" signifies, variously, a magician's prop, a typewriter, a short story, a novel, and an elusive artifact, a black bird better known as the Maltese Falcon. It also signifies a funny-looking portable seat used by hunters, and though this usage of "dingus," unlike the others, has nothing directly to do with writing, perhaps it emphasizes, by associating them with portable chairs, how curious Hammett thought the things of writing to be.

For "thing" is what "dingus," related by way of Dutch to the German *Ding*, more or less means. Like "whatchamacallit," "thingamajig," "gizmo," and "doodad," "dingus" acts as a linguistic place-holder, a way of noting the "thingly" quality of some thing whose adequate designation is unknown, avoided, or caught on the tip of the tongue. At the same time, saying "dingus" rather than simply "thing" makes fun of the process of naming, feigns catching it midstride, before thing and noun are fused: once upon a time, "dingus" seems to say, words like potholder or parrot or plasma, or pen or pencil or paper, may have sounded equally awkward. Like "gizmo," however, "dingus" calls attention as much to the peculiarity of the thing not named as to the speaker's inability to name it. "Dingus" is not merely a place-holder or parody of naming, but the beginnings of a bemused or a mildly contemptuous specification.

For instance when Hammett, in correspondence with his editor at Knopf, said of his recently revised novel *The Dain Curse* "the dingus is still undoubtedly rather complicated," he no doubt had the words "novel" and "book" at his command.[20] By recourse to the phallic diminutive "dingus," he diffidently deprived the thing he had just revised of a small portion of its dignity. But what, for Hammett, makes a short story, or novel, or black falcon a dingus? These literary dinguses share a proximity, for Hammett, to the problem of conceiving the artifact he produces as *one* thing at all. In other words, dingus *is* complication, in the root sense of "thing" as the product of combination or of a "folding together." Insofar as an artifact is seen as a plurality, it becomes difficult for Hammett to think of it as a thing after all, for he will trouble the movement—*e pluribus unum*—in which what is conceivable as a number of things is also conceivable as one thing. Calling his literary artifact a dingus, then, at once draws attention to and questions the artifact's status as a individual thing.

Take, for instance, *The Dain Curse*. It had originally been published serially in four issues of *Black Mask* and, according to Knopf editor Harry Block, still fell "too definitely into three sections" as a novel (quoted in Johnson, *Hammett*, 74). These three "sections" no doubt endure as the three "parts" of the published book—the first two corresponding more or less to the first two magazine segments, the third a combination of the last two magazine segments. Still bearing the traces of its serial origins, what it needed, thought Block, was a "connecting thread."

Block's aspirations for *The Dain Curse* are familiar enough: a demand for unity in any artistic project has been one of the more common demands of prescriptive aesthetics. In the case of *The Dain Curse*, however, the editor's prescription of unity is thematized in the central question driving the novel, namely, whether the "theory that there [is] some connecting link" in a number of murders—note the similarity between "connecting link" and Block's "connecting thread"—will hold up to scrutiny.[21] Hammett's unnamed detective, the Continental Op, who has "stopped believing in accidents" (138), thinks it will, and the question then becomes what "connecting link" he will uncover. The "Dain curse" is adduced by several characters to explain as supernatural the common source of a number of murders that occur in the vicinity of Gabrielle Leggett, whose mother was a Dain. The Continental Op sets himself the task of finding a more "tangible, logical and jailable answer than any curse" (188)—namely, a human being, one body and "one mind" with a "system that he likes, and sticks to" (169).

This "one mind," as it turns out, belongs to Hugh Fitzstephen, a novelist who looks conspicuously like Hammett did. Such coy self-reflexivity suggests a familiar analogy between the author who presides over his created world, endowing it with coherent intention, and the will of God Himself. That the answer to the question "whodunit?" in *The Dain Curse* is "the author" does, however, reinforce the notion that the novel interrogates the possibility of its own unity. Form and theme converge in *The Dain Curse*, since the potential unity the novel ponders is conspicuously its own. Its possibility hinges on the ability to map to a single person the novel's discrete parts—conceivable now either formally as "sections" of the book or thematically as its numerous murders. Appropriately enough, this person is both a murderer and a novelist. When at the end of part one the Op says "[W]e [at the Agency] wrote *Discontinued* at the bottom of the Leggett record" (66), the question of continuity that would bother Block is inscribed, indeed italicized, in the pages of the novel itself. When a few sentences later the Op is told that " 'the Leggett matter is active again' " (67) because someone else has been murdered, this announces at once the continuation of the Leggett record, the continuation of the novel *The Dain Curse*, and the renewed search for the single person who forces both of these narratives onward.

But can either the Op or the text itself find this single person? A conversation between the Op and the novelist Fitzstephen, the former concerned with realities, the latter with representations, suggests that discovering this unity will be difficult:

> "Are you—who [as a detective] make your living snooping—sneering at my curiosity about people and my attempts to satisfy it?"
>
> "We're different," I said. "I do mine with the object of putting people in jail, and I get paid for it, though not as much as I should."
>
> "That's not different," he said. "I do mine with the object of putting people in books, and I get paid for it, though not as much as I should."
>
> "Yeah, but what good does that do?"
>
> "God knows. What good does putting them in jail do?"
>
> "Relieves congestion," I said. "Put enough people in jail and cities wouldn't have traffic problems." (22)

For all the apparent similarities between the "snooping" detective and the "curious" novelist, then, "putting people in books" only makes flesh into representations that, as the Op would say, are not "jailable." So even if the Op succeeds in jailing the single body responsible for the murders, the novel itself only ambiguously succeeds in locating the individual author/ murderer that will guarantee its own unity. The convergence of the formal and the thematic in *The Dain Curse* is held, that is, in a state of incompletion. Fitzstephen may be the origin of the murders in the book, but as he tells the Op, in court the "number of my crimes will be to my advantage, on the theory that nobody but a lunatic could have committed so many. And won't they be many? I'll produce crimes and crimes, dating from the cradle" (220). The Op (to Fitzstephen's dismay) does in fact think the novelist is a lunatic. The sheer number of the novelist's crimes makes the category of intentionality useless for the Op, and the body that is sent to the prison-psychiatric hospital will not have the status of a responsible, intending subject. The (moral) unconsciousness implied by Fitzstephen's insanity, then, mirrors his necessary unconsciousness of the formal problems in the novel of which he is a part. Only a representation of an author, he may not be held responsible for resolving its formal pluralities. Beyond the Op's grasp, the real author is present in the world of the novel only as phantom, something like the "writhing"—or is that "writing"?—"indescribable thing," who appears to the Op in a chapter entitled, pointedly enough, "God." This chapter tells of the Op's adventures in the temple of the "Holy Grail Cult" run by the novelist Fitzstephen:

> Not more than three feet away, there in the black room, a pale bright thing like a body, but not like flesh, stood writhing before me. . . . Its feet—it had feet, but I don't know what their shape was. They had no shape, just as the thing's legs and torso, arms and hands, head and face, had no shape, no fixed form. They writhed, swelling and contracting, stretching and shrinking. . . . The legs were now one leg like a twisting pedestal, and then three, and then two. No feature or member ever stopped twisting, quivering, writhing long enough for its average outline, its proper shape, to be seen. The thing was a thing like a man who floated above the floor. (92–93)

Whether this figure signifies the author/god, evident in the novel in the form of the shifting effects of his cause, or the unreality of fictional character as such (What are these beings in books but a kind of ghost?), or the disunity of the novel itself—the dingus, as Hammett would put it, is still undoubtedly rather complicated. In the more practical terms of editors and authors, the unresolved problem of the unity of the novel reveals itself in Hammett's criticism, upon receiving last galley proofs, of Block's editorial efforts: "I had my hands full trying to make it look like all the work of the same writer" (quoted in Johnson, *Hammett*, 77).

What is fascinating about this problem, the problem of multiplicity, is how faithfully it is mirrored in the criticism surrounding Hammett's first two novels. Widespread opinion held that they were, like the writhing ghost itself, almost too chaotic to comprehend. And what is curious about these judgments is the ambiguity they evince with respect to the source of the chaos. About Hammett's first novel, *Red Harvest* (1929), for instance, there was considerable uncertainty as to whether this chaos resulted from its excessive number of murders or its excessive number of characters. *Red Harvest* was at first to be called "Poisonville," a pun on the name of the crowded city of Personville, and suggestive at the same time of a novel problematically inhabited by many characters. So, too, Donald Willsson, the captain of industry who "was Personville," who "owned Personville heart, soul, skin and guts," is a single person inhabited by many. The task of the Op will be, in a sense, to cure this individual of the poisonous social occupation of his identity represented visually by the crowd of consonants in his name.[22] One reviewer, who seems to be bothered more by the novel's number of murders than by its "crowd of characters," is canny enough to see the necessarily intimate or economic relation of the two:

> There has been in detective stories a decided increase in the number of murders deemed necessary to complete the story. Such an appetite will certainly be glutted in "Red Harvest." It is crowded with characters—it had to be to supply

material for the murders—the action moves dizzily and when it's all over,
the reader wonders just what it was all about. (quoted in Layman, *Shadow
Man*, 97)

Only numerous characters can "supply material" for numerous murders.
Since they are necessarily simultaneous, it is often unclear which of the
two is really at issue. Immediately after complaining that *The Dain Curse*
falls "too definitely into three sections," Block, like this dizzied critic, complains about the "violence" that "is piled on a bit thick" and about its
"immense number of characters, which is so great as to create confusion"
(quoted in Johnson, *Hammett*, 74). Blanche Knopf finds about *Red Harvest* that "so many killings on a page make the reader doubt the story,
and instead of the continued suspense and feeling of horror, the interest
slackens" (70). Knopf, however, only repeats the Op's observation of an
excess of killing *within* the novel: "[T]here's been what? A dozen and a
half murders since I've been here. Donald Willsson; Ike Bush; the four
wops at Cedar Hill . . . [etc.]. That's sixteen of them in less than a week,
and more coming up."[23] Hammett himself, roughly when he was assuring
Blanche Knopf that removing a few murders from *Red Harvest* would "relieve the congestion" of *killing*, was making the Continental Op in *The
Dain Curse* claim with the same phrasing that the value of his profession
is to "relieve [the] congestion" of *persons* in cities.

What are we to make of this odd convergence of bothersome pluralities?
I am suggesting here that Hammett's problem with manyness is a symptom
of his uneasiness with his place as an author in a commercial culture Henry
James had characterized by its "multiplication, multiplication of everything . . . multiplication with a vengeance."[24] He must serve, as an author
of popular fiction, the multitude, a reversal of authority Hammett, typical
of his time, found disturbing. For Gertrude Stein, for example, the very
idea of a social relation between writer and audience, which forces the
writer to hear not him- or herself but "what the audience hears one say"
(147), disables her pursuit of the lofty thing-in-itself. This notion can put
a surprising spin on the question of Hammett's style. Indeed, rejecting the
notion that the famed Hemingwayesque sparseness of his prose represents
the language of the common "man on the street," Hammett averred that
the language of the street is in fact "not only excessively complicated and
repetitious, but almost purposeless in its lack of coherence," while "simplicity and clarity . . . are the most elusive and difficult of literary accomplishments" (quoted in Johnson, *Hammett*, 54). Hammett suggests here
that he intended the sparseness of his prose to resist the incoherence of the
man on the street for whom he nonetheless wrote.[25] Similarly, producing
many characters represents the many, while murdering them symbolically
resists the imposition of a social relation between writer and audience. In

this construction the purer realm of "literature" is not so much realized in the work as produced as its timeless negative image, an uninhabited, asocial space.

Hammett was indeed, if anything, more severe in adhering to these Symbolist values than was his fellow hard-boiled antisentimentalist, Ernest Hemingway. While neither writer would admit to an excessive interest in the other, there are indeed some important similarities between the two that extend beyond either their panicked hypermasculinity or their development of the hard-boiled style. Both writers present case studies in the conversion of personal experience into authority. Indeed, Hemingway understood better than anyone since Stephen Crane the value of *experiential capital* for a writer—so important to the World War generation that would often stake its claim to authority (as Crane never could) on its personal experience of battle.

Dashiell Hammett was not, as is frequently reported, an ambulance driver like Hemingway, Dos Passos, Cummings, and the rest. He fell ill in training camp and never left the United States. He did, however, capitalize on having actually worked as a Pinkerton's Detective agent for a brief time. This allowed him to pull rank on Van Dine and the others who could only imagine what detective work was all about. In his initial correspondence to Knopf he wrote: "By way of introducing myself: I was a Pinkerton's National Detective Agency operative for a number of years; and, more recently, have published fiction."[26] Later, discussing appropriate titles for *Red Harvest* with Blanche Knopf, he wrote that his only "prejudice . . . in this connection is against the word 'case' used where my sleuth would use 'job.' " All of Van Dine's titles contained the word "case."[27] Publicity materials for *The Thin Man* (1934) touted Hammett's "unsurpassed first-hand knowledge of the underworld, gained through many years as an actual operative of the Pinkerton Detective Agency."[28]

And yet the idea of experiential capital won by personal risk influences the form of his novels, and indeed of all hard-boiled detective fiction, more profoundly still: the signal feature of the hard-boiled detective novel, over against the purely "analytical" tradition of Poe, Conan Doyle, and Van Dine, is not only that the detective becomes a professional but that his body is placed at constant risk as he goes about solving the crime. Only incidentally does the brainy analytical detective have a body, and his position as aristocratic amateur sets him above the fray. Not so with grizzled professionals like the Op and Sam Spade, who do not lose the role of analyst of clues but who add to this the role of fighter.

Hemingway's professionalism is manifest in the obsessive ethic of sentence craftsmanship that has been his most influential legacy to subsequent generations of "serious" writers (especially those who emerge from writing programs). Hemingway wanted to "cut out the scroll-work" and

write "one true word," and this, no less than for Hammett, was to resist a
kind of rhetorical "feminization." But this "most elusive and difficult of
literary accomplishments"—simplicity—was for Hemingway as useful for
appealing to the masses as for resisting them: an early letter to the publisher of *In Our Time* touts its linguistic austerity as something that "would
be praised by the highbrows and could be read by the lowbrows."[29]

And indeed, for all the seeming ease with which the Nobelist Hemingway
came to be understood as a novelist-artist, a work like *The Sun Also Rises*
(1926) suggests a standard for the art-novel somewhat easier to meet than
Hammett's theological rejection of the commerce in representations in his
lowly detective fiction:

> Romero never made any contortions, always it was straight and pure and natural
> in line. The others twisted themselves like cork-screws, their elbows raised, and
> leaned against the flanks of the bull after his horns had passed, to give a faked
> look of danger. Afterward, all that was faked turned bad and gave an unpleasant
> feeling. Romero's bull-fighting gave real emotion, because he kept the absolute
> purity of line in his movements and always quietly and calmly let the horns pass
> him close each time.[30]

Assuming, as seems reasonable, that this description of Romero's "purity
of line" in the bullfight can be understood, on another level, as Hemingway's *ars poetica*, this ideal of writing asks for "truth" in a common,
not an ultimate, sense. Hemingway's truth is like "truth in advertising"—
honesty, an absence of "commercial" lies. It is strictly opposed neither to
commerce *as such* nor to money, wanting only a "[s]imple exchange of
values. You give them money. They give you a stuffed dog" (78). Never
for a moment is it doubted that young Romero is paid handsomely for his
honest work; his *aficion* means simply that he does not fight *only* to be
paid, any more than the modernist writer writes only to be paid.

Neither, though he remains a Catholic, does the Hemingway-like character Jake Barnes seem to have any real problem with civic commercialism
on the Ben Franklin model: indeed, he is an obsessive participant in it—a
purchaser of women, wineskins, coffee, taxicabs, and hotel rooms. Nothing
is more remarkable in this novel than how rigorously it keeps its accounts:
"I discovered I had a balance of $1832.60" (38), Jake tells us, implying
that he can afford the fun he will have in Pamplona. The characters this
novel most admires are those, all of them men, who do not live on credit
and who do not decline to pay for what they get. " 'Don't we pay for all
the things we do, though?" (34), asks Brett Ashely, but it is Jake who,
realizing he "had been getting something for nothing" (152), will finally
settle his and her bill.

At least in this respect, Hammett's literary "Catholicism" was stricter
than Hemingway's. His detective's demands for payment are meant to

suggest a brutal, if honest, cynicism, and the commerce in representations in Hammett is a ultimately sign of fallenness. As a form of representation, fiction is an inherent lie, a bunch of "colored bubbles" with which one fools one's customers. For Hammett there is no "one true word." I believe we should read the pursuit of the grail-like statuette in *The Maltese Falcon*, an object centuries old but now lost, in this context, for the falcon's very pricelessness suggests that its value, if realized, would transcend the logic of exchange. When Sam Spade asks Gutman what the "maximum" value of the "dingus" might be, Gutman refuses "to guess. You'd think me crazy. I don't know. There's no telling how high it could go, sir, and that's the one and only truth about it."[31]

It is probably no accident that the novel that produces an image of "timeless" value in the falcon is precisely the novel of Hammett's upon which literary history begins, though tentatively, to confer the status of "literature." *The Maltese Falcon* has relatively few characters, and its small number of murders all occur "off-stage." Its formal unity, as one biographer puts it, "[makes] no concessions to magazine publication" (Layman, *Shadow Man*, 107) and like that of the grail itself resists periodicity as such, or "timely" social history.[32] Thus we might say that the *Maltese Falcon as novel* aspires to the absolute value, or unity, of the Maltese Falcon *as object*.[33]

But, notoriously, the object actually acquired in the novel turns out to be a fake, not the real thing. And this suggests, first, that the falcon remains merely a commodity, trapped in the logic of commodity fetishism as described by Marx. In this familiar account the commodity provokes, but never truly satisfies, a desire for the existential plenitude it represents. Thus Spade says to Gutman, demanding payment for his services even though the falcon has turned out to be fake: "You got your dingus. It's your hard luck, not mine, that it wasn't what you wanted" (203). This counterfeit continues Hammett's distinction between the "colored bubbles" he produces in his fiction and the transcendental thing to which he aspires, and which no accumulation of riches won by his writing can buy for him.[34] The sarcasm Hammett heaps upon the novelist Fitzstephen's Holy Grail Cult in *The Dain Curse* could in this context be read as a measure of his sense that the time of a legitimate theological culture has passed and that the obvious religious preoccupations of his own work as a novelist can unfold only in the similarly debased form of the dingus. Thus Hammett traces a constitutive "lack" at the center of individual identity—as in the psychoanalytical account of Jacques Lacan—to its origins in the social and historical realm, where in dialectical turn it is seen to produce the constitutive discrepancy internal to the individual representation.[35]

Predictably, then, *The Maltese Falcon*, a study in narrative economy, ultimately collapses back into the multiplicity so evident in the earlier novels. When the treacherous woman Brigid O'Shaughnessy begs Sam Spade to admit that he loves her, he does so, but only to state the impotence of his love in the face of the sheer multiplicity of practical reasons she should be hanged, which Spade proceeds to list. His seventh reason is a question of odds, since he doesn't "even like the idea of thinking that there might be one chance in a hundred that" he's being "played . . . for a sucker." His last reason is the "eighth—but that's enough. . . . Maybe some of them are important. I won't argue about that. But look at the number of them" (214).

This confession of failure to find the One is precisely what in retrospect might make Hammett appear so much the shadow modernist, the producer of "literature." Indeed, even as for Hammett access to high culture institutions meant the unification of his serial fragments in the form of the beautiful Knopf book, for T. S. Eliot the hermetic "heap of broken images" of *The Waste Land* (1922) had become the proper form of modern poetry. In the context of a certain strain of elite modernism, that is, something like the chaos of Hammett's first two novels, so bothersome to his editors and critics, could be revalued as a sign of modernism's critique of romantic unities and traditional forms. Without denying the obvious differences between the two texts, then, we can see the degree to which protocols of reading determine what is normally asserted to be a quality inherent in the object itself. In Eliot's case the high culture reader could be asked to supply, as an erudite hermeneut, the spectral unity of *The Waste Land*'s fragments. The comparatively "low" Hammett, speaking to the many, was required to make sense.

Inspired, he tells us, by his reading of Jessie Weston's analysis of the grail legend in *From Ritual to Romance*, which Weston argues has its origins in ancient rites surrounding the harvest, Eliot figures London life in *The Waste Land* as a bleak urban desert, deprived of spiritual nourishment. In the Unreal City of his poem, "A crowd flowed over the London Bridge, so many, / I had not thought death had undone so many"—an image that in a sense looks forward to the carnage, the "red harvest," of the many characters of Personville.[36] And while Hammett declined to pursue the project of Christian cultural renewal that Eliot would take up in later years, Lillian Hellman gives evidence that Hammett was reading *The Waste Land* around the time he wrote *The Maltese Falcon* (we know as well that Eliot was a fan of detective fiction). Both works make conspicuous use of the timeless value of the Holy Grail as a measure of the inauthenticity of the merely "representational" market culture in which they are produced, and which in turn produces them, not as single artifacts able to do the work of God and Mammon at once, but as two seemingly different *kinds* of object.[37]

The transposition of the high/low division from the "American mind" to the realm of objects themselves is perhaps the most important and ultimately disabling legacy of modernism's "failure" to merge the high and low in a single object. As John Guillory, following Pierre Bourdieu, demonstrates in *Cultural Capital*, what we mean by "highness" is best understood not as a quality of certain objects, but as a privileged *relation* to knowledge; in this view, for instance, a "sophisticated" account of even the most resolutely "popular" text might have the effect of reconstituting this low text as exclusive intellectual property. The texts I have been examining here, following the example of Poe's purloined letter, had the virtue at least of partly recognizing this fact, though they tended to understand it not as an outrage but as an opportunity: an opportunity to produce intellectual social distinctions within the "common" space of mass culture.

In later years, Eliot became less concerned to champion the necessary pleasures of the popular, as he had in the essay "Wilkie Collins and Dickens," less concerned to figure the dissociation of the high and low as the unfortunate rupture of a single thing.[38] Increasingly, as in his 1936 introduction to Djuna Barnes's *Nightwood*, he became the impassioned spokesman for elite culture he is now remembered to have been. The cultural-hierarchical complexities his later career presents are worth pondering, however, since even as he began to speak in the unambiguous accents of privilege, he was raised to the status of popular modernist icon, departing the rarified milieu of the little magazines to appear, in 1950, on the cover of *Time*. "No one thinks of me as a poet any more," Eliot would lament, "but as a celebrity."[39]

This irony is in many ways reciprocal to that of the low modernist Dashiell Hammett, the would-be beacon of "Literature" flashing from the mire of the mass market. Recently Hammett's collected works have been republished in the prestigious and handsomely bound Library of America series, certainly as close a physical approximation to the spiritual status of canonical "literature" as he could have wished for, and a long way from the literal and symbolic trashiness of the pulps where he began. Reversing the case of Willard Huntington Wright in more ways than one, Hammett might have said, "I used to be a lowbrow but look at me now."

a f t e r w o r d

Möbius Fictions

> When we speak of technique, then, we speak of nearly
> everything.
> —Mark Schorer, "Technique as Discovery"

> This gravitation of the highbrows to the universities is fairly
> recent.
> —Russell Lynes, *The Tastemakers*

> Gliding from fellowship to fellowship, Raskolnikov may now
> end life as a sober professor of literature.
> —Irving Howe, "Mass Society and Postmodern Fiction"

In the story called "Frame Tale," which opens his collection of
short fiction, *Lost in the Funhouse* (1968), John Barth instructs the reader
to "Cut on dotted line. Twist end once and fasten AB to ab, CD to cd."
Along the right hand margin, in large type framed by the letters AB and
CD, one reads the words "ONCE UPON A TIME THERE." Turning the page one
finds along the left margin, framed now by the letters ab and cd, "WAS A
STORY THAT BEGAN."[1] I don't know how many readers have taken the bait
and constructed with scissors and tape the Möbius band that would now
read "ONCE UPON A TIME THERE WAS A STORY THAT BEGAN ONCE UPON A TIME
THERE WAS A STORY THAT BEGAN ONCE UPON A TIME THERE WAS A STORY THAT
BEGAN ONCE UPON A TIME THERE WAS A STORY THAT BEGAN ONCE UPON A TIME
. . . [etc]." I suspect few have done so; one does not need scissors to get
the idea, which is that the single-sided text so constructed could be read
not repetitively, but continuously and interminably. Supposing that we
entered the fictive "space," such as it is, that the tale constructs, no narrative line or logic could possibly lead us back to the "outside." The sense
of an ending could come only by readerly fiat, a decision, which is also an
admission, that one will not have read the "Frame Tale" to its conclusion.
"The only way to get out of a mirror-maze," as Barth puts it elsewhere in
the volume, "is to close your eyes" (108). It was Henry James who, in the
preface to *The Portrait of a Lady,* described the institution of the novel as
a "house of fiction." In John Barth the house of fiction has become a funhouse of fiction, an infinitely regressive hall of mirrors that one enters
without hope of satisfactory egress.

Still less, it would seem, given the paucity of "content" the "Tale" offers, could one tie it in any meaningful way to the "real world" with which fiction is conventionally understood, at least to some degree, to engage. If there could be such a thing as abstract fiction, a fiction of pure form, hermetically sealed from any domain of reference, surely this empty "Tale" is it. And yet, we might insist, in fact there cannot be such a thing. And indeed, as one begins to historicize the rise of that particular species of postmodern fiction called "metafiction," a fairly convincing reading of such a tale might present itself.

For how might one describe the "postmodernism" of John Barth? Efforts have been made to define postmodern fiction at the level of internal formal analysis, distinguishing it, typically, from an antecedent experimental modernist narrative.[2] These formalist definitions might be countered, however, by an account that emphasizes the institutional space in which Barth's metafiction evolved, which, put briefly, might go something like this: the version of postmodernism produced by a writer like Barth is one thing that happens to modernist fiction when some of its practitioners are absorbed by the university after the Second World War. This account is obviously of limited application, serving well for the work of Barth, Donald Barthelme, Robert Coover, William Gass, and Vladimir Nabokov, but not quite stretching to cover experimental writings by such as Thomas Pynchon, William Burroughs, and Kathy Acker.[3] Unlike poetry, which, as a profession at least, has become all but entirely dependent on the patronage of the university, the art-novel's strong and continuing ties to economically viable readerships have kept it from so complete an absorption by the school. And yet it is the case that, come the 1950s, as Malcolm Cowley observes in his study of postwar fiction, "There has never been a time when so many practicing writers [of fiction] were attached to the staffs of American universities."[4] The extraordinary novelty of this situation is seconded by Alfred Kazin, who notes the "very great change" represented by the postwar "university's friendly hospitality to writers," its eagerness "to play the active role of patron—to support the creation of literature, to take writers into the academic community, and thus to show that it regards them as assimilable, harmonious—and necessary."[5] John Barth, for instance, became an instructor of English at Penn State in 1952, and his career as a novelist is entirely coincident with his career as a professor. By 1966, symptomatically, he would produce a novel, *Giles Goat-Boy, or The Revised New Syllabus*, founded on a pun that collapses the distinction between the *universe* and the *university* and that, or so the reader is told, might have been written by the West Campus computer itself.[6] Raymond Olderman is surely on to something when, in an essay called "The Grail Knight Goes to College," he argues that the modernist cityscape of Eliot's *The Waste Land* is transposed by Barth, in this novel, onto the university campus.[7] The production of postmodern fiction in the university coincides with, and is in a sense doubled by, the consecration of earlier modernist novels placed in this period on the university syllabus.

Symptomatically, then, one finds a tendency in postmodern fiction to define itself not against its supposed predecessor, modernist fiction, but *with* modernist fiction against nineteenth-century realist fiction, as in this passage from Barth's story "Lost in the Funhouse":

> Initials, blanks, or both were often substituted for proper names in nineteenth-century fiction to enhance the illusion of reality. It is as if the author felt it necessary to delete the names for reasons of tact or legal liability. Interestingly, as with other aspects of realism, it is an *illusion* that is being enhanced, by purely artificial means. (69–70)

Reading this disillusioning passage, where fiction, as metafiction, has become rhetorically indistinguishable from literary criticism, one is tempted to say that the programmatic "technicality" of the metafictional experiments of American professor-writers such as Barth and Barthelme and Coover should be read, in a sense, as *instances* of the bureaucratic-technical discourse produced in the postwar American university—even as they must also be seen as *aestheticizations* of that discourse.

One of the purest literary-critical expressions of this attraction to the technical—and conveniently, for my purposes, one that transposes it to the specific domain of the novel—must surely be Mark Schorer's 1948 essay, "Technique as Discovery."[8] This essay touts the "exacting scrutiny of literary texts" on the part of modern literary critics even as it demands "the most exacting technical scrutiny" (67) of their subject matter by novelists themselves. Suffused with the terminology of "tools" and "materials" and "objectivity" and "technique," the essay mimes the language of the laboratory, seeming to make a bid for the validity of literary criticism, and especially criticism of the novel, as an academic pursuit.[9] It does so even as its arguments for "technique" in the novel—which hard term Schorer prefers to the fluffier "form"—are barely distinguishable from those made by Henry James some fifty years earlier. The only significant addition he makes to James had already been made by T. S. Eliot when, in his 1937 introduction to Djuna Barnes's "poetic" novel *Nightwood*, he drew attention to its use of what Schorer calls "the resources of language" that are a "part of the technique of fiction" (68).

Schorer's indebtedness to James, touched with a patina of technicist terminology and supplied with an ear for the linguistic effects of poetry, is expressed mostly by proxy, in a thorough thrashing of the ultimate novelist as antiartist, James's one-time friend and eventual nemesis, H. G. Wells. Here Schorer settles accounts in a forty-year-old dispute, consigning Wells to the dustbin of literary history. Whereas James had insisted to Wells that

it is "art that *makes* life, *makes* interest," Schorer states in somewhat more
sedate, professorial terms that "technique alone objectifies the materials of
art; hence technique alone evaluates those materials." He finds the messy
"social historian" Wells sadly wanting on those grounds. Whereas James,
in "The Art of Fiction," had complained that the novel in his time was a
thing with "no air of having a theory, a conviction, a consciousness of
itself behind it," Schorer asserts that "modern fiction at its best has been
peculiarly conscious of itself and of its tools" (86). In Mark Schorer—but
not only in Mark Schorer—James's high aesthetic aspirations for the novel
are *institutionalized*. This paves the way for Philip Rahv's emphatic 1956
declaration that "the novel is at the present time universally recognized as
one of the greater historic forms of literary art."[10] At last—although even
in 1956 it is still worth the effort of saying so—the novel is secure in the
accredited pantheon of the fine arts: it is a golden bowl.

Seen in the light of this call to technical self-consciousness, the funhouse
"enclosure" in which John Barth finds himself trapped might then be read,
allegorically, as the *institutional* enclosure represented by the school itself,
which now mediates the relation between the tenured experimental writer
and the literary market. Reading Barth, we can see a modernist writer
troubled by his paradise gained. The vertiginous mirror-effects of the "Literature of Exhaustion" are perhaps best explained, that is, as symptoms
of the institutionalization of modernist fiction.[11] As such, they are best
described not as revolutionary but as *ultraconventional*:

> Plot and theme: notions vitiated by this hour of the world but as yet not success-
> fully succeeded. . . . The worst is to come. Everything leads to nothing: future
> tense; past tense; present tense. Perfect. Can't stand any more of this. . . . Oh
> God comma I abhor self-consciousness. I despise what we have come to; I loathe
> our loathsome loathing, our place our time our situation, our loathsome art, this
> ditto necessary story. (102,110)

Modernist narrative in United States, when it had been produced earlier
in the century by James, Faulkner, Stein, et alia, had not issued from and
circled back to the institutional space of the university. The modernist
writer of the early-twentieth century was not typically "in residence," and
neither were his or her texts resident on the college syllabus. And thus,
arguably, did the "self-consciousness" of modernist fiction typically take
a form different from that in metafiction, in which the establishment of a
modernist aesthetic is everywhere marked by its violent engagement with
external hostile forces, with others and with objects that are understood
to *impede* the pure self-consciousness that will become John Barth's bane.
So, too, we might say, did the pathos of modernism shape itself differently,

since the "despair" in which it occasionally trafficked was as often as not directed at the "mass market" or "mass culture" in which it felt itself to be enclosed.

Thus, when we encounter another evocation of the idea of Möbius fiction, written this time by a writer who came of age in the twenties, Dashiell Hammett, its significance is quite different from what it will be for Barth:

> Tony gave a little gurgle of delight when I said topology, as if I had mentioned an old friend. He used to listen one winter when Gus and I gave dimensions back to the sculptors and spent hours talking about painting having to do with the relationship in space of the surfaces of objects and nothing else. I liked topology: a few years before I had written a story on a Möbius band, designed to be read from any point on it on around to that point again, and to be complete and sensible story regardless of where you started. It had worked out pretty well—I don't mean perfectly; what story ever does that? But pretty well.[12]

This notional single-sided artifact appears in Hammett's unfinished novel "Tulip," written in 1952, the same year as John Barth's entry into the professoriat. In contrast to Barth, Hammett had not received even a high school diploma, and not unrelatedly thought himself trapped, as a writer of "trashy" popular fiction, in the unprotected space of the literary market. When Hammett, in this passage, refers to a body of technical knowledge called "topology," and when he casually refers to himself as an ideologue of painterly abstraction, these are the gestures of a popular writer concerned, indeed somewhat ashamed, by his lack of certification by the school. He is showing off. Hammett's experiment with the Möbius strip—not "perfect," but not bad—bespeaks not the despair of the "perfectly" self-conscious enclosure of the university funhouse. If anything, it bespeaks the despair of a would-be modernist aspiring to the privilege of avant-garde experimentation—aspiring, that is, to the self-containment and aesthetic "autonomy" toward which his Möbius tale gestures. Between Hammett and Barth, we might say, the cultural polarities have been reversed, the paradise of one having become the prison of the other.

Thus, in Barth, and in metafiction generally, we have something like an image of what happens when modernism gets what it wants: a heightened (never total) autonomy from an all-engulfing mass market, and from its traffic in realist representations. That this could be true even as the G.I. Bill radically altered the social composition of universities; even as the brute historical force of Cold War containment policies undergirded and permeated university life; even as, with the eruption of campus protest against the war in Vietnam, the university seemed, to some, not at the periphery but the center of "real world" politics; that a newly institutionalized status for modernist writing should be registered so forcefully in and as "metafiction" says a lot for the vulgar materialist dimensions of cultural form that I have emphasized in this account of the emergence of the modernist, and now postmodernist, art-novel.

Not that it says *too* much for these dimensions: the institutionalization of modernist fiction as "metafiction" is perhaps only partly explained in terms of economies of institutional support. And indeed metafiction itself is only one small formation in a more general and dazzlingly heterogenous development of the art-novel after the Second World War. This study concludes with a glance at the, in retrospect, somewhat minor literary-historical moment of professorial metafiction not only to mark an end—the end of a certain period in the modernist novel. It does so also because the structural narcissism of metafiction is a helpful way of acknowledging at last, and for what it's worth, its own condition of self-enclosure. In brief, it can now be admitted that the institutionalization of modernism in the university that produced metafiction has also made this scholarly work on modernism possible—even as it has necessarily, in so doing, circumscribed the infinity of its possibilities.

I make this acknowledgment "for what it's worth" because, really, insofar as this has been a work of literary scholarship, the strength or weakness, truth or falsity, of its many positive claims can be judged without recourse to their origins—without recourse, that is, to genetic fallacies. And should this work be submitted to some other, more dialectical, criterion of judgment—even then the value of this gesture of self-reflection would be uncertain. Pointing to the very worldly circumstances (I really need to clean this office) of its own production, it would humbly acknowledge its constitutive limitations, institutional and otherwise, and invite the reader to read with an eye to what lies beyond. At the same time, learning something from modernism, it would begin to claim even these most intimate matters of fact for mind. Evincing in its own way the uncanny "consciousness of itself" that James hoped would be brought to bear on the novel, the argument of this book would come to a perfect circle, glittering, vanishing at last into a higher dimension altogether.

Thus—for what it's worth—I would say that this afterword is also a misplaced foreword that would, if this book were perfectly consistent (which thankfully it is not), twist itself over now and fasten itself to page 1.

n o t e s

Introduction
The Rise of the Art-Novel and the Question of Class

1. T. S. Eliot, introduction to *Nightwood*, by Djuna Barnes (New York: New Directions, 1937), xi-xii.

2. "Modernist novel"—which term I prefer to specify as much as possible in this study as the "art-novel"—is best thought of as a "simple abstraction" in the Marxian sense elaborated by Michael McKeon, who describes this feature of dialectical materialism as "a deceptively monolithic"—though perhaps conceptually necessary—"category that encloses a complex historical process." See Michael McKeon, *The Origins of the English Novel, 1600–1740* (Baltimore: Johns Hopkins University Press, 1987) 14–22.

3. This will entail a certain prudent resistance to a recent tendency in sociological literary studies to remain at the surface of the literary work, thus to avoid a suspiciously worshipful "New Critical" enterprise of close reading. A strong argument against moving from context to a reading of modernist texts is presented in Lawrence Rainey, *Institutions of Modernism: Literary Elites and Public Culture* (New Haven: Yale University Press, 1998), where Rainey demonstrates, for instance, how thoroughly *The Waste Land* was understood to speak for the modernist poetic avant-garde before any of its potential publishers had even seen the text to read it. But while, for Rainey, one problem with performing readings of literary texts is that it suggests a retrograde New Critical humility before the aesthetic artifact, another is that "juxtaposing the analysis of specific works with discussion of institutional networks would encourage, however inadvertently, a vulgar materialism" he also wants to "disclaim" (6–7). For reasons that will become increasingly clear, I am happy to call my approach in this book "vulgar materialist," though that seems to me too tendentious a term for a form of analysis that attends to (among many other things) the projections and displacements of various economic and other contextual dilemmas into the production of modernist texts. Some of the potential of this mode of reading is suggested by Rainey himself, who, directly after disclaiming vulgar materialism, provides a brief but compelling reading of *Ulysses* as representing not "aimless wandering about the city of Dublin, as is often reported, but in tireless search for patrons and patronage" (7), a signal concern of Joyce himself.

4. See Terry Lovell, *Consuming Fiction* (London: Verso, 1987). Lovell's helpful study marks the novel's transition from "commodity" to "literature" as occurring somewhere between 1820 and 1840, but does not cite any period discourse on the status of the novel to support this claim. The programmatic bid for respect made by James and others toward the end of the century suggests that for them, at least, the novel still had some ways to go in being considered "literature," and perhaps

even more so in being considered "fine art." Of course, if James and his contemporaries were wrong in their beliefs about the historical status of the novel as they received it, this would in a way be even more interesting and telling than the contrary in that it would plainly suggest some of the constructive self-interest involved in falsely imagining oneself as among the first artist-novelists.

5. Henry James, "The Art of Fiction" in *Literary Criticism: Essays on Literature, American Writers, English Writers* (New York: Library of America, 1984), 44–65.

6. H. G. Wells, *Experiment in Autobiography* (New York: Macmillan, 1934), 410–11, quoted in Nicholas Delbanco, *Group Portrait: Joseph Conrad, Stephen Crane, Ford Madox Ford, Henry James* (New York: Caroll and Graf, 1984), 32.

7. The analogy of novel and painting would be pursued most famously by Virginia Woolf in *To the Lighthouse* (1927), but it was also a constant presence in the criticism of Willa Cather and would feature prominently in much modernist fiction. See Deborah Schnitzer, *The Pictorial in Modernist Fiction from Stephen Crane to Ernest Hemingway* (Ann Arbor: UMI Research Press, 1988).

8. Charles Dudley Warner, *The Complete Writings* (Hartford, CT: American Publishing, 1904), 251–75.

9. See Michael Anesko, *"Friction with the Market": Henry James and the Profession of Authorship* (New York: Oxford University Press, 1986).

10. Quoted in Henry Nash Smith, *Democracy and the Novel: Popular Resistance to Classic American Writers* (New York: Oxford University Press, 1978), 12. Oliphant's remarks were made in the context of an 1855 critique of Nathaniel Hawthorne's excessive intellectualism. Some account of Hawthornian romance as a precursor to the art-novel is given here in chapter 1.

11. In an utterance more interesting for its inadvertent proposal of solutions than for its self-pitying statement of the problem, Harold Stearns expressed a sense of the intellectual's existential domination by the culture of the undifferentiated social mass—he calls it the "crowd"—that might have been shared by almost any artistically ambitious novelist of the early-twentieth century:

> Increasingly the only method [one] can employ for the expression of his individuality is through the crowd. He must use an instrument which in a sense is a denial of his original purpose. To express his individuality he must employ the very thing that is by nature designed to smother it.

In Stearns's account the ambitious individual, thoroughly dominated by the crowd, must somehow turn his master into an "instrument" for producing his distinction within this crowd. Absent in this scenario, we notice, is any plan or even hope of escape from this sorry state of affairs. But note that while it is depressive, this complaint is also reflexively resourceful, turning impediments into instruments, problems into solutions: the crowd *shall* be employed as a method of individual expression. See Harold Stearns, *America and the Young Intellectual* (New York: Doran, 1921), 64.

12. See for instance, Thomas Strychacz, *Modernism, Mass Culture, and Professionalism* (New York: Cambridge University Press, 1993); Rainey, *Institutions of Modernism*; Joyce Wexler, *Who Paid for Modernism? Art, Money, and the Fiction of Conrad, Joyce, and Lawrence* (Fayetteville: University of Arkansas Press, 1997); Kevin J. H. Dettmar and Stephen Watt, eds., *Marketing Modernisms: Self-*

Promotion, Canonization, and Rereading (Ann Arbor: University of Michigan Press, 1996); an account of the constitutive interrelation of modernism and mass culture in painting is available in Thomas Crow, *Modern Art in the Common Culture* (New Haven: Yale University Press, 1996).

13. Andreas Huyssen, *After the Great Divide: Modernism, Mass Culture, Postmodernism* (Bloomington: Indiana University Press, 1986), vii. See also Fredric Jameson, *The Political Unconscious: Narrative as a Socially Symbolic Act* (Ithaca: Cornell University Press, 1981), 207. Lawrence Levine, similarly, speaking to the specifically American context, describes how at the turn of the century an elite "highbrow" culture, reacting to the shock of mass immigration, began to define itself in opposition to the "lowbrow" culture of the unruly multitude. What had been a "rich shared public culture" was replaced in this period, he argues, by a view of culture that increasingly excluded any commerce between the sacred art of the elite and the profane entertainments of the mass. See Lawrence Levine, *Highbrow/Lowbrow: The Emergence of Cultural Hierarchy in America* (Cambridge: Harvard University Press, 1988), 9.

14. That implication is of course a fact, but so too is it a fact that modernist texts were only rarely, at least at the time of their production, "authoritative" or "powerful" ones in any obvious sense. The question will always be "authoritative to whom?" or "powerful in what way?" Introducing a rhetoric of disguise, Strychacz runs the risk here of reinstalling the category of the "inauthentic" he has just been at pains to transcend. Perhaps least of all were modernist texts authoritative in the eyes of the university literature departments against which modernism defined itself almost as insistently as it did against mass culture. My argument with this aspect of Strychacz's important account of modernism is taken up again in chapter 4.

15. Michael North, *The Dialectic of Modernism: Race, Language, and Twentieth-Century Literature* (New York: Oxford University Press, 1994); see also Elazar Barkan and Ronald Bush, eds., *Prehistories of the Future: The Primitivist Project and the Culture of Modernism* (Stanford, CA: Stanford University Press, 1995).

16. William Empson, *Some Versions of Pastoral* (New York: New Directions, 1960).

17. See Jack Conroy, *The Disinherited* (Columbia: University of Missouri Press, 1991).

18. Neither, I should say, do I mean to make too many claims about the more literal (and typically nonexperimental) realist tradition of "business fiction" or "white collar portraiture" examined, for instance, in Christopher P. Wilson's *White Collar Fictions: Class and Social Representation in American Literature, 1885–1925* (Athens: University of Georgia Press, 1992).

19. On some of the philosophical and methodological complexities bequeathed by James to latter-day academic literary critics see Mary Poovey, "Beyond the Current Impasse in Literary Studies," *American Literary History* 11, no. 2 (Summer 1999): 354–77.

20. Parallel to this major pastoral tradition is the subgenre that directly narrates the formation and position of the of writer/artist in the early-twentieth century. The best known of these is of course James Joyce's *Portrait of the Artist as a Young Man* (1916). American examples include Jack London, *Martin Eden* (New York:

Macmillan, 1909); Stephen French Whitman, *Predestined: A Novel of New York Life* (New York: Scribner's, 1910); Theodore Dreiser, *The Genius* (New York: John Lane, 1915); Willard Huntington Wright, *A Man of Promise* (New York: John Lane, 1916); Floyd Dell, *Mooncalf* (New York: Knopf, 1920); and Carl Van Vechten, *Peter Whiffle* (New York: Knopf, 1922). Edith Wharton made a late, fascinating entry into this genre with her novels *Hudson River Bracketed* (New York: Appleton, 1929) and *The Gods Arrive* (New York: Appleton, 1932), which trace at great length the formation and development of the fictional male novelist Vance Weston. Part of my strategy in this book is to read some of the concerns expressed in these portraits of the artist back into novels where they are encoded as pastoral representations of the simpleton, and as innovations of literary form.

21. Wyndham Lewis, "The Revolutionary Simpleton" first published in *The Enemy: A Review of Art and Literature*, no. 1 (Jan. 1927; reprint, Santa Clara, CA: Black Sparrow Press, 1994), 27–182.

22. One might also consider James's *What Maisie Knew* (1897), in which the simple consciousness of a young child is interwoven with that of a more sophisticated narrator, in terms of the "child-cult."

23. Friedrich Nietzsche, *On the Genealogy of Morals and Ecce Homo*, trans. Walter Kaufmann (New York: Vintage, 1989), 26.

24. See, for instance, Pierre Bourdieu, *The Rules of Art: Genesis and Structure of the Literary Field*, trans. Susan Emanuel (Stanford, CA: Stanford University Press, 1996), 214–23.

25. An excellent account of the realist dimension of the Jamesian novel—yoking its transformation of the novel of manners tradition to period developments in anthropology—is available in Nancy Bentley, *The Ethnography of Manners: Hawthorne, James, Wharton* (New York: Cambridge University Press, 1995).

26. William Dean Howells, *Criticism and Fiction and Other Essays* (New York: New York University Press, 1959), esp. 85–87.

27. José Ortega y Gassett, *The Dehumanization of Art and Notes on the Novel*, trans. Helene Weyl (Princeton: Princeton University Press, 1948), 5, quoted in Pierre Bourdieu, *Distinction: A Social Critique of the Judgment of Taste*, trans. Richard Nice (Cambridge: Harvard University Press, 1984), 31.

28. Richard Poirier, "The Difficulties of Modernism and the Modernism of Difficulty," *Humanities in Society* 1 (1978): 271–82.

29. C. Wright Mills, "The New Middle Class 1," in *The New Middle Classes: Lifestyles, Status Claims, and Political Orientations*, ed. Arthur J. Vidich (New York: New York University Press, 1995), 189–202.

30. Barbara Ehrenreich and John Ehrenreich, "The Professional Managerial Class," *Radical America* 2, no. 2 (March–April 1977): 13.

31. See, for instance, Alfred D. Chandler, *The Visible Hand: The Managerial Revolution in American Business* (Cambridge: Harvard University Press, 1977).

32. See Jennifer Wicke, *Advertising Fictions: Literature, Advertisement and Social Reading* (New York: Columbia University Press, 1988). See also William Marling, *The American Roman Noir: Hammett, Cain, and Chandler* (Athens: University of Georgia Press, 1995), which contains a rich description of the relation between literature, consumerism, and advertising in the 1920s and 1930s.

In *Consuming Fiction*, Terry Lovell dates the advent of "consumer capitalism" much earlier than the late-nineteenth century, arguing in effect that the "Protestant ethic" of productive thrift described by Weber is only one side of a Janus-faced capitalism that also must solicit the desire to consume. This is no doubt latently true in theory, but still it seems necessary to note that the discourse of consumerism, most importantly the advertisement, undergoes a staggering proliferation beginning at the end of the nineteenth century. For instance, as Richard Ohmann demonstrates in *Selling Culture: Magazines, Markets, and Class at the Turn of the Century* (London: Verso, 1996), to compare the typographical sobriety of magazine ads in, say, 1880 to the riotously appealing spreads of, say, 1910 is to see what looks like the advent of an entirely new world—our world.

33. McKeon, *The Origins of the English Novel*, 212–72.

34. Reprinted in Richard Ruland, ed., *A Storied Land: Theories of American Literature* (New York: E. P. Dutton, 1976), 2:312.

35. Quoted in Anne T. Margolis, *Henry James and the Problem of the Audience: An International Act* (Ann Arbor: UMI Research Press, 1985), 8. It is the unapologetic, "beyond good and evil" nature of this "immorality" that distinguishes the modernist novel from the novel as such, which had of course throughout its history been deemed by its critics immoral, a charge rarely if ever accepted by novelists themselves.

36. See Wexler, *Who Paid For Modernism?* 13–18.

37. Jonathan Freedman, *Professions of Taste: Henry James, British Aestheticism, and Commodity Culture* (Stanford, CA: Stanford University Press, 1996); Strychacz, *Modernism, Mass Culture, and Professionalism*; Louis Menand, *Discovering Modernism: T. S. Eliot and His Context* (New York: Oxford University Press, 1987). See also Burton J. Bledstein, *The Culture of Professionalism: The Middle Class and the Development of Higher Education in America* (New York: Norton, 1976).

38. George Saintsbury, "The Present State of the English Novel," in *Collected Essays and Papers, 1875–1920* (London: J. M Dent, 1923), 3:120–50. The term "ordinary tradesman" is what is missing from the binary schematic developed by Wexler in *Who Paid For Modernism?*, which opposes the heroically independent "artist" unconcerned with money to the "professional" who makes his or her living by writing. To figure the opposition this way diminishes the degree to which the discourse of professionalism mediated the romantic ideal of the artist and the low-status wage labor of the tradesman, and thus incorporated (variably dominant) elements of both.

39. The classic account of status elevation arising from distance from pure market forces is found in Max Weber, "Class, Status, Party," *From Max Weber: Essays in Sociology*, trans. and ed. H. H. Gerth and C. Wright Mills (New York: Oxford University Press, 1958), 180–95.

40. See Rainey, *Institutions of Modernism*.

41. Quoted in John Tebbel, *Between Covers: The Rise and Transformation of Book Publishing in America* (New York: Oxford University Press, 1987), 85.

42. See Stuart Culver, "Representing the Author: Henry James, Intellectual Property, and the Work of Writing" in *Henry James: Fiction as History*, ed. Ian F. A. Bell (London: Barnes and Noble, 1984), 114–36.

43. Gertrude Stein, *Everybody's Autobiography* (1937; reprint Cambridge, MA: Exact Change, 1993), 41.

44. Carlos Baker, *Ernest Hemingway: A Life Story* (New York: Collier, 1969), 143.

45. Quoted in Delbanco, *Group Portrait*, 181; see also Anesko, *"Friction with the Market,"* 61–78.

46. A more nuanced account of the changing relation between professional group identity and artistic individualism than I give here is available in Menand, *Discovering Modernism*, 97–132.

47. See Malcolm Cowley, *Exile's Return: A Literary Odyssey of the 1920s* (New York: Penguin, 1994), 5.

48. Henry Harrison Brown, *Concentration: The Road to Success: A Lesson in Soul Culture* (Philadelphia: David McKay, 1907); Christian D. Larson, *Brains and How to Get Them* (Los Angeles: New Literature, 1914); A. Victor Segno, *The Law of Mentalism* (Los Angeles: American Institute of Mentalism, 1902); an analysis of the New Thought movement is available in Gail Thain Parker, *Mind Cure in New England, from the Civil War to World War I* (Hanover, NH: University Press of New England, 1973).

49. See, for instance, Jennie A. Kassanoff, "Extinction, Taxidermy, Tableaux Vivants: Staging Race and Class in *The House of Mirth*," *PMLA* 115, no. 1 (January 2000): 60–74, which tries hard to make Wharton's text seem interestingly involved with questions of race.

50. Marriage was of course another means of class mobility and access. Even here, though, the tendency of such works as James's *The Portrait of a Lady* and Edith Wharton's *The House of Mirth* is to conceive the pursuit and practice of marriage precisely in terms of a woman's "career."

51. Joseph Pieper, *Leisure: The Basis of Culture*, intro. T. S. Eliot, trans. Alexander Dru (New York: Pantheon, 1952), 24.

52. Marcus Klein, *Foreigners: The Making of American Literature, 1900–1940* (Chicago: University of Chicago Press, 1981), 7–16. This account is supported by E. Digby Baltzell, *The Protestant Establishment: Aristocracy and Caste in America* (New York: Vintage, 1964).

53. Pierre Bourdieu, *In Other Words*, trans. Matthew Adamson (Stanford, CA: Stanford University Press, 1990), 180.

54. Gertrude Stein, *The Making of Americans* (1925; reprint, Normal, IL: Dalkey Archive, 1995), 34.

55. See Perry Anderson, *The Origins of Postmodernity* (London: Verso, 1998), 103.

56. See, for instance, Alan Swingewood's observation that in "the purely documentary sense, one can see the novel as dealing with much the same social, economic, and political textures as sociology." Diana T. Laurenson and Alan Swingewood, *The Sociology of Literature* (London: MacGibbon and Kee, 1971), 12. The relation between Bourdieu's sociology and Flaubert's fiction is discussed in John Guillory, "Bourdieu's Refusal," *Modern Language Quarterly* 58, no. 4 (December 1997): 367–98.

57. Quoted in Sergio Perosa, *American Theories of the Novel, 1793–1903* (New York: New York University Press, 1985), 148; Howells's appreciation of Veblen is reprinted in Howells, *Criticism and Fiction*, 339–42.

58. Alfred Gell, "The Technology of Enchantment and the Enchantment of Technology," in *Anthropology, Art and Aesthetics*, ed. Jeremy Coote and Anthony Shelton (Oxford: Clarendon Press, 1992), 40–63. The critical potential of philistinism has been intelligently debated in a recent series of essays in the *New Left Review*: see Dave Beech and John Roberts, "Spectres of the Aesthetic," *New Left Review*, no. 218 (July–August 1996): 102–27; Malcolm Bull, "The Ecstasy of Philistinism," *New Left Review*, no. 219 (September–October 1996): 22–41; J. M. Bernstein, "Against Voluptuous Bodies: Of Satiation without Happiness," *New Left Review*, no. 225 (September–October 1997): 89–104; Dave Beech and John Roberts, "Tolerating Impurities: An Ontology, Genealogy, and Defence of Philistinism" *New Left Review*, no. 227 (January–February 1998): 45–71.

59. John Guillory, *Cultural Capital: The Problem of Literary Canon Formation* (Chicago: University of Chicago Press, 1993), 152.

60. Which is not to say that these things—essential superiority and the institutional reproduction of social superiority—are necessarily incompatible, since membership in a family or admission to a school can be taken as evidence of an inborn essence that is only cultivated, not produced, by the institution itself.

61. Joseph Frank, *The Widening Gyre: Crisis and Mastery in Modern Literature* (New Brunswick, NJ: Rutgers University Press, 1963), 3–62.

62. See the beginning of "The Revolutionary Simpleton" (1927), where Lewis claims:

> The profession of the "timeless" doctrine, in any average person, always seems to involve this contradiction: that he will be much more the slave of Time than anybody not so fanatically indoctrinated. An obsession with the temporal scale, a feverish regard for the niceties of fashion, a sick anxiety directed to questions of time and place (that is, of *fashion* and *milieu*), appears to be the psychological concomitant of the possession of a time-theory that denies time its normal reality. (33)

This is a rather large "contradiction" to swallow at the beginning of an account of the period that critiques its romantic submission to temporality. Still, as always, Lewis is on to something important in noticing the ironic link between these theories of timelessness and contemporary (intellectual) fashion.

63. Georg Lukács, *The Theory of the Novel: A Historico-Philosophical Essay on the Forms of Great Epic Literature*, trans. Anna Bostock (Cambridge: MIT Press, 1971).

64. See Fredric Jameson's cogent discussion of this problem in *Marxism and Form: Twentieth-Century Dialectical Theories of Literature* (Princeton: Princeton University Press, 1971), 180.

65. Erin Carlston, *Thinking Fascism: Sapphic Modernism and Fascist Modernity* (Stanford, CA: Stanford University Press, 1998). See also Margaret Bockting, "The Great War and Modern Gender Consciousness: The Subversive Poetics of Djuna Barnes," *Mosaic* 3, no. 1 (September 1997): 21–38; Georgette Fleischer, "Djuna Barnes and T. S. Eliot: The Politics and Poetics of *Nightwood*," *Studies in*

the Novel 30, no. 3 (Fall 1998); Diane Chisholm, "Obscene Modernism: Eros Noir and the Profane Illumination of Djuna Barnes," *American Literature* 61, no. 1 (March 1997): 167–206.

Chapter One
The Mind's Eye and Mental Labor

1. Henry James, *The Golden Bowl* (1909; reprint, New York: Penguin, 1987), 113–19.
2. Quoted in Gore Vidal, introduction to James, *The Golden Bowl*, 11.
3. F. O. Matthiessen, *Henry James: The Major Phase* (New York: Oxford University Press, 1944), 82.
4. Laurence B. Holland, *The Expense of Vision: Essays on the Craft of Henry James* (1962; reprint, Baltimore: Johns Hopkins University Press, 1982), 337.
5. W. J. T. Mitchell, *Picture Theory* (Chicago: University of Chicago Press, 1994), esp. 111–81.
6. Joseph Conrad, preface to *The Nigger of the "Narcissus"* (New York: Norton, 1979), 147.
7. Joseph A. Kestner, *The Spatiality of the Novel* (Detroit: Wayne State University Press, 1978), 87–95.
8. John T. Irwin, *The Mystery to a Solution: Poe, Borges, and the Analytic Detective Story* (Baltimore: Johns Hopkins University Press, 1994), 22.
9. These are collected in John P. Muller and William J. Richardson, eds., *The Purloined Poe: Lacan, Derrida, and Psychoanalytic Reading* (Baltimore: Johns Hopkins University Press, 1988).
10. In his reading of the novel, Leo Bersani notes that prevalence of another kind of triadic formation in James, in which "betrayal takes the form of an [observed] intimacy which excludes its witness." Here, however, exclusion is precisely what makes for intimacy, and so one could note that more primary still than either exclusion or intimacy is a triadic logic that insists on the other as embodied, or other *insofar as* embodied. See Leo Bersani, "The Jamesian Lie," in *A Future for Astyanax: Character and Desire in Literature* (Boston: Little, Brown, 1976), 133.
11. See Philip Horne, *Henry James and Revision: The New York Edition* (Oxford: Oxford University Press, 1990), 5.
12. See Michael Anesko, *"Friction with the Market": Henry James and the Profession of Authorship* (New York: Oxford University Press, 1986), 141–62.
13. On the photographic frontispieces to the New York Edition, see Ira B. Nadel, "Visual Culture: The Photo Frontispieces to the New York Edition," in *Henry James's New York Edition: The Construction of Authorship*, ed. David McWhirter (Stanford, CA: Stanford University Press, 1995), 90–108.
14. A brief account of James and illustration is available in J. Hillis Miller, "The 'Grafted' Image: James on Illustration," in McWhirter, *Henry James's New York Edition*, 138–41.
15. Charles Dudley Warner, *The Complete Writings* (Hartford, CT: American Publishing, 1904), 169; Henry James, "The Art of Fiction," in *Literary Criticism: Essays on Literature, American Writers, English Writers* (New York: Library of America, 1984), 100–110; George Saintsbury, "The Present State of the English

Novel," in *Collected Essays and Papers, 1875–1920* (London: J. M. Dent, 1923), 3:127.

16. The exception, appropriately enough, is the frontispiece to volume 13, containing *The Reverberator*, James's story of obnoxiously intrusive journalism, which gives a glimpse inside one of the hotels of the "hotel-world" that James found to be disturbingly open to an indistinct public.

17. In a brilliant account of James and consumer culture Jean-Christophe Agnew refers to this as a "consuming vision," a formulation that underemphasizes the degree to which Jamesian vision was understood to be *productive* vision, that is, an act not merely of consumption, but also of mental labor. See Jean-Christophe Agnew, "The Consuming Vision of Henry James," in *The Culture of Consumption: Critical Essays in American History, 1880–1980*, ed. Richard Wightman Fox and T. J. Jackson Lears (New York: Pantheon, 1983), 65–100.

18. See the epigraph to this chapter. Regis Debray, "The Book as Symbolic Object," in *The Future of the Book*, ed. Geoffrey Nunberg (Berkeley and Los Angeles: University of California Press, 1996), 139–52.

19. Howells, "The Man of Letters as a Man of Business" in *Criticism and Fiction and Other Essays* (New York: New York University Press, 1959), 298–309.

20. Michael McKeon, *The Origins of the English Novel, 1600–1740* (Baltimore: Johns Hopkins University Press, 1987).

21. Ian Watt, *The Rise of the Novel: Studies in Defoe, Richardson, and Fielding* (Berkeley and Los Angeles: University of California Press, 1957).

22. The conservatism of romance ideology is downplayed in favor of its utopian potential in Fredric Jameson's important essay on genre, "Magical Narratives: On the Dialectical Use of Genre Criticism," in *The Political Unconscious: Narrative as a Socially Symbolic Act* (Ithaca: Cornell University Press, 1981), 103–50.

23. See D. A. Miller, *The Novel and the Police* (Berkeley and Los Angeles: University of California Press, 1988); and Mark Seltzer, *Henry James and the Art of Power* (Ithaca: Cornell University Press, 1984).

24. Nathaniel Hawthorne, *The Complete Novels and Selected Tales* (New York: Modern Library, 1937), 243.

25. Richard Chase, *The American Novel and Its Tradition* (Baltimore: Johns Hopkins University Press, 1980).

26. A helpful analysis of the history and function of the concept of "romance" in twentieth-century American literary criticism—understanding it, in essence, as a reiterated argument for the irrelevance of the question of class and class conflict in American cultural history—is available in William Ellis, *The Theory of the American Romance: An Ideology in American Intellectual History* (Ann Arbor: UMI Research Press, 1989).

27. Nina Baym, "Melodramas of Beset Manhood: How Theories of American Fiction Exclude Women Authors," in *The New Feminist Criticism: Essays on Women, Literature, and Theory*, ed. Elaine Showalter (New York: Pantheon, 1985), 63–80; Jane Tompkins, *Sensational Designs: The Cultural Work of American Fiction, 1790–1860* (New York: Oxford University Press, 1985).

28. Terry Lovell, *Consuming Fiction* (London: Verso, 1987). Another critique of Watt is available in Tony Bennett, *Outside Literature* (New York: Routledge, 1990).

29. See, on the internationality of the "romance" in the nineteenth century, Edwin M. Eigner, *The Metaphysical Novel in England and America: Dickens, Bulwer, Melville, and Hawthorne* (Berkeley and Los Angeles: University of California Press, 1978).

30. Indeed, he seems to offer a textbook case of the respective ideological valences of realism and romance that Watt and McKeon describe: in his relatively impecunious youth, Bulwer was a radical reformist member of Parliament and an author mainly of novels; when in midlife he inherited the family seat in Knebworth, he became a conservative member of Parliament and an author of what he, like Hawthorne, called "Romances."

31. This is already true to the extent that, in Hawthorne as in Bulwer, romance seems to be produced in self-conscious reaction to the perceived dominance of novelistic realism, suggesting that under the umbrella term of "prose fiction" romance competes in, and for, the same cultural space as the novel. As this space is colonized in the name of the novel, we might say, romance finds itself surrounded, eventually appearing merely as a kind of novel. Of course it is not quite this simple. In the work of Marie Corelli, for instance—staggeringly successful author of *A Romance of Two Worlds* (1886) and *The Sorrows of Satan* (1895) but, like Bulwer, virtually erased from literary history except as a foil for Joyce—romance clings to a combative, if vestigial, generic autonomy. But a work such as Conrad and Ford's jointly authored *Romance: A Novel* (1903) suggests, even in its title, the more common state of affairs: the novel dominates, incorporates.

32. Clayton Hamilton, *Materials and Methods of Fiction*, rev. and enl. (New York: Doubleday, 1918).

33. One already sees this splitting begin to occur in a work like Eliot's *Daniel Deronda*, where the speculative metaphysics and mysticism of what Trilling called "the Jewish part" of the novel seems inexplicably to erupt in a text, indeed in a career, otherwise comfortably situated within the parameters of realism. And from this perspective it might be as accurate to say that romance invades the novel, or critiques it from within, as to say that romance is colonized by the novel. Call it the return of the repressed: the attacks on romance that persist in the discourse of realism well into the nineteenth century begin to seem, from this perspective, like symptomatic overkill, as though the spectral authority of romance continues to hover over realism even in its moment of triumph.

34. R. A. Scott-James, *Modernism and Romance* (New York: John Lane, 1908).

35. Frank Norris, *The Responsibilities of the Novelist and Other Literary Essays* (London: Grant Richards, 1903), 211–20.

36. Quoted in Sergio Perosa, *American Theories of the Novel, 1793–1903* (New York: New York University Press, 1985), 147.

37. John Erskine, *The Moral Obligation to Be Intelligent and Other Essays* (Indianapolis, IN: Bobbs-Merrill, 1915).

38. Henry James, *The American* (New York: Norton, 1978), 5.

39. I would agree with Franco Moretti, who has suggested that the oft-noted "fragmentation" of the subject into phenomenological bits in modernism is anything but a sign of the "relativist" humility of the modernist author with respect to the "truth." See Franco Moretti, "The Long Goodbye: *Ulysses* and the End of

Liberal Capitalism," in his *Signs Taken for Wonders*, rev. ed. (London: Verso, 1988), 182–208.

40. Consider, then, the powerful ironies attendant to the staging of *The American* as a play. Leon Edel reports that in order to satisfy provincial audiences, James was forced by producer Edward Compton to, as James put it, "basely gratify their artless instincts" by rewriting the ending so that Newman and Claire will marry. See James, *The American*, 477. Further account of James's agonized relation to the theater, and to the aggressive, quasi-authorial agency of the popular theater audience, is given here in chapter 2.

41. Compare this to Edith Wharton's description of Dick (seen through the eyes of his mother) in the early novella *Sanctuary* (1903):

[H]is enjoyment of beauty was of that happy sort which does not generate the wish for possession. As long as the inner eye had food for contemplation, he cared very little for the deficiencies of his surroundings; or, it might rather be said, he felt, in the sum-total of beauty around him, an ownership of appreciation that left him free from the fret of personal desire. (Edith Wharton, *Madame de Treymes and Three Novellas* [New York: Scribner's, 1995], 158)

42. That Maggie acts as an "artist" of sorts in the second volume of the novel, and that James therefore is drawing a strong analogy between what she does and what he does, has been noted by several critics, including J. A. Ward, who writes that "there are many . . . metaphors that relate Maggie's maneuvers to art. They are neither hyperbolic nor strained, for Maggie really is an artist, one who seeks the ideal fusion of the appearance and the content of her marriage." See J. A. Ward, *The Search for Form: Studies in James's Fiction* (Chapel Hill: University of North Carolina Press, 1967), 213.

43. See, for instance, Philip Weinstein's discussion of this issue: "There is in fact something appalling in the uncritical use of the author's relation to his characters as a model for Maggie's relation to her family. . . . [One shouldn't however undervalue] the beauty and weird sincerity of Maggie's plan, the passion with which James could invest her imaginative concern for 'serenities and dignities and decencies,' for the forms in life." See Philip Weinstein, *Henry James and the Requirements of the Imagination* (Cambridge: Harvard University Press, 1971), 183.

44. A brilliant account of consciousness in James is offered by Sharon Cameron in her *Thinking in Henry James* (Chicago: University of Chicago Press, 1989). By contrast to the account I am giving here, in which consciousness and the property it produces are understood to differentiate persons, Cameron emphasizes the way, for James, consciousness seems to be shared between or across persons.

45. Alternatively, later in the century the trope of incest will reappear in the discourse of American nativism as a means precisely of *retaining* differences between people—in particular between races of people—where it is imagined that incestuous procreation needn't risk the admixture of different kinds of blood. See Walter Benn Michaels, *Our America: Nativism, Modernism, Pluralism* (Durham, NC: Duke University Press, 1995), 1–12.

46. In *Social Formalism: The Novel in Theory from Henry James to the Present* (Stanford, CA: Stanford University Press, 1998), 21–63, Dorothy J. Hale pieces through the complexities of Jamesian perspectivism more patiently than I do here.

See also Sara Blair's helpful "Henry James and the Paradox of Literary Mastery," *Philosophy and Literature* 15 (1991): 89–102.

Chapter Two
Social Geometries

1. Edwin A. Abbott, *Flatland: A Romance of Many Dimensions, by A. Square* (New York: Penguin, 1987).

2. While Abbott uses the term "second dimension," he often seems rather to be describing a minimally three-dimensional world—i.e., "flat" like a (three-dimensional) piece of paper. Hence, in the passage quoted above, the awkward equivocation of "on or in"—neither of which is able to express a two-dimensional relation to a surface. If one removes the requirement that objects must have mass—as in the case of objects of thought, or shadows conceived as objects, or indeed any visual data (light) before they have been cognitively processed as the revelation of a solid object—then one can speak coherently of objects of fewer than three dimensions. Abbott's enterprise has difficulty abiding by this restriction, however, in wanting to represent the existence in Flatland of such things as the apparatus of vision itself (eyes, etc.) and solid bodies in general.

Michel Butor, "The Space of the Novel," in *Inventory*, ed. Richard Howard (New York: Simon and Schuster, 1969), 31–38. There is, by now, an extensive critical literature on the problem of space in the novel. Accounts that I have found particularly helpful include W. J. T. Mitchell, "Spatial Form in Literature: Toward a General Theory," in *The Language of Images*, ed. W.J.T. Mitchell (Chicago: University of Chicago Press, 1980), 271–99; James M. Curtis, "Spatial Form in the Context of Modernist Aesthetics," in *Spatial Form in Narrative*, ed. Jeffrey R. Smitten and Ann Daghistany (Ithaca: Cornell University Press, 1981), 161–78; Joseph A. Kestner, *The Spatiality of the Novel* (Detroit: Wayne State University Press, 1978). While distinct, in emphasis, from either these works or my own, Michael Fried's *Realism, Writing, Disfiguration: On Thomas Eakins and Stephen Crane* (Chicago: University of Chicago Press, 1987) includes an account of the operation of "surface effects" in Crane's writing that has been crucially enabling of my project here.

Though it does not address the question of the virtual interior of fiction as such, Joseph Frank's essay "Spatial Form in Modern Literature," discussed at some length in the introduction to this book, was seminal in initiating inquiry into the question of space in modernist fiction, arguing that modernism's rejection of realist temporal forms in favor of an idea of abstract spatial co-presence (for instance, the "timeless" world of myth) is a symptom of "man's" existential discomfort with history. See Frank, *The Widening Gyre: Crisis and Mastery in Modern Literature* (New Brunswick, NJ: Rutgers University Press, 1963), 3–62.

3. We understand, for instance, that it is of fundamental importance to Eugene in Balzac's *Le Pere Goriot*—fundamental to who Eugene becomes—that he leaves the provinces not for Poughkeepsie but for Paris, that he lodges not somewhere but in Balzac's meticulously described Pension Vacquer. For an account of the question of setting in the novel see Philip Fisher, *Hard Facts: Setting and Form in the American Novel* (New York: Oxford University Press, 1985).

4. As Butor puts it: "Of course, it is first of all in the space of representations that the novel introduces its essential modification, but who can fail to see how information influences both routes and objects [in real space]; how, in fact, beginning with an invention in a novel, objects can be effectively shifted, and the order of trajectories—journeys, voyages, passages, and paths—can be transformed?" Butor, "Space of the Novel," 38.

Texts I have found helpful in understanding the concept of social space—as opposed to representational space (though the relation between the two is what I am trying to get at here)—include David Harvey, *The Condition of Postmodernity* (Cambridge: Blackwood, 1990), 201–307; Philip Fisher, "Appearing and Disappearing in Public: Social Space in Late-Nineteenth-Century Literature and Culture," in *Reconstructing American Literary History*, ed. Sacvan Bercovitch (Cambridge: Harvard University Press, 1986), 155–88; Philip Fisher, "Democratic Social Space: Whitman, Melville, and the Promise of American Transparency," in *The New American Studies: Essays from Representations*, ed. Philip Fisher (Berkeley and Los Angeles: University of California Press, 1991), 70–111. A much darker account of the idea of abstract social space examined by Fisher, in which it becomes a technology of oppressive social regulation, is found in Mary Poovey, "The Production of Abstract Space," in her *Making a Social Body: British Cultural Formation, 1830–1864* (Chicago: University of Chicago Press, 1995), 25–54. Also see Gilles Deleuze and Felix Guattari's influential *A Thousand Plateaus: Capitalism and Schizophrenia*, trans. Brian Massumi (Minneapolis: University of Minnesota Press, 1987), which suggests a remarkably precise materialist inversion of the transcendental project of Abbott's *Flatland*.

5. Clement Greenberg, *The Collected Essays and Criticism*, ed. John O'Brian, 4 vols. (Chicago: University of Chicago Press, 1986–1993). Passages quoted here are from "Towards a Newer Laocoon" (1940), 1:35.

6. In "Towards a Newer Laocoon" Greenberg disables any notion of the naivete of his position when he writes that "it is quite easy to show that abstract art like every other cultural phenomenon reflects the social and other circumstances of the age in which its creators live, and that there is nothing inside art itself, disconnected from history, which compels it to go in one direction or another" (23). The margin of uncertainty that remains in this important qualification of his account of abstract art's self-purification revolves around the word "reflects." Things become more complicated when one argues that abstraction actively *partakes* in and, to a degree, *produces* the circumstances in which it dwells, which makes the theoretical difficulties surrounding the idea of the *social production of asociality* that much clearer.

7. The first two quotations in this sentence are from Clement Greenberg, "Avant-Garde and Kitsch," in his *Collected Essays* 1:9; the last is from Greenberg, "Towards a Newer Laocoon," 1:27.

8. Quoted in Roberto Bonola, *Non-Euclidean Geometry: A Critical and Historical Study of Its Development* (New York: Dover, 1955), 67.

9. Morris Kline, *Mathematics in Western Culture* (New York: Oxford University Press, 1953), 413.

10. Quoted in Linda Dalrymple Henderson, *The Fourth Dimension and Non-Euclidean Geometry in Modern Art* (Princeton: Princeton University Press, 1983), 19.

11. Hermann von Helmholtz, *Popular Lectures on Scientific Subjects*, 2d ser. (London: Longman's, 1881), 35.

12. D. H. Lawrence, "Morality and the Novel," in *Calendar of Modern Letters, March 1925–July 1927*, vol. 2, *September 1925–February 1926*, ed. Edgell Rickward and Douglas Garman (New York: Barnes and Noble, 1966), 269.

13. Wendell Harris, *The Omnipresent Debate: Empiricism and Transcendentalism in Nineteenth-Century English Prose* (DeKalb: Northern Illinois University Press, 1981).

14. This was the central contention of Mme Blavatsky's Theosophy and of "occult" thinkers in general, whose wide influence in the emergence of modernism has tended to be downplayed by later critics. Although attention to the fourth dimension is not notable in the writings of Blavatsky, for her successor P. D. Ouspensky the fourth dimension would become the central concept in his critique of the spiritual poverty of empiricism, elaborated in his *Tertium Organum: The Third Canon of Thought: A Key to the Enigmas of the World* (1920; reprint, New York: Vintage, 1981). For an account of the role of the occult in the emergence of modernism see Leon Surette, *The Birth of Modernism: Ezra Pound, T. S. Eliot, W. B. Yeats, and the Occult* (Montreal: McGill-Queen's University Press, 1993).

15. Henri Bergson, *Matter and Memory*, trans. Nancy Paul and W. Scott Palmer (London: Allen and Unwin, 1911), vii. See, on this aspect of Pater, F. C. McGrath, *The Sensible Spirit: Walter Pater and the Modernist Paradigm* (Tampa: University of South Florida Press, 1986).

16. Friedrich Nietzsche, *On the Genealogy of Morals and Ecce Homo*, trans. Walter Kaufmann (New York: Vintage, 1989), 26.

17. See also Joseph Conrad and Ford Madox Ford's novel *The Inheritors* (1901), where the fourth dimension is a space inhabited by Fabian revolutionaries, i.e., the forces of modernity.

18. E. M. Forster, *Aspects of the Novel* (New York: Harcourt, Brace, 1927), 65–82.

19. More directly, though, Forster lifted the critical concept for which he is most famous from one of the more prominent aesthetic theorists of the late-nineteenth century, Vernon Lee (Violet Paget). In the late essay " 'Imagination Penetrative,' " in her *The Handling of Words and Other Studies in Literary Psychology* (New York: Dodd and Mead, 1923), 280–81, Lee had already spoken of "what I can only call [the] *otherness*," of certain kinds of characters, "of that third dimension in which alone change can take place and life expand." A few years before this the early champion of Henry James, Percy Lubbock, had spoken of the "imaginative faculties" of the reader that allow him or her to give characters "dimensions, to see round them, to make them 'real,' " that "common gift . . . by which we turn . . . flat impressions . . . into solid shapes." See Lubbock, *The Craft of Fiction* (New York: Peter Smith, 1943), 9.

20. Wyndham Lewis, *Time and Western Man*, ed. Paul Edwards (Santa Rosa, CA: Black Sparrow, 1993), 12.

21. Wyndham Lewis, "Henry James, The Arch-Enemy of 'Low Company,' " in *Men without Art* (Santa Rosa, CA: Black Sparrow, 1987), 118. Lewis continues: "It is as a rule not difficult, in fact, by scratching a little the intelligence snob, to find beneath the unlovely veneer that even less commendable sentimentalist out of the Book of Snobs. For no one can really be today a social snob alone. All who in sleepier times would have been simply that, have today become intellectualist. The intellectual world, as much as the Church, provides a refuge for these homeless instincts of the uprooted 'bourgeois.' "

22. It is probably not an accident that at precisely the time James was discovering the power of intellectual distinction, the whole question of innate intelligence and of the "intelligence quotient" was being taken up by figures such as Alfred Binet and others. As I will discuss at length in chapter 4, what this focus on innate intelligence managed is the construction of a meritocratic essentialism, a romance of intelligence, since the blood of higher intelligence could not be suffused in the common schools.

23. Or, for that matter, even of James's friend H. G. Wells, in whose science fiction of the 1890s the question of dimension is a more or less constant presence. Take, for instance, Wells's "The Plattner Story" (1897), in his *The Plattner Story and Others* (London: Methuen, 1897), 2–28. Gottfried Plattner, ignorant instructor of boys, stands before a chemistry class, teaching them nothing. He merely fiddles with a powder, mysterious and green. The scene Wells portrays is as representative of the history of popular elementary education in England, in which teaching had been largely a low-status, uncredentialed occupation, as it is shaded with personal irony. A child of the lower-middle class, Wells was a student of remarkable talent, and owed his social advancement entirely to his education. Something of Wells's memory of obstructions overcome, but also of his good luck, is remembered in the figure of Plattner, who, when the mysterious green powder suddenly explodes, finds his world turned inside out. There is, we are told, an "exoteric" side of Plattner's story, the tale of his disappearance from the schoolroom, of his return nine days later, and of the amazing reversal of all his body parts—heart beating on the wrong side of his chest—as though his mirror image had walked into the world. The esoteric side of Plattner's story is his weird time in a spiritualized "fourth dimension," the higher reality that is not exactly divided from, but interpenetrates the normal world. From this perspective the ghostly higher-dimensional Plattner sees through material obstructions to the hidden truths of his town. This esoteric side of the story, however, cannot be verified by common means.

24. Though my reading of *The Princess Casamassima* departs from theirs in several crucial respects, I have found the accounts of this novel by Lionel Trilling, Mark Seltzer, and Michael Anesko particularly helpful in developing my argument. See Lionel Trilling, *The Liberal Imagination: Essays on Literature and Society* (New York: Viking, 1950), 58–92; Mark Seltzer, *Henry James and the Art of Power* (Ithaca: Cornell University Press, 1984); Michael Anesko, *"Friction with the Market": Henry James and the Profession of Authorship* (New York: Oxford University Press, 1986), 101–18.

25. Henry James, *The Princess Casamassima* (1886; reprint, London: Penguin, 1987), 54.

26. Charles Dudley Warner, "The Novel and the Common School," in *The Complete Writings* (Hartford, CT: American Publishing, 1904), 249–76.

27. The classic account of literacy and readership in England is Richard Altick's *The English Common Reader* (Chicago: University of Chicago Press, 1957). Importantly, one rationale given for the Education Act was explicitly the prior extension by Parliament of the franchise, and thus political power, to the lower classes. When he introduced the bill into Parliament on February 17, 1870, W. E. Forster argued that

> upon this speedy provision depends . . . I fully believe, the good, the safe working of our constitutional system. To its honour, Parliament has lately decided that England shall in future be governed by popular government. I am one of those who would not wait until the people were educated before I would trust them with political power. If we had thus waited we might have waited long for education; but now that we have given them political power we must not wait any longer to give them education.

In this view, education is a way to encourage the masses to use their political power rationally. The characteristic response of the literary elite I am discussing (see the quotation of Edmund Gosse, above) is to deny this notion, suggesting that education simply gives the masses more power in the exertion of their irrationality. This rhetorical move is managed by shifting the terms of the debate from the question of literacy to the quality of the education the masses receive: in this view the masses are not truly civilized in primary schools but merely "quarter-educated." In other words, a little knowledge is dangerous.

28. The most striking response, in this time, to the horror of this intrusion is no doubt George Gissing's *New Grub Street* (1895), which James admired.

29. Henry James, preface to *The Golden Bowl* (1909; reprint, New York: Penguin, 1987).

30. Thus does Hyacinth seem so useful as a potential assassin, since he will be able to gain physical proximity to his target without being noticed as "out of place." The dissonant relation between James's description in the preface and what we see in the novel provides further support, I would argue, for my suggestion below that Hyacinth's penetration of exclusive spaces is understood by James to be in an important sense "fictional" or hallucinatory.

31. Hyacinth is thus, as the preface will make explicit, a sort of alter ego of James himself, his abjected, excluded, lower-class self, with all the complexity of identification and repulsion that relation implies. See Anesko, *"Friction with the Market,"* 101–18. Interestingly enough, 1886 also saw the first appearance of Robert Louis Stevenson's Mr. Hyde, the suddenly unhidden, déclassé double—complete with a flat in the wrong part of town, but with a key to the back door of the lab—of the esteemed Dr. Jekyll. Hyde enters the lab and the life of the respectable Jekyll from the same dirty London streets plied by James's pretty little bookbinder.

32. Henry James, "The Future of the Novel" in *Literary Criticism: Essays on Literature, American Writers, English Writers* (New York: Library of America, 1984), 100.

33. It seems obvious, with a little scrutiny, that the apparently empirical place that James sees crowded with massive novels, a place called "the Anglo-Saxon world," is itself in some measure a virtual entity. No less than in the earlier Malthusian version of overpopulation paranoia—which Frances Ferguson has de-

coded as a concern with the multiplication of politically assertive consciousness, rather than of bodies—the referent of James's "Anglo-Saxon world" is more likely to be found in the social imaginary than in a place in which books are literally "everywhere." See Frances Ferguson, "Malthus, Godwin, Wordsworth, and the Spirit of Solitude," in her *Solitude and the Sublime* (New York: Routledge, 1992), 114–28.

34. Marion Crawford, *The Novel: What It Is* (New York: Macmillan, 1893). An earlier description of the novel-as-theater had been made in the United States by G. A. Lathrop, who in 1874 described the novel as a "portable drama, requiring no stage, no actors, no lights or scenery, and no fixed time of enactment." See Lathrop, "The Novel and Its Future," *Atlantic Monthly* 34 (September 1874), 313.

35. Walter Besant, *The Art of Fiction* (New York: Brentano, 1902), 18–19.

36. Howells, *Criticism and Fiction and Other Essays* (New York: New York University Press, 1959), 87.

37. See John Goode, "The Art of Fiction: Walter Besant and Henry James," in *Tradition and Tolerance in Nineteenth-Century Fiction: Critical Essays on Some English and American Novels*, ed. David Howard (London: Routledge, 1966), 251–62, cited in Anesko, *"Friction with the Market,"* 230n.

38. It is, glancing ahead, precisely this fantasy of friendship that is criticized by Q. D. Leavis in 1930, when the modernist attack on the mass market and the mass reader is given its most systematic elaboration. In Q. D. Leavis, *Fiction and the Reading Public* (London: Chatto and Windus, 1967) the naive mass reader will be disdained on the ground of his "confusion of fiction with life," and with his "co-operat[ing] to persuade himself that he is in contact with 'real people' " who might be his friends. By contrast, the highbrow novelist Leavis champions, if he or she " 'creates' character at all is apt to produce personalities that . . . do not lend themselves to [such] fantas[ies of friendship]" (59–60).

39. Perhaps the purest version of the mass reader who learns from books in *The Princess* is the prostrate Rose Muniment, who never leaves her bed, and about whom it is said, " 'It's very wonderful: she can describe things she has never seen. And they're just like the reality' " (151).

40. In chapter 3 of this work I will be able to take up a crucial feature of the rise of the mass reader I am not addressing here: the fact that this reader is often perceived, by James and Crawford among others, to be female, indeed a young, newly literate female. The problem of gender, one may have noticed, was already troubling and complicating the problem of class identity as elaborated in Abbott's *Flatland*.

41. A well-known instance of this kind of reversal of spatial values is the Symbolist-modernist ideal of poetic "impersonality," where a form of transcendence ("escape from personality" is how Eliot put it) is thought to be gained by authorial self-exclusion from the formerly esoteric spaces of representation.

42. Another tactic, which we have already glimpsed in Leavis's characterization of modernist narrative in *Fiction and the Reading Public*, is to alter representations of literary character such that it becomes ever-more difficult to conceive of these characters as "friends." This, I would argue, is the technique elaborated in the novels of Wyndham Lewis, such as *Tarr*, where the relentless awfulness of the people he represents would disable the reader's habits of identification.

43. H. G. Wells, *The Invisible Man* (London: Collins, 1959), 79, 82.

44. On the increasing anonymity of author/reader relations in the late-nineteenth century, and on the relation between theatricality and authorship, see Barbara Hochman, "Disappearing Authors and Resentful Readers in Late-Nineteenth-Century American Fiction: The Case of Henry James," *ELH* 63 (1996): 177–201.

45. Henry James, *Guy Domville: A Play in Three Acts with comments by Bernard Shaw, H. G. Wells, Arnold Bennett, preceded by biographical chapters from Henry James: The Dramatic Years, by Leon Edel,* ed. Leon Edel (London: Rupert Hart-Davis, 1961), 212–13.

46. In merging the roles of manager and lead actor, George Alexander became for James a figure of the literary character run amok, as though this character has arisen from the prison of the page and begun to dictate his own terms. It was Alexander, for instance, who insisted, against James's objections, that the play be called *Guy Domville*, after the character he would play. One should also note the play's interweaving of political and professional nostalgia: The central dilemma driving the plot—shall the aristocrat Guy retire to the priesthood or shall he be a procreating man of the world, saving the family seat from the hands of the "pack of village bastards" fathered by his uncle?—echoes on a number of levels: we are reminded both of the half-French, illegitimate son of an aristocrat, the reader Hyacinth, who takes possession of the theatrical house of fiction and who threatens to revolt, and of James's professional quandary, playwright and novelist figuring, respectively, as career positions "in" and "out" of the world, since the job of playwright required confronting the "deadly vulgarity and illiteracy of the world one enters, practically, in knocking at a manager's door" (*Domville*, 55).

47. Edmund Gosse, "What Is a Great Poet" in his *Questions at Issue*, quoted in Leavis, *Fiction and the Reading Public*, 190.

48. The beginning of this transition, a sort of retraction of his texts from the space of social performance, can be seen in the preface to the first volume of James's *Theatricals* (London: Osgood, 1894), where James managed to publish the plays that no one wanted to perform:

The covers of the book may, in a seat that costs nothing, figure the friendly curtain, and the legible "lines" the various voices on the stage; so that if these things manage at all to disclose a picture or drop a tone into the reader's ear the ghostly ordeal will in a manner have passed and the dim foot-lights faced. (vi)

49. Henry James, *What Maisie Knew* (Oxford: Oxford University Press, 1980), 268.

50. Floyd Dell, *Intellectual Vagabondage* (New York: Doran, 1926), 208.

51. My account thus differs in emphasis from Ross Posnock's valuable discussion of James as a culture critic, *The Trial of Curiosity: Henry James, William James, and the Challenge of Modernity* (New York: Oxford University Press, 1991), where it is argued that in imagining a "politics of non-identity," James in some respects prefigures the positions taken up by leftist cultural critics later in the century. Posnock makes much of openness-to-the-unpredictable suggested in James's claim, in the first of his "American Letters" (1898), that the uncertain implications of the rise of the mass market audience "suggest for the critic—even for the critic least sure of where the chase will bring him out—a delicious rest from

the oppressive *a priori*" (James, *Literary Criticism*, 651). While this does make James appear a rather game observer of the suddenly "huge, homogenous and fast-growing population from which the flood of books issues and to which it returns" (651)—we should also note the proto-Leavisite nature of James's fantasy, a few pages later, of what this situation might produce:

> It is . . . just from the very force of the conditions making for reaction in spots and phases that the liveliest appeal of future American production may spring— reaction, I mean, against the grossness of any view, any taste or tone, in danger of becoming so extravagantly general as to efface the really interesting thing, the traceability of the individual. Then, for all I know, we may get individual publics positively more sifted and evolved than anywhere else, shoals of fish rising to more delicate bait. (654)

In other words, the best that James can hope for the undifferentiated, deindividualizing mass culture is that it will make things *so generally bad* that a "more delicate" literature, and a more delicate "public," will be produced in reaction to it. Thus, while James does not go in here for the elitist hysteria of Edmund Gosse (quoted above), ranting about the "revolution against taste," his view of mass culture nonetheless seems explicitly, even technically, reactionary.

Chapter Three
Downward Mobilities

1. That the project of Howells and other American realists was one of "masculinizing" the novel is argued by Michael Davitt Bell in *The Problem of American Realism: Studies in the Cultural History of an Idea* (Chicago: University of Chicago Press, 1993); accounts of modernism as a remasculinization of culture include Sandra M. Gilbert and Susan Gubar, *No Man's Land: the Place of the Woman Writer in the Twentieth Century*, 3 vols. (New Haven: Yale University Press, 1988–94); Ann Douglas, *Terrible Honesty: Mongrel Manhattan in the 1920s* (New York: Farrar, Straus and Giroux, 1995); and Andreas Huyssen, *After the Great Divide: Modernism, Mass Culture, Postmodernism* (Bloomington: Indiana University Press, 1986), 44–64.

2. Henry James, *The Princess Casamassima* (1886; reprint, London: Penguin, 1987), 79.

3. Mark Seltzer, *Bodies and Machines* (New York: Routledge, 1992).

4. Hyacinth is said to be "*ab ovo* a revolutionary," and he does sign on with a group of anarchists, and yet it is the "nature of his mind" to be "perpetually, almost morbidly, conscious that the circle in which he lived was an infinitesimally small, shallow eddy in the roaring vortex of London." Thus, though he remains a laborer on the outside of books, he seems a natural born "insider," or perhaps "outsider"— in any case a writer—in that his "imagination plunged again and again into the waves that whirled past it and round it, in the hope of being carried to some brighter, happier vision—the vision of societies in which, in splendid rooms" distinguished people "talked about art, literature, history" (145). But that this active imagination is said to be *in his nature*, it might seem that James entirely violates the tenets of naturalism when, soon enough, the real world seems with uncanny servitude to respond to its demands, carrying Hyacinth into the very "splendid

rooms" from which he was supposed to have been shut out. He befriends the Princess Casamassima, who encloses him in a womb of luxury only ambiguously continuous with the "outer world" that, when Hyacinth explores the glorious rooms of the Princess's house, Medley, he "forgot." The point, however, is that in naturalizing the imagination, placing it on equal footing with natural fact, James has made both the project of naturalism and the life of Hyacinth somewhat incoherent, suffusing both with a volatile mix of fiction and fact, of internal and external sources of causality, whose relation can no longer be understood, let alone legislated.

5. See James's observation that " 'L'Assommoir' had not been one of the literary things that creep humbly into the world. Its 'success' may be cited as almost insolently prompt, and the fact remains true if the idea of success be restricted, after the inveterate fashion, to the idea of circulation." Henry James, *Literary Criticism: French Writers, Other European Writers, the Prefaces to the New York Edition* (New York: Library of America, 1984), 882.

6. Mark Seltzer, *Henry James and the Art of Power* (Ithaca: Cornell University Press, 1984), 19.

7. This critique of Foucauldian criticism was lodged early on by Gerald Graff in "American Criticism Left and Right," in *Ideology in Classic American Literature*, ed. Sacvan Bercovitch and Myra Jehlen (New York: Cambridge University Press, 1986), 114–15. See also David Swartz, *Culture and Power: The Sociology of Pierre Bourdieu* (Chicago: University of Chicago Press, 1997), 79n.

8. The evident affinities, personal and theoretical, between Foucault and Pierre Bourdieu have no doubt retarded the recognition that Bourdieu's sociology implicitly questions the tendency, on the part of Foucauldian literary criticism to exaggerate the power of its object—as though the discourse of literature, disclaiming its investment in power, weren't to some degree, as a matter of historical fact, taken at its word. And yet Bourdieu's sociology seems to me less compelling as a strong critique of the Foucauldian account of the "art of power" than as a goad to a more interesting, because more highly textured, history.

9. See, for instance, Pierre Bourdieu, *The Rules of Art: Genesis and Structure of the Literary Field*, trans. Susan Emanuel (Stanford, CA: Stanford University Press, 1996), 114–20.

10. A sustained account of James's relation to naturalism is available in Lyall H. Powers, *Henry James and the Naturalist Movement* (Michigan: Michigan State University Press, 1971).

11. In 1876 James had observed of Zola that, "[u]nfortunately the real, for him, means exclusively the unclean, and he utters his crudities with an air of bravado which makes them doubly intolerable" (*French Writers*, 861). A few years later, in his review of *Nana* (1880), James demanded to know "[o]n what authority does M. Zola represent nature to us as a combination of the cesspool and the house of prostitution? On what authority does he represent foulness rather than fairness as the sign we are to know her by?" (*French Writers*, 866).

12. Stephen Crane, *Maggie: A Girl of the Streets* (1893/1896; reprint, New York: Norton, 1979), 3–4.

13. Howard Horwitz has recently used this opening passage to work through the antinomies of agency in what he calls the "sociological paradigm" in the late-nineteenth century, where a belief in passive environmental determinism coincides

with sociological dreams of transcendent agency. My account of Crane and other New York writers will harmonize with this argument to a degree, with the difference that I will be emphasizing how cultural narrative in this period, while it is understood to explain or control the subject, also is seen as a vehicle and object of aspiration *for* the subject. See Howard Horwitz, "*Maggie* and the Sociological Paradigm," *American Literary History* 10 (Winter 1998): 606–63.

14. Jacob A. Riis, *How the Other Half Lives: Studies among the Tenements of New York* (New York: Dover, 1971), 13.

15. Stephen Crane, *Letters*, ed. R. W. Stallman and Lillian Gilkes (New York: New York University Press, 1960).

16. O. Henry [William Sydney Porter], *41 Stories* (New York: Signet, 1984).

17. Edith Wharton and Ogden Codman, Jr., *The Decoration of Houses* (New York: Scribner's, 1897).

18. Edith Wharton, *The House of Mirth* (New York: Penguin, 1985), 287.

19. A helpful account of the cultural context of Will Porter's fiction is available in Christopher Wilson, "One over the Counter: O. Henry and the Loyal Employee," in his *The Labor of Words: Literary Professionalism in the Progressive Era* (Athens: University of Georgia Press, 1985), 25–55.

20. See, for instance, R. W. B. Lewis, *Edith Wharton: A Biography* (New York: Harper and Row, 1975); on the nexus of gender and vocation in *The House of Mirth* see Candace Waid, *Edith Wharton's Letters from the Underworld: Fictions of Women and Writing* (Chapel Hill: University of North Carolina Press, 1991), 15–50.

21. Elaine Showalter, "The Death of the Lady (Novelist): Wharton's *House of Mirth*," in *Edith Wharton: Modern Critical Views*, ed. Harold Bloom (New York: Chelsea House, 1986), 142.

22. Christopher Benfey, *The Double Life of Stephen Crane* (New York: Knopf, 1992). See also James B. Colvert, *Stephen Crane* (New York: Harcourt Brace Jovanovich, 1984); and Michael Robertson, *Stephen Crane, Journalism, and the Making of Modern American Literature* (New York: Columbia University Press, 1997). Robertson argues that what had been a blanket hostility to journalism in the generation of James and Howells is transformed after Crane into an acceptance of the journalist as a fellow literary artist. Rather, one would want to argue that in the discourse of the novel there had always been, and continued to be, an agonized relation between journalism and the realist novel as two discourses of truth. Robertson can sustain his narrative of status conversion only by changing the terms of the argument in midcourse, deciding by critical fiat, for instance, to discount Hemingway's strong sense of the status difference between his journalism and his fiction as kinds of writing. He thus misses the subtler manipulations of status involved in Hemingway's explaining (to himself and others) how a prose style that did indeed bear a strong resemblance to terse newspaper prose was actually the highest and purest literary form.

23. See Huyssen, *After the Great Divide*, 44–64.

24. As for the obscurities of Crane's creed: Why, for instance, if it is acknowledged as a "substitute" for nature, does "art" remain beholden to nature?

25. See Michael Fried, *Realism, Writing, Disfiguration: On Thomas Eakins and Stephen Crane* (Chicago: University of Chicago Press, 1987).

26. Luce Irigaray, *Speculum of the Other Woman*, trans. Gillian C. Gill (Ithaca: Cornell University Press, 1985), 229.

27. I take it that Seltzer's "logistics" is meant to scale down the totalizing pretensions of earlier New Historicist conceptions of a cultural "logic," and yet one can see the case in precisely the reverse terms: not explicable in terms of anything other than itself, the body-machine complex achieves something like the authority of the poem in New Criticism, which is violated by the "heresy of paraphrase." Foreclosing, in advance, the possibility of finding a historical explanation of the body-machine complex he describes, Seltzer reinstalls, as negation, the totalizations he wants to criticize. And yet surely the point is that *we don't know* if we can find an adequate and useful historical explanation for the body-machine complex, and *we won't know* unless we are allowed to try.

28. I allude to Crane's "Experiment in Misery" (in Stephen Crane, *"The Red Badge of Courage," "Maggie: A Girl of the Streets," and Other Selected Writings*, ed. Phyllis Frus and Stanley Corkin [Boston: Houghton Mifflin, 2000], 130–38), the newspaper piece he wrote after impersonating a member of the "other half." This and other acts of class-passing are analyzed by Eric Shocket in "Undercover Explorations of the 'Other Half,' or The Writer as Class Transvestite," *Representations* 64 (Fall 1998): 109–33.

29. Quoted in Alfred Kazin, *On Native Ground: An Interpretation of Modern American Prose Literature* (New York: Reynal and Hitchcock, 1941), 5.

30. William Dean Howells, *A Hazard of New Fortunes* (New York: New American Library, 1965), 17.

31. John Dos Passos, *Manhattan Transfer* (Boston: Houghton Mifflin, 1953).

32. John Dos Passos, *One Man's Initiation, 1917* (Lanham, MD: University Press of America, 1969), 8.

Chapter Four
Highbrows and Dumb Blondes

1. Anita Loos, *Gentlemen Prefer Blondes: The Illuminating Diary of a Professional Lady* (London: Penguin, 1992), 13.

2. H. L. Mencken, "The Sahara of the Bozart" (1920), collected in *A Mencken Chrestomathy* (1949; reprint, New York: Vintage, 1982), 184.

3. A interesting precursor to, and gender inversion of, *Gentlemen Prefer Blondes* is Ring Lardner's *You Know Me Al* (1914), which is organized as a collection of letters home from a dimwitted, egotistical baseball player.

4. Susan Hegeman, "Taking Blondes Seriously," *American Literary History* 7 no. 3 (Fall 1995): 530.

5. See Hegeman, "Taking Blondes Seriously," 531.

6. Willard Huntington Wright, *The Creative Will: Studies in the Philosophy and Syntax of Aesthetics* (New York: John Lane, 1916), 140–41.

7. Wyndham Lewis, *Time and Western Man*, ed. Paul Edwards (Santa Rosa, CA: Black Sparrow Press, 1993), 55–60.

8. Alfred Kazin, "The Writer and the University," in his *The Inmost Leaf: A Selection of Essays* (New York: Harcourt, Brace, 1955), 244.

9. Thomas Strychacz, *Modernism, Mass Culture, and Professionalism* (New York: Cambridge University Press, 1993).

10. It is an oft-noted irony that New Critical methodologies, accused of an anti-historical and elitist formalism, owed some of their success to their sociological efficiency in the context of expanded access to the university. Staging a close encounter with the literary text, New Criticism suggests that the meaning of this text is derivable without the cumbersome apparatus of traditional, "gentlemanly" erudition. See, for instance, Gerald Graff, *Professing Literature: An Institutional History* (Chicago: University of Chicago Press, 1987), 163.

11. Henry Adams, *The Education of Henry Adams*, intro. Leon Wieseltier (New York: Vintage, 1990), 56.

12. Carl Van Vechten, *The Blind Bow-Boy* (New York: Knopf, 1923).

13. F. Scott Fitzgerald, *The Beautiful and Damned* (New York: Scribner's, 1922), 257.

14. See Graff, *Professing Literature*, 147.

15. H. L. Mencken, *H. L. Mencken's "Smart Set" Criticism*, ed. William H. Nolte (Washington, DC: Gateway, 1987), 20.

16. See Graff, *Professing Literature*, 121–79.

17. See, for instance, John G. Richardson, "Historical Sequences and the Origins of Common Schooling in the American States," in *Handbook of Theory and Research for the Sociology of Education*, ed. John G. Richardson (New York: Greenwood, 1986), 35–64.

18. Wyndham Lewis, *The Art of Being Ruled* (Santa Rosa, CA: Black Sparrow, 1989), 105.

19. S. N. Behrman, introduction to *"The Smart Set": A History and Anthology*, by Carl Dolmetsch (New York: Dial, 1966), xxi.

20. Willard Huntington Wright, *I Used to Be a Highbrow, but Look at Me Now* (New York: Scribner's, 1929)

21. The history of intelligence testing is examined in Stephen Jay Gould, *The Mismeasure of Man*, rev. and exp. [to include a critique of Charles Murray's *The Bell Curve*] (New York: Norton, 1996); and in Raymond E. Fancher, *The Intelligence Men: Makers of the IQ Controversy* (New York: Norton, 1985).

22. Charles Spearman, *The Nature of "Intelligence" and the Principles of Cognition* (London: Macmillan, 1927), 15.

23. John Erskine, *The Moral Obligation to Be Intelligent and Other Essays* (Indianapolis, IN: Bobbs-Merrill, 1915), 3–34.

24. Henry Herbert Goddard, *The Kallikak Family* (New York: Macmillan, 1914), 101–2.

25. Anita Loos, *But Gentlemen Marry Brunettes: The Illuminating Diary of a Professional Lady* (New York: Penguin, 1992), 10.

26. See Fancher, *Intelligence Men*, 5–18.

27. E. Digby Baltzell, in *The Protestant Establishment: Aristocracy and Caste in America* (New York: Vintage, 1964), describes a general tendency of American elites in this period to move from ideologies of "class" to ideologies of "caste."

28. Carl C. Brigham, *A Study of American Intelligence* (Princeton: Princeton University Press, 1923), 210.

29. This notion became the fulcrum of an acrimonious debate between Walter Lippmann and Lewis Terman in the *New Republic*. Lippmann was quick to point out the absurdity of the notion that the "average adult intelligence of a representative sample of the nation is that of an immature child in that same nation. The average adult intelligence cannot be less than the average adult intelligence." See N. J. Block and Gerald Dworkin, eds., *The IQ Controversy: Critical Readings* (New York: Pantheon, 1976), 4–44.

30. See Walter Benn Michaels, *Our America: Nativism, Modernism, and Pluralism* (Durham, NC: Duke University Press, 1995); and Michael North, *The Dialect of Modernism: Race, Language, and Twentieth-Century Literature* (New York: Oxford University Press, 1994).

31. It would not be too much of a stretch, pursuing this logic into *Gentlemen Prefer Blondes*, to see in Lorelei Lee's white trash blondeness the inverted mark of a pseudo-blackness, an explicit racial identity that is transposed to her maid, Lulu, for whom Lorelei shows a liberal regard:

> I told Lulu to let all the house work go and spend the day reading a book entitled "Lord Jim" and then tell me all about it, so that I would improve my mind while Gerry is away. But when I got her the book I nearly made a mistake and gave her a book by the title of "The Nigger of the Narcissus" which really would have hurt her feelings. I mean I do not know why authors cannot say "Negro" instead of "Nigger" as they have their feelings just the same as we have. (33)

It hardly needs to be said that, with Mark Twain, Conrad was perhaps the writer that Mencken most admired. That it is Lulu who will actually read *Lord Jim* and then tell Lorelei about it echoes Mencken's sentiment that such worthwhile culture as *has* emerged from the South in recent years has been produced by Negroes of "mixed blood, usually with the white predominating."

32. Gertrude Stein, *Three Lives* (New York: Vintage), 200, 86.

33. Werner Sollers, *Neither Black nor White yet Both: Thematic Explorations of Interracial Literature* (New York: Oxford University Press, 1997).

34. Indeed, it is useful to compare the neurotic complexity and intelligence of Melanctha, as imagined by a former psychological researcher and medical student, to the simplicity of Lorelei, who when she is brought to see "Dr Froyd" in Vienna proves incapable of being assimilated to his depth psychology: "So Dr Froyd and I had quite a long talk in the english landguage. So it seems that everybody seems to have a thing called inhibitions, which is when you want to do a thing and you do not do it." Discovering that Lorelei has neither inhibitions nor dreams, Freud calls in his "assistance and he pointed at me and talked to his assistance in the Viennese landguage. So then his assistance looked at me and looked at me and it really seems as if I was quite a famous case. So then Dr Froyd said that all I needed was to cultivate a few inhibitions and get some sleep" (118–19).

35. Lucien Lévy-Bruhl, *How Natives Think*, trans. Lilian A. Clare (1925; reprint, New York: Arno Press, 1979), 19. The anthropological discourse of the "primitive mind," as it relates in particular to the formation of T. S. Eliot, is helpfully discussed by Ronald Bush in "The Presence of the Past: Ethnographic Thinking/Literary Politics," in *Prehistories of the Future: The Primitivist Project and the*

Culture of Modernism, ed. Elazar Barkan and Ronald Bush (Stanford, CA: Stanford University Press, 1995), 23–41.

36. North, *The Dialect of Modernism*, 73.

37. Gertrude Stein, "Portraits and Repetition," in *Writings, 1932–1946* (New York: Library of America, 1998).

38. John T. Matthews, *The Play of Faulkner's Language* (Ithaca: Cornell University Press, 1982), 73.

39. Noel Polk, *Children of the Dark House: Text and Context in Faulkner* (Jackson: University Press of Mississippi, 1996), 105.

40. Polk, *Children of the Dark House*, 101.

Chapter Five
Faulkner's Ambit

1. Cleanth Brooks, *William Faulkner: The Yoknapatawpha Country* (New Haven: Yale University Press, 1963), 2.

2. William Faulkner, *The Marble Faun* (Boston: Four Seas, 1924), 6.

3. John Dos Passos, *The Major Nonfictional Prose*, ed. Donald Pizer (Detroit: Wayne State University Press, 1988), 36–37.

4. Malcolm Cowley, introduction to *The Portable Faulkner*, rev. ed. (New York: Penguin, 1967), vii.

5. See Lawrence H. Schwarz, *Creating Faulkner's Reputation: The Politics of Modern Literary Criticism* (Knoxville: University of Tennessee Press, 1988). While he does not discuss the long thread of attempts to ground Faulkner in his "native soil," stretching from Stone to Cowley to Brooks and beyond, that I am following here, Schwarz's study is a model of its kind, ably discussing the Cold War recruitment of Faulkner to a New Critical modernist aesthetic emphasizing the freedom of individual expression under capitalism.

6. Malcolm Cowley, *Exile's Return: A Literary Odyssey of the 1920s* (New York: Penguin, 1994), 27.

7. Allen Tate, "Remarks on the Southern Religion," in *I'll Take My Stand: The South and the Agrarian Tradition* (New York: Harper and Brothers, 1930), 171, quoted in Frederick J. Hoffman, *The Twenties: American Writing in the Postwar Decade*, rev. ed. (London: Free Press, 1962), 176.

8. Michael Grimwood, *Heart in Conflict: Faulkner's Struggles with Vocation* (Athens: University of Georgia Press, 1987). While it is tied to a somewhat distracting (to me) superstructure derived from Eriksonian psychology, Grimwood's is an extremely compelling and plausible reconstruction of the "pastoral" contradictions informing Faulkner's career as a Southern modernist, and of the way these contradictions are made manifest in the fiction.

9. William Faulkner, *A Green Bough* (New York: Harrison Smith, 1933), 67. Quoted in Joseph Blotner, *Faulkner: A Biography*, 1-vol. ed. (New York: Vintage, 1991), 69.

10. See also Andre Bleikasten, *The Ink of Melancholy: Faulkner's Novels from "The Sound and the Fury" to "Light in August"* (Bloomington: Indiana University Press, 1990), 1–37. Further accounts of Faulkner's early years are available in

Martin Kreiswirth, *William Faulkner: The Making of a Novelist* (Athens: University of Georgia Press, 1983); and Michael Kreyling, *Inventing Southern Literature* (Jackson: University of Mississippi Press, 1998), 126–36.

11. Carolyn Porter, *Seeing and Being: The Plight of the Participant Observer in Emerson, James, Adams, and Faulkner* (Middletown, CT: Wesleyan University Press, 1981), 207.

12. William Faulkner, *Sartoris* (New York: Random House, 1956), 375, an edited version of the novel eventually published in complete form as *Flags in the Dust* (New York: Vintage, 1974).

13. William Faulkner, *Early Prose and Poetry*, ed. Carvel Collins (Boston: Atlantic–Little, Brown, 1962), 94.

14. A useful parallel to Faulkner's career move toward his Southern "home" would be Thomas Wolfe's version of the same in *Look Homeward, Angel* (1929).

15. William Faulkner, *Light in August* (New York: Vintage, 1972), 5.

16. Quoted in Blotner, *Faulkner: A Biography*, 123.

17. James B. Meriwether and Michael Millgate, eds., *Lion in the Garden: Interviews with William Faulkner, 1926–1962* (New York: Random House, 1968), 255.

18. Doreen Fowler, introduction to *Faulkner and the Southern Renaissance: Faulkner and Yoknapatawpha, 1981*, ed. Doreen Fowler and Ann J. Abadie (Jackson: University Press of Mississippi, 1982), viii. See also Kreyling, *Inventing Southern Literature*, 127.

19. W. J. Cash, *The Mind of the South* (New York: Vintage, 1941), vii.

20. F. R. Leavis, *Mass Civilisation and Minority Culture* (Cambridge: Minority Press, 1930).

21. Floyd C. Watkins, "What Stand Did Faulkner Take?" in Fowler and Abadie, *Faulkner and the Southern Renaissance*.

22. Reprinted in M. Thomas Inge, ed., *William Faulkner: The Contemporary Reviews* (Cambridge: Cambridge University Press, 1995), 27.

23. The same would be true after World War II, when, as discussed by Schwarz, Faulkner's regional racination would enable his global circulation as a poet of the universal "nature of man." On Faulkner's relation to and participation in 1920s discourses of American nativism, see Walter Benn Michaels, *Our America: Nativism, Modernism, and Pluralism* (Durham, NC: Duke University Press, 1995).

24. William R. Taylor, *Cavalier and Yankee: The Old South and the American National Character* (New York: Oxford University Press, 1993).

25. William Faulkner, *Absalom, Absalom!* (New York: Vintage, 1990).

26. On the relation of regionalism to nationalism, see Roberto Maria Dainotto, " 'All the Regions Do Smilingly Revolt': The Literature of Place and Region," *Critical Inquiry* 22 (Spring 1996): 486–505.

27. Myra Jehlen, *Class and Character in Faulkner's South* (New York: Columbia University Press, 1976), 9.

28. See also Hugh Kenner, "Faulkner and the Avant-Garde," in *Faulkner: A Collection of Critical Essays*, ed. Richard H. Brodhead (Englewood Cliffs, NJ: Prentice-Hall, 1983), 62–73.

29. This is the difficulty that Floyd Watkins is bumping against when he says that, "[s]trangely, Faulkner and the Fugitive-Agrarians all preached anti-intellectualism even though they were themselves intellectuals" (53). For systematic ac-

countings of Faulkner's connections to the modernist movement, see Thomas L. McHaney, "Faulkner and Modernism: Why Does It Matter?" eds. Doreen Fowler and Ann J. Abadie, *New Directions in Faulkner Studies: Faulkner and Yoknapatawpha, 1983* (Jackson: University Press of Mississippi, 1984), 37–60; Daniel J. Singal, *William Faulkner: The Making of a Modernist* (Chapel Hill: University of North Carolina Press, 1997).

30. Evelyn Scott, *On William Faulkner's "The Sound and the Fury"* (New York: Cape and Smith, 1929), 5.

31. An informative account of the career opportunities represented by regional fiction in the late-nineteenth century is found in Richard H. Brodhead, "Regionalism and the Upper Class" in *Rethinking Class: Literary Studies and Social Formations*, ed. Wai Chee Dimock and Michael T. Gilmore (New York: Columbia University Press, 1994), 150–74.

32. Malcolm Cowley, *The Portable Malcolm Cowley* (New York: Viking, 1990), 349.

33. William Faulkner, *Selected Letters*, ed. Joseph Blotner (New York: Vintage, 1978), 90.

34. On Faulkner's investment in anticommercial "Cavalier ideology" see Kevin Railey, "Cavalier Ideology and History: The Significance of Quentin's Section in *The Sound and the Fury*," *Arizona Quarterly* 48, no. 3 (Autumn 1992): 77–94.

35. See, for instance, Eric Sundquist, *Faulkner: The House Divided* (Baltimore: Johns Hopkins University Press, 1983), 123.

36. William Faulkner, *The Unvanquished: The Corrected Text* (New York: Vintage, 1991), 140–41.

37. See for instance Andre Bleikasten, "Faulkner and the New Ideologues," in *Faulkner and Ideology: Faulkner and Yoknapatawpha, 1992*, ed. Donald M. Kartiganer and Ann J. Abadie (Jackson: University Press of Mississippi, 1995), 3–21.

38. William Faulkner, *Mosquitoes* (New York: Liveright, 1997), 52.

39. A thorough accounting of the influences and allusions in Faulkner's second novel is available in Edwin Arnold, *Annotations to Faulkner's "Mosquitoes"* (New York: Garland, 1989).

40. William Faulkner, *The Sound and the Fury: The Corrected Text* (New York: Vintage, 1990), 94, italics in original.

Chapter Six
Making "Literature" of It

1. On Poe's relation to mass culture see Jonathan Elmer, *Reading at the Social Limit: Affect, Mass Culture, and Edgar Allan Poe* (Stanford, CA: Stanford University Press, 1996).

2. Quoted in John Loughery, *Alias S. S. Van Dine* (New York: Scribner's, 1992), 180.

3. Willard Huntington Wright, *A Man of Promise* (New York: John Lane, 1916), 111.

4. S. S. Van Dine, *I Used to Be a Highbrow, but Look at Me Now.* See Loughery, *Alias S. S. Van Dine*, 203.

5. S. S. Van Dine, *The Benson Murder Case* (New York: Scribner's, 1926), 15.

6. See Van Dine, *Benson Murder Case*, 84; S. S. Van Dine, *The "Canary" Murder Case* (New York: Scribner's, 1927).

7. Van Wyck Brooks, *America's Coming of Age* (Garden City, NY: Doubleday Anchor, 1958), 1–19.

8. D. A. Miller, *The Novel and the Police* (Berkeley and Los Angeles: University of California Press, 1988).

9. Gertrude Stein, *Writings and Lectures, 1911–1945* (London: Peter Owen, 1967), 149.

10. Waldo Frank, *Chalk Face* (New York: Boni and Liveright, 1924).

11. Quoted in Joan Shelley Rubin, *The Making of Middlebrow Culture* (Chapel Hill: University of North Carolina Press, 1992), xix; see also Janice A. Radway, *A Feeling for Books: The Book-of-the-Month Club, Literary Taste, and Middle-Class Desire* (Chapel Hill: University of North Carolina Press, 1997).

12. For the some of the philosophical implications of Symbolist self-inclusion, see John T. Irwin, *The Mystery to a Solution: Poe, Borges, and the Analytic Detective Story* (Baltimore: Johns Hopkins University Press, 1994).

13. Quoted in Diane Johnson, *Dashiell Hammett: A Life* (New York: Ballantine, 1983), 72.

14. Alfred A. Knopf, Inc., Papers (Dashiell Hammett), Harry Ransom Humanities Research Center, University of Texas at Austin.

15. See Willa Cather et al., *Alfred Knopf: Quarter Century* (New York: Doubleday Anchor, 1958), 10.

The antecedents of modernism's concern with the material forms of publication are of course several, and difficult to trace into the twentieth century with precision. This is especially true in the case of Hammett, who had little formal education, and whose reputedly voracious autodidactic efforts remain only partially documented and specified. But one's attention is drawn, for instance, to Mallarmé's influential and obsessive attention to printing, typography, and the book, discussed briefly in chapter 2. This concern was also pursued in England, though on somewhat different grounds, by William Morris. The juxtaposition of Hammett and Mallarmé, odd as it may at first seem, would be tempting, if only for their shared literary paternity in the figure of Poe. In his essay on the material forms of publication, "The Book: A Spiritual Instrument" (1895), Mallarmé harshly criticizes debased periodical forms like the newspaper, claiming instead that "all earthly existence must ultimately be contained in a book," a unified Book of Life that can be "observe[d] with the eyes of the divinity." This divine, totalized vision is to be achieved not by representation, as in the ideal of the encyclopedia, but in the resonating interstices of the materiality of the Symbolist text itself. At this level, Mallarmé suggests, the separate identities limned by language break down and merge in the larger unity of an occult Being. This Being is not "periodical"—that is, conditioned by the temporal exigencies of history—but "timeless." See Stephane Mallarmé, *Selected Prose Poems, Essays, and Letters* (Baltimore: Johns Hopkins University Press, 1956). Mallarmé was thus at least one important source of the difficult, totalizing terms that would inform so much of what we now think of as the modernist project, including Gide's aspiration in *The Counterfeiters* "to put everything into" his novel, "everything I see, everything I know." This "everything"

NOTES TO CHAPTER SIX

NOTES TO CHAPTER SIX   **211**

even encompasses, to dizzying reflexive effect, the composition of a novel called *The Counterfeiters*. It is in this apparently unlikely context, I think, that we can make sense of Hammett's aspiration to "take the detective story seriously"—to "make 'literature' of it"—as well.

16. W.H., "The Peak of Mystery Fiction" *Courier Journal* (January 28, 1934); Anonymous, *Kansas City Journal Post* (January 7, 1934). These clippings are contained in the Hammett Papers, Harry Ransom Humanities Research Center, University of Texas at Austin.

17. Dashiell Hammett, *The Big Knockover: Selected Stories and Short Novels* (New York: Vintage, 1989).

18. Q. D. Leavis, *Fiction and the Reading Public*, 59.

19. Dashiell Hammett, *The Maltese Falcon* (New York: Vintage, 1992).

20. Quoted in Richard Layman, *Shadow Man: The Life of Dashiell Hammett* (New York: Harcourt Brace Jovanovich, 1981), 103.

21. Dashiell Hammett, *The Dain Curse* (New York: Vintage, 1989), 39.

22. Two other titles Hammett pondered for what eventually became *Red Harvest*—"The Seventeenth Murder" and "Murder Plus"—would have indicated the mathematical sublimity of this bloody project.

23. Dashiell Hammett, *Red Harvest* (New York: Vintage, 1989), 154.

24. Quoted in Lawrence Levine, *Highbrow/Lowbrow: The Emergence of Cultural Hierarchy in America* (Cambridge: Harvard University Press, 1988), 171.

25. See William Marling, *The American Roman Noir: Hammett, Cain, and Chandler* (Athens: University of Georgia Press, 1995), 116–18.

26. Letter dated February 11, 1928, Hammett Papers, Ransom Humanities Center.

27. Letter dated March 20, 1928, Hammett Papers, Ransom Humanities Center.

28. Hammett Papers, Ransom Humanities Center

29. Carlos Baker, *Ernest Hemingway: A Life Story* (New York: Collier, 1969), 143.

30. Ernest Hemingway, *The Sun Also Rises* (New York: Scribner's Paperback), 171.

31. Dashiell Hammett, *The Maltese Falcon* (New York: Vintage, 1992), 130.

32. About high literature's resistance to time, Gertrude Stein observes that "the word timely as used in our speech is very interesting but you can any one can see that it has nothing to do with a master-piece. . . . The word timely tells that masterpieces have nothing to do with time" (Stein, *Writings and Lectures*, 153).

33. While the first two novels are written in the first person, in *The Maltese Falcon* Hammett for the first time in his career uses third-person narration. This narratological shift allows Hammett to present his named detective, Sam Spade, as a visible body, an object. Thus are we told that "the steep, rounded slope of [Spade's] shoulders made his body seem almost conical—no broader than it was thick" (4), which suggests the ontological intimacy of the object that Samuel Spade is, the object that he as an author-figure pursues, and the object, in this case named after an object, which is the novel itself. The novel's "quest," no less than Gide's in *The Counterfeiters* to include its own authorship, is thus a quest for the reconstituted unity of author and book in the transcendental object that Gertrude Stein

describes as serving God: "Now serving god for a writer who is writing is writing anything directly, it makes no difference what it is but it must be direct, the relation between the thing done and the doer must be direct. In this way there is completion" (Stein, *Writings and Lectures*, 38).

34. On these grounds I would dispute James Naremore's claim that Hammett "managed to reconcile some of the deepest contradictions in his culture." See James Naremore, "Dashiell Hammett and the Poetics of Hard-Boiled Detection," in *Art in Crime Writing: Essays on Detective Fiction*, ed. Bernard Benstock (New York: St. Martin's, 1983), 49.

35. In this Hammett appears precursive, in some respects, of the Marxism of Fredric Jameson, who similarly reads modern culture as a sort of Fall into market relations. See Fredric Jameson, *The Political Unconscious: Narrative as a Socially Symbolic Act* (Ithaca: Cornell University Press, 1981), 285.

36. T. S. Eliot, *The Complete Poems and Plays, 1909–1950* (New York: Harcourt, Brace, 1980), 39.

37. See John Guillory, *Cultural Capital: The Problem of Literary Canon Formation* (Chicago: University of Chicago Press, 1993).

38. Writing in 1927, T. S. Eliot claims that the divergence of high and low narrative forms occurred in the early-twentieth century, the result of a "dissociation of the elements of the old three-volume melodramatic novel into the various types of the modern 300-page novel." But, as Eliot's use of the term "dissociation" makes clear, the "distinction of *genre* between such-and-such a profound 'psychological' novel of today and such-and-such a masterly 'detective' novel of today" (409) is not a promising sign of the seriousness of the post-Jamesian novelist but lamentable evidence of cultural unhealth. See T. S. Eliot, *Selected Essays* (New York: Harcourt, Brace and World, 1967). See, on Eliot's relation to mass culture, David Chinitz, "T. S. Eliot and the Great Divide," *PMLA* 110, no. 2 (1995): 236–47.

39. Lyndall Gordon, *Eliot's New Life* (Oxford: Oxford University Press, 1988), 192.

Afterword
Möbius Fictions

1. John Barth, *Lost in the Funhouse* (New York: Bantam, 1981), 1–2.

2. It has been argued by Brian McHale, for instance, that whereas modernist narrative is most preoccupied with epistemology—hence its elaboration of "stream of consciousness" narrative, etc.—postmodernist fiction turns its attention to ontology. See Brian McHale, *Postmodernist Fiction* (New York: Methuen, 1987).

3. Pynchon, though, is an ambiguous example of the non-academic postmodernist. One of his most formative influences, for instance, was the ultrareflexive professor-novelist Vladimir Nabokov, and much of the high science component of Pynchon's early fiction seems to be an infusion from science classes he took at Cornell University.

4. Malcolm Cowley, *The Literary Situation* (New York: Viking, 1958), 50.

5. Alfred Kazin, *The Inmost Leaf: A Selection of Essays* (New York: Harcourt, Brace, 1955), 244, 243, 243–44.

6. John Barth, *Giles Goat-Boy, or The Revised New Syllabus* (New York: Doubleday, 1966).

7. Raymond M. Olderman, *Beyond the Waste Land: A Study of the American Novel in the Nineteen-Sixties* (New Haven: Yale University Press, 1972), 72–93.

8. Mark Schorer, "Technique as Discovery," *Hudson Review* 1, no. 1 (Spring 1948): 67–87.

9. John Guillory makes a similar point about the symptomatic nature of de Manian deconstruction, arguing that its suffusion by a language of analytical "rigor" is the defensive reflection of a crisis in the institutional conditions and perceived legitimacy of literary-academic labor in the science-oriented university. See John Guillory, *Cultural Capital*, 176–265. This picture is completed (though with less—dare I say—rigor than Guillory) by Hal Foster, who draws out another, seemingly contradictory but historically complementary, significance to the Theory boom that began in the 1970s: the way the playful and confusing Derridean critical text, retaining "such values as difficulty and distinction," has "served as a secret continuation of modernism by other means" and also, in its more overtly politicized forms, as "secret continuation of the avant-garde by other means." Hal Foster, *The Return of the Real: The Avant-Garde at the End of the Century* (Cambridge: MIT Press, 1996), xiv.

10. Philip Rahv, "Fiction and the Criticism of Fiction," *Kenyon Review* 18, no. 2 (Spring 1956): 276–99.

11. John Barth, "The Literature of Exhaustion," in *The Friday Book: Essays and Other Nonfiction* (New York: G. P. Putnam, 1984), 62–76.

12. Dashiell Hammett, "Tulip," in *The Big Knockover: Selected Stories and Short Novels* (New York: Vintage, 1989), 329–330.

index

Abbott, Edwin A., *Flatland: A Romance of Many Dimensions by A. Square*, 57–61, 63–64, 66, 75–76,194n.2, 195n.4
abstract art, 153
Acker, Kathy, 178
Adams, Henry: *Democracy*, 141; *The Education of Henry Adams*, 113, 115
Agnew, Jean-Christophe, 191n.17
Altick, Richard, 198n.27
American Mercury, 108–9
Anderson, Margaret. See *Little Review*
Anderson, Perry, 19, 188n.55
Anderson, Sherwood: *Dark Laughter*, 109; *Double Dealer*, 117; *Winesburg, Ohio*, 130
Anesko, Michael, 36, 184n.9, 190n.12, 197n.24, 198n.31
anthropology, 131, 186n.25, 206–7n.35
Arnold, Edwin, 209n.39
art-novel: aesthetic forms of, 2, 4, 9–10, 29; and class, 2,4; as cultural capital, 78, 133; definition of, 172, 183n.2; dialectical account of, 9; emergence and rise of, 5–6, 11, 19, 23, 43–44, 129, 182; as pastoral, 8, 13, 19; precursors of, 184n.10; and professionalism, 15; and reading public, 5; tradition of, 130. *See also* modernist novel
Atherton, Gertrude, 12
Atlantic Monthly, 103
Austen, Jane, 45, 50; *Northanger Abby*, 50, 94
avant-garde, 7, 59, 76, 93, 153, 181, 183n.2, 213n.9

Baltzell, E. Digby, 188n.52, 205n.27
Balzac, Honoré de, *Le Pere Goriot*, 194n.3
Barkan, Elazar, 185n.15
Barnes, Djuna, *Nightwood*, 1, 4–5, 13, 27–29, 175, 179
Barth, John, 178–81; *Giles Goat-Boy, or The Revised New Syllabus*, 178; *Lost in the Funhouse*, 177, 179–80

Barthelme, Donald, 178–79
Baym, Nina, 46
Beech, Dave, 189n.58
Behrman, S. N., 116
Bell, Michael Davitt, 201n.1
Benfey, Christopher, 91
Bennett, Tony, 119n.28
Bentley, Nancy, 186n.25
Bergson, Henri, 63–64
Bernstein, J. M., 189n.58
Bersani, Leo, 190n.10
Besant, Walter, "The Art of Fiction," 3, 68, 70, 75
Binet, Alfred, 118, 197n.22
Bixler, Paul, 148, 153
Black Mask, 117–18, 161, 164, 167
Blair, Sara, 193–94n.46
Blavatsky, Madame H. P., 196n.14
Bledstein, Burton J., 187n.37
Bleikasten, Andre, 207n.10, 209n.37
Block, Harry, 167, 169–70
Block, N. J., 206n.29
Blotner, Joseph, 138, 144, 150
Bockting, Margaret, 189n.65
Boni, Charles, 14, 109
Bookman, 14
Bourdieu, Pierre, 9, 18–19, 22, 83, 92, 175, 186n.24, 188n.56, 202 nn. 8 and 9
Bradley, F. H., 114
Brigham, Carl, *A Study of American Intelligence*, 125–26
Brodhead, Richard H., 209n.31
Brooks, Cleanth, 135, 137, 144, 152
Brooks, Van Wyck, 114; "'Highbrow' and 'Lowbrow',"" 162–63
Brown, Henry Harrison, *Concentration: The Road to Success*, 16
Bull, Malcolm, 189n.58
Bulwer-Lytton, Edward, 46, 192 nn. 30 and 31
Burroughs, William, 178
Bush, Ronald, 6, 185n.15, 206–7n.35
Butor, Michel, 57–58, 195n.4